The Politics of Display

The *Heritage: Care–Preservation–Management* programme has been designed to serve the needs of the museum and heritage community worldwide. It publishes books and information services for professional museum and heritage workers, and for all the organizations that service the museum community.

Editor-in-chief: Andrew Wheatcroft

The Politics of Display

Museums, science, culture

Edited by Sharon Macdonald

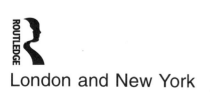

London and New York

First published 1998
by Routledge
11 New Fetter Lane, London EC4P 4EE

Simultaneously published in the USA and Canada
by Routledge
29 West 35th Street, New York, NY 10001

First published in paperback 1998

Typeset in Garamond by Keystroke, Jacaranda Lodge, Wolverhampton
Printed and bound in Great Britain by Biddles Ltd, Guildford and King's Lynn

British Library Cataloguing in Publication Data
A catalogue record for this book is available from the British Library

Library of Congress Cataloguing in Publication Data
The politics of display : museums, science, culture / edited by Sharon
 Macdonald.
     Includes bibliographical references and index.
     1. Museum exhibits–Political aspects. 2. Science museums–
Exhibitions–Political aspects. 3. Exhibitions–Political aspects.
4. Popular culture–Political aspects. 5. Political correctness.
I. Macdonald, Sharon.
AM151.P65   1998
069'.5–dc21   97–3319

ISBN 0–415–15325–5 (hbk)
ISBN 0–415–15326–3 (pbk)

Contents

Figures

Contributors

Steven W. Allison-Bunnell is an independent scholar and media producer based in Missoula, Montana, USA. A product of Cornell University's Department of Science and Technology Studies, his Ph.D. dissertation examined constructions of nature in natural history museum exhibitions in the twentieth century.

Ken Arnold has a Ph.D. in History, on the subject of cabinets of curiosity, from Princeton University. He is exhibitions manager at the Wellcome Trust, where he has been involved in creating a number of innovative and sometimes controversial exhibitions.

Andrew Barry lectures in Sociology at Goldsmiths' College, London University. He is co-editor of *Foucault and Political Reason* (1996). He is currently working on a book called *Unstable Borders: Technologies and the Dispersion of Politics*.

Jim Bennett was Curator of the Whipple Museum of the History of Science in Cambridge for 15 years until 1995, when he became Keeper of the Museum of the History of Science, University of Oxford.

Tony Bennett is Professor of Cultural Studies and Foundation Director of the Institute for Cultural Policy Studies in the Faculty of Humanities at Griffith University, Australia. His books include *The Birth of the Museum: History, Theory, Politics* (Routledge, 1995).

Mary Bouquet is a social anthropologist who has held research and teaching posts at the Universities of Exeter, Lisbon, Amsterdam and Oslo. Her publications include *Reclaiming English Kinship: Portuguese Reflections of English Kinship Theory* (1993). She has been involved in creating anthropological exhibitions in Portugal, the Netherlands and Norway.

Nélia Dias is Professor of Social Anthropology at the University of Lisbon, Portugal. She is author of *Le Musée d'Ethnographie du Trocadéro (1878–1908): Anthropologie et Muséologie en France* (1991) and many papers on the history of anthropological museums.

Thomas F. Gieryn is Professor of Sociology at Indiana University and Director of the Program on Scientific Dimensions of Society. His book *Cultural*

Cartography of Science: Episodes in Boundary-work, Sociologically Rendered will appear in 1998. His current work explores the cultural and architectural aspects of sites for scientific work – specifically, the connections between place and truth. In 1996/7, he was the Ralph and Doris Hansmann Member of the School of Social Science, Institute for Advanced Study in Princeton, New Jersey, where his chapter 'Balancing Acts' was written.

Penelope Harvey is Senior Lecturer in Social Anthropology at Manchester University. Her publications include (as co-editor) *Sex and Violence: Issues in Representation and Experience* (Routledge, 1994) and *Hybrids of Modernity: Anthropology, the Nation-state and the Universal Exhibition* (Routledge, 1996).

Sharon Macdonald lectures in Social Anthropology in the Department of Sociological Studies, Sheffield University. Her publications include (as co-editor) *Theorizing Museums* (1996) and *Reimagining Culture* (1997).

Tracy Lang Teslow is completing a Ph.D. on representations of race in natural history museums at the Morris Fishbein Center for the History of Science and Medicine, University of Chicago.

Preface

a recreation, an educational experience, a monument to humankind's struggle
to rise from the muck and the goo, and get an upperhand over its environment . . . Planes, trains, all sorts of weird objects, various exhibits, a huge
model railroad, and stuff too numerous to mention.
(Museum Guide voice-over in *The Museum of Science and Industry Story*,
David Mamet 1988: 96)

In David Mamet's play, *The Museum of Science and Industry Story*, a man called
Albert gets locked in Chicago's Museum of Science and Industry one night.
He finds a remarkable life behind the scenes. Former workers from disbanded
industries and university escapees live in a twilight world between reality and
fantasy, working the exhibits, 'reminiscin'', squabbling, and consuming Pepsi and
Snickers from the vending machines. The play is a clever and subtle commentary
on the ironies of the museum's celebrations and silences. Laid-off miners tending
the mining exhibits are a reminder that this industry, monumentalized in display,
is in terminal decline. Boomerang-throwing Potowatamies, struggling to make
their presence felt, illustrate museums' marginalization of some cultures and
their technologies. And a German U-boat radioman, presiding over his highly
destructive technology, comments shrewdly on the power of the museum to
make history: 'Zis building is a monument to science . . . Zis building is a monument to orderly understanding, and a stark affront to all ze ravages of Time . . .
it has some *weight*' (Mamet 1988: 118; emphasis in original).

   This book explores museums' celebrations and silences, their life behind the
scenes, and the consequences of their 'weight'. It looks at the processes involved
in, and the political consequences of, museum display. Its focus is on museums
and exhibitions of science, broadly conceived, for, of all types of public display,
it is these that have most frequently presented themselves as, and been thought
to be, outside – or above – politics.

   In recent years there has been a flourishing of interest in cultural perspectives
on both museums and science as part of a broader critique of modernity and its
technologies of truth production. At the same time, there has also been a
clamour of often heated public and academic debate over the role of science and

of museums in contemporary culture. This has sometimes been expressed in the phrases 'Culture Wars', 'History Wars' and 'Science Wars'. Museums and exhibitions of science are potential – and, increasingly frequently, actual – battlegrounds for the waging of all of these types of wars. They are contestable (if not necessarily contested) sites in which knowledge and truth are defined and offered up to 'the public'.

As yet, however, there has been relatively little theoretically informed research focused on museums of science. It is as a contribution to this research that this book is intended. All of the chapters are based on detailed empirical research which entails either historical documentary analysis or contemporary observation and involvement. They are written by scholars from a range of disciplines – history, anthropology, sociology and STS (science and technology studies) – so providing a rich reservoir of cross-disciplinary insight; and they share a concern with analysing science and technology as part of, rather than separate from, culture. That is, they see science and technology as entailing cultural assumptions and social relationships, and as playing active roles in the ongoing processes of defining cultural worlds and social difference. They see exhibitions as implicated in such processes; and as potentially powerful arenas for reflecting upon them.

To focus on politics, and to draw on critical perspectives, is not to denigrate the intellectual fascination and achievements of either science or museums. On the contrary, it is hoped that this book will convey a sense of the importance and complexity of both science and exhibitions in contemporary life, as well as of the broader cultural understandings that can be derived from attention to them.

At the end of *The Museum of Science and Industry Story* Albert falls out of a fire-door and finds himself on the street. He pounds on the door and screams to be let back in. Two policemen gaze on incredulously: 'I never *seen* this . . . some kind of *culture* junkie . . . [to Albert:] Go home, go read a book, something' (Mamet 1988: 124; emphases in original). Life behind the scenes of the museum, with its political skirmishes and contradictions, has, it seems, been compelling. While this book may not lead to people hammering on the doors of science museums, it is hoped that it will contribute to the awareness of their cultural significance and fascination.

This book began life as a special issue of the journal *Science as Culture* – a journal dedicated to the analysis of science in society. Many of the chapters originally published there have been revised – Andrew Barry has expanded a short review into a full-length chapter; and additional chapters by Nélia Dias, Tony Bennett, Ken Arnold and Tom Gieryn have been added. This book also includes an introduction which seeks to provide a framework and a schematic history for the study of museums and exhibitions of science; and an afterword which addresses debates about the role of contemporary science museums.

As editor of the collection I extend particular thanks to the editors and editorial board of *Science as Culture* for inviting me to act as guest editor for the journal, for helpful editorial comments and for permitting the republication of articles originally published in the special issue. I would also like to thank contributors for hanging in there and helping to make it all happen in the end.

Sharon Macdonald

REFERENCE

Mamet, D. (1988) *Five Television Plays*, New York: Grove Weidenfeld.

Chapter 1

Exhibitions of power and powers of exhibition

An introduction to the politics of display

Sharon Macdonald

In recent years politics has erupted publicly into the imagined sanctity of science and of museums on an increasing number of occasions. Two cases which have caused world-wide ripples of concern are the controversy over the representation of the *Enola Gay* – the aircraft which dropped the atomic bomb on Hiroshima in World War II – and the *Science in American Life* exhibition, both at the Smithsonian Institution in Washington (see Gieryn, Chapter 12 this volume). Although most science exhibitions have not achieved the same notoriety, the questions that were raised in the controversies can be asked of other exhibitions too. Who decides what should be displayed? How are notions of 'science' and 'objectivity' mobilized to justify particular representations? Who gets to speak in the name of 'science', 'the public' or 'the nation'? What are the processes, interest groups and negotiations involved in constructing an exhibition? What is ironed out or silenced? And how does the content and style of an exhibition inform public understandings?

This book is concerned with these questions. It explores the political nature, uses and consequences of representations of science and technology for the public in exhibitions; and shows that exhibitions and science are productive arenas in which to investigate questions of cultural production and knowledge more generally. The focus is on museums and exhibitions that are identified as broadly scientific and are concerned with some aspect of science and technology. This includes museums of science and industry, natural history, geology, anthropology and medicine, as well as universal exhibitions (which deal with industry, technology and their own peculiar anthropology) – all of which are referred to here as either museums or exhibitions of science. The volume contains a mix of historical and present-day examples, for the aim is to show that science displays are never, and have never been, just representations of uncontestable facts. They always involve the culturally, socially and politically saturated business of negotiation and value-judgment; and they always have cultural, social and political implications. This is the case not only for recent examples which have sparked such controversy, but also for other and earlier exhibitions which have not been publicly contested.

Exploring the politics of exhibitionary selections, styles and silences is not, however, an easy matter. Exhibitions tend to be presented to the public rather as do scientific facts: as unequivocal statements rather than as the outcome of particular processes and contexts. The assumptions, rationales, compromises and accidents that lead to a finished exhibition are generally hidden from public view: they are tidied away along with the cleaning equipment, the early drafts of text and the artefacts for which no place could be found. Likewise, exhibitions rarely seek to explain their contents in terms of a broader social and political context; and this may be something which even those involved in making exhibitions tend to overlook as they concentrate upon the intellectual, aesthetic and practical details of the task at hand. Generally invisible too, through paucity of research, are the understandings of exhibitions and science by those who visit. By analogy with the use of the term 'black box' (borrowed from cybernetics) in the sociology of science to describe those technical objects or scientific principles which are taken as given by scientists without any knowledge of their background or workings,[1] we might suggest that exhibitions tend to be presented as 'glass-cased' – that is, as objects there to be gazed upon, admired, and understood only in relation to themselves. Research, however, must seek to move beyond this.[2]

In order to move towards a more thorough understanding of the potentials, difficulties and consequences of putting science on display we need to look analytically at the contents of exhibitions in relation to their production, contexts and reception. Clearly, it is rarely possible to do all of these within any one study (evidence of what visitors thought of historical exhibitions, for example, is scant). Nevertheless, by bringing together a range of careful, probing studies which each tackle various of these dimensions, this book provides a collective vision of what is possible.

In this introduction my aim is to set out some issues involved in the analysis of the politics of the public display of science and to provide a framework in relation to which the studies might be located. I do this partly through a schematic history of the exhibition of science and technology which seeks to highlight the changing relations between museums, science, publics and power.

MUSEUMS, KNOWLEDGE AND POWER

In this book, we bring museums and science together not just to explore the politics and cultural operations of each, but also to highlight the discursive inter-relationships between the two. Museums which deal with science are not simply putting science on display; they are also creating particular kinds of science for the public, and are lending to the science that is displayed their own legitimizing imprimatur. In other words, one effect of science museums is to pronounce certain practices and artefacts as belonging to the proper realm of 'science', and as being science that an educated public ought to know about. Moreover, some museums are sites of scientific research, and some collections have been formed as part of the development of particular scientific disciplines. In this way, they have played important roles in the constitution of scientific knowledge (see Allison-Bunnell, Dias, and J. Bennett, Chapters 5, 3 and 10 this volume) and have helped to define and perform scientific conceptions of 'truth' and 'objectivity'. At the same time, museums of science are widely conceived of as 'scientific' institutions in the sense that they are regarded as organized according to orderly and authoritative principles – principles conceived of as separate from power and politics.

Seeing 'truth' and 'values', 'science' and 'politics', and 'knowledge' and 'power' as divided off from one another is characteristic of ways of thinking which, in the Western tradition, have their roots in the seventeenth century, but which crystallized in the nineteenth century. From the late nineteenth century, however, with thinkers such as Nietzsche and Heidegger, and gathering pace dramatically since around the 1960s, there has been a growing number of cultural and historical analyses which have sought to subject these divisions to critical analysis rather than take them as given. Questions have been asked about their formation and effects: how did such separations come about and what are their consequences? This has opened up many fields of research exploring the workings of power in different domains of knowledge and practice, including modern science.[3]

In this book, we are concerned with 'politics' in this broad sense of the workings of power. As Foucault has argued, power and knowledge are thoroughly mutually implicated: power is involved in the construction of truths, and knowledge has implications for power (see Foucault 1977, 1979). The production, distribution and consumption of knowledge are always political in this sense. 'Knowledge' here does not only mean that which is displayed in an exhibition as formal knowledge, of course. It also includes the knowledges (including unreflected-upon assumptions) of different parties involved in exhibition-making, their attempts to, for example, gather knowledge about visitors, and the understandings of visitors themselves.[4] These do not always work neatly with one another. Politics is, therefore, a matter of (often implicit) negotiation: a dynamic power-play of competing knowledges, intentions and interests. Moreover, if we view knowledge and power as intertwined, politics is not restricted to particular events or institutions; rather, it has ramifications throughout social life and cultural practice. Even where our concern is with what Foucault calls 'governmentality' – the administration of individuals and populations – we should look towards the detailed tactics, or 'semio-techniques', by which this may operate (Foucault 1977, 1991). Politics, in other words, lies not just in policy statements and intentions (though these are important) but also in apparently non-political and even 'minor' details, such as the architecture of buildings, the classification and juxtaposition of artefacts in an exhibition, the use of glass cases or inter-actives, and the presence or lack of a voice-over on a film. This is not to say that we will necessarily be able to detect the direct influence of, say, 'the State' in the design of such details; and it is likely in many cases that we will not even be able to say from where we draw our assumptions that particular display techniques are appropriate.[5] There will, however, be 'local' assumptions, claims and statements of intention – e.g. that exhibitions should 'speak to the eyes' or that labels should be designed for different 'levels' of reading skill and interest among the public. The task of the analyst, as the later chapters demonstrate, is to explore these beliefs and rationales, and to see how they are associated with – perhaps reflecting or opposing – wider historically located cultural logics and political rationalities.

The task is also to explore the consequences of particular forms of representation in terms of the distribution of power: who is empowered or disempowered by certain modes of display? Within the cultural study of museums, one of the most productive theoretical developments has been the analysis of museums as 'texts' or as 'media'; and this is an approach that can usefully be harnessed to questions of the politics of display. While sometimes focused narrowly on content, in its more interesting forms this approach has sought to open up questions about production (encoding/writing) and consumption (decoding/ reading), as well as content (text) and the interrelationships between these.[6] It is an approach which leads to important questions about the determination of meaning and the distribution of the power to define in exhibitions. For example, who authors exhibitions? How much agency does an exhibition-maker have? What state political or economic interests impinge? How is the audience imagined? Who is excluded? To what extent do visitors to an exhibition define it in their own terms? And how do certain exhibitionary forms or techniques enable certain kinds of readings? More specifically, this is an approach which can lead to questions about interrelationships between particular kinds of producers, exhibitions and audiences, and the different distributions of power these might entail and enable.

In many of the later chapters we see the interrelationship between exhibition production, content and imagined and/or actual audiences, and the positioning of these in relation to science and technology. That our focus is on museums of science is important, for it is by no means clear that the politics of production and reception necessarily work in the same ways for different media and genres of display. The strategies and techniques of, say, television, and the nature of the authority relationships that audiences have with it, are not the same as those of museums; likewise, the kinds of positioning of audiences through notions of taste, and the nature of appeals to authority, in art museums may well be different from those in museums of science. As Chapters 4 and 7 (by Teslow, and Macdonald) illustrate, a science museum trying to present an exhibition as 'art', or attempting to offer visitors choice, may easily be misunderstood. So, too, may understandings of science presented in the context of a museum differ from the understandings that the public may form in other contexts. Research into the public understanding of science has highlighted the importance to lay people of the perceived morality and trustworthiness of those who speak about science: judgments about the reliability of scientific knowledge and assessments of risk are made at least in part on the basis of estimations about the personal and institutional qualities of those providing the information (Irwin and Wynne 1996; Wynne 1996). Museums, as later chapters suggest, tend to be invested with cultural authority as trustworthy scientific witnesses – though increasingly, it seems, they have to work hard to maintain this status through rhetorical assertions of political impartiality and balance (see Gieryn, Chapter 12 this volume).

Of course, there are also variations between different types of science exhibition. Expectations of a national museum differ from those of smaller provincial museums or of universal exhibitions; assumptions about geology exhibitions may differ from those about modern technology or medical history. Likewise, certain exhibitionary styles – hands-on or hands-off, employing realism, hyperrealism, historical artefacts or reconstructions – also have consequences for the authority of producers in relation to consumers, and for the types of meanings that it is possible to inscribe. Roger Silverstone has suggested that we might explore such specificities in relation to the ways in which different media articulate time and space (1992), and in terms of their thematic, poetic and rhetorical strategies (1989). An emphasis on time and space would direct us to consideration of such matters as the authority effects of the temporal stability of most museum exhibitions, many of which are in place for years; and to the implications of their spatial fixity and the fact that visitors literally must move through them. The interest here would be in how such features might limit or expand the definitional power of institutions and of audiences. Thematics concerns genre – what are the socio-political propulsions towards, and implications of, particular representational forms? Poetics focuses on the aesthetic strategies of display, those intended to bring pleasure; and rhetoric on the mechanisms of persuasion, those intended to instruct. Of course, these may well overlap in practice, and indeed such overlap – the blurring of the aesthetic and the rhetorical, say – itself has implications for the politics of representation as various later chapters illustrate. Nevertheless, such a framework is useful in helping analysis of museums move towards a more informed sense of the implications of particular display strategies. It will also help highlight the kinds of difficulties that might be encountered in trying to use exhibitions themselves to disrupt assumptions about, say, divisions between 'art' and 'science', and 'power' and 'knowledge'.

A SCHEMATIC HISTORY OF MUSEUMS OF SCIENCE

Museums of science can be regarded as cultural technologies which define both certain kinds of 'knowledge' (and certain knowledges as 'Knowledge' or 'science') and certain kinds of publics. Museums of science have not, however, remained constant over time: the types of science displayed, the types of public enlisted, the representational strategies and the institutional contexts, political motivations and effects have all undergone transformation. The aim of the next part of this introductory chapter is to provide a brief schematic account of some of these historical patterns and developments. There is, inevitably, much that is not touched on here, but my intention is to select examples in order to highlight some of the major continuities and shifts involved. In doing so, I divide the account into three unequal periods. The first deals with early modern museums of science, the growth of collecting during the Renaissance and the beginnings of 'scientific' ways of knowing in the seventeenth century. The next part considers the expansion of public museums of science and the development of world fairs, from the late eighteenth and more especially the nineteenth century; and the third part concerns a period, particularly since the 1960s, which has seen changing forms of display in science museums and the growth of industrial heritage and science centres.

Early modern museums of science: collecting, seeing and knowing

Histories of museums and, more specifically, of museums of science, generally trace their origins to the curiosity cabinets of Renaissance princes and scholars.[7] These were but one manifestation of a broader fascination with collecting which emerged in the fifteenth century out of 'an attempt to manage the empirical explosion of materials that wider dissemination of ancient texts, increased travel, voyages of discovery, and more systematic forms of communication and exchange had produced' (Findlen 1994: 3). Such an empirical profusion posed problems for ways of knowing that had centred upon the inscribed wisdom of the Bible and of the ancients: here was material that was neither contained within nor immediately accountable by them. In response to this, collecting developed as a 'way of maintaining some degree of control over the natural world and taking its measure. If knowledge of the world could no longer be contained in a set of canonical texts, then perhaps it could be displayed in a museum' (ibid.: 4).

Although these collections often contained fanciful artefacts, such as unicorns' horns and the remains of dragons, their attempt was to represent and comprehend 'nature' through the collection and interpretation of material culture, and to this extent it is useful to consider them in relation to the emergence of conceptions of science. However, as Findlen makes clear, there was at this time no identifiable category of 'science' congruent with that which we would today label as such: Renaissance natural philosophers' understanding of their activities was more 'expansive' and 'encyclopaedic' than this (ibid.: 9). Moreover, although their attempts to devise epistemologies based on observation of the natural world might be seen as a precursor of later scientific ideas, the ways in which they formed and ordered knowledge was also marked by major differences (ibid.; Hooper-Greenhill 1992). In the sixteenth century, according to Foucault (1970; see also Hooper-Greenhill 1992 and Prösler 1996), knowledge was based upon notions of 'similitude' and 'resemblance'. As Martin Prösler explains:

Things as well as words were God's creation, bearing his signature at a 'deeper level'. These signs were laid down at the moment of the Creation, so that ultimately man might reveal its secrets. The form of knowing therefore corresponded to an *interpretation of signs* and of the resemblances that arose among them. Just as words and things meshed together seamlessly, so in the description of natural phenomena no distinction was made between observation, document and fable. The task of a natural historian like Aldrovandi, writing a natural history based upon his collection, was to represent this complex system – to draw together all that was known about an animal or plant and to present it in terms of the semantic relationships that connected it into the world.

(Prösler 1996: 30; emphasis in original)

To later observers, cabinets often appeared haphazard, so unfamiliar are the principles according to which they are ordered. Moreover, by the seventeenth century natural philosophers were dismissing the principles of similitude and resemblance, and replacing them with ideas of *comparison*, of which, Foucault argues, there were two forms: measurement and order ('mathesis' and 'taxonomia') (Foucault 1970: 71). 'Henceforth, no longer did one search for signs of covert resemblance and affinity, but rather, through *observation*, isolated those characteristics whose comparison betrayed the identity, or diversity, of cosmic creations' (Prösler 1996: 30; emphasis in original). This was a 'project of a general science of order' (Foucault 1970: 71); and it was one in which *vision* became prioritized over other senses:

Observation, from the seventeenth century onward, is a perceptible knowledge furnished with a series of systematically negative conditions. Hearsay is excluded . . . but so too are taste and smell, because their lack of certainty and their variability render impossible any analysis into distinct elements that could be universally acceptable. The sense of touch is very narrowly limited to the designation of a few fairly evident distinctions . . . which leaves sight with an almost exclusive privilege, being the sense by which we perceive extent and establish proof, and, in consequence, the means to an analysis *partes extra partes* acceptable to everyone.

(Foucault 1970: 132–3)

Museums and collections had a vital role in this new project of observation and comparison. Francis Bacon recommended that learned gentlemen should, as part of their scholarly endeavours, have at their disposal 'a goodly huge cabinet, wherein whatsoever the hand of man by exquisite art or engine has made rare in stuff, form or motion; whatsoever singularity, chance and the shuffle of things hath produced; whatsoever Nature has wrought in things that want life and may be kept; shall be sorted and included' (Bacon *Gesta Grayorum* (1594) quoted in Impey and MacGregor 1985: 1). Such a cabinet would provide 'in small compass a model of the universal nature made private' (ibid.); and on the basis of this 'world in microcosm' (Prösler 1996), the natural philosopher would be able to learn to 'read' the 'book of nature' (Findlen 1994: 55). It was to this end that early modern scientific collections, such as the Repository of the Royal Society, established in London in the 1660s, were set up. However, as Eilean Hooper-Greenhill describes, such collections mostly failed in their aim to provide a complete 'visual grammar of nature' (Hooper-Greenhill 1992: 157) because of the eclectic nature of collections (which were largely formed out of chance donations) and because 'The aim of cataloguing the whole of nature was too ambitious' (ibid.: 163).

The seventeenth century also saw the beginning of other changes in the criteria for authenticating and validating scientific findings. Prior to this period, the principal criterion of authenticity seems to have been the worthiness and gentlemanly status of the scientist (Shapin 1994). In other words, you could take a finding as true if it came from a noble fellow. During the seventeenth century, however, this was increasingly questioned and was partly replaced by the idea of authentication in terms of particular *methods* carried out in defined spaces, notably laboratories. These were spaces of 'observation' in which 'truth' came to be defined as flowing not from worthy persons, but from specified procedures. In theory, any person (properly equipped) would be capable of replicating these truths. However, as Steven Shapin argues, the repudiation of personal testimony as the basis for truth did not mean that the association between personal identity and truth was severed; although publicly dismissed, it remained (and remains) influential within scientific knowledge producing domains (ibid.: chapter 8).

Museums, which themselves had earlier validated their collections largely in terms of the worthiness of their donors, became important technologies for performing this new conception of truth. As Nélia Dias argues (Chapter 3 this volume), craniological collections assembled by nineteenth-century anthropological museums not only helped shape the craniological knowledge produced, they also helped to instantiate the new ideas about scientific method. In particular, what the museum offered was a site in which scientific findings were theoretically (and to a lesser extent practically) open to a general public as well as to a community of scientists: here, 'anybody' might come and survey the evidence of science.

The Repository of the Royal Society, like most other collections prior to the late eighteenth century, was not intended for the general public. It served primarily as a scientific research centre, a locus for gentlemanly scholars (Hooper-Greenhill 1992: 145). There were a few exceptions to the restricted access of scientific collections at this time: collections of natural and artificial curiosities in mid-sixteenth century Florence and Bologna, and mid-seventeenth century Copenhagen (the collections of Cesalpini, Aldrovandi and Worm, respectively) were 'public' collections according to Bedini (1965), though the majority of those who visited seem to have been of high social status and had usually been preceded by a letter of introduction.[8] Indeed, it seems that such visitors were also enlisted as part of the establishment of authoritative knowledge via personal nobility. As Findlen notes, seventeenth-century visitors' books 'immortalised the fame of a museum and its creator by recording their connection to the social, political and intellectual centers of power' (1994: 137); and, as such, they helped define the knowledge contained within the museum as authoritative knowledge.

The period between the Renaissance and the eighteenth century, then, sees considerable transformation in conceptions of knowledge and of museums. In the seventeenth century we see the beginnings of the growth of a particular kind of taxonomic knowledge based upon ideas of objective observation, visibility, mathematization and the ambitions of a science of order. While many of these ideas remain important, the period from the late eighteenth century sees further changes, in particular an 'opening up' of the museum to a much broader public, which is connected in part with changing conceptions of scientific authority. As we shall see in the next section, however, this is not the only impetus to the growth of the public museums, and the nineteenth century sees further changes in the nature of scientific knowledge – changes in which the museum again has an important formative role.

Modern museums of science: diagnosis, publics and progress

Particularly important to the shaping of the museum in this modern period are the following: the formation of nation-states – 'imagined communities' which sought to define and enlist a bounded citizenship (Anderson 1983); colonialist expansion – which both provided 'material' for display and territories requiring governance; the further development of 'scientific' and more specifically 'museological' ways of seeing the world, and the extension of these to other domains of life. The museum is not, however, merely a product of or a site for displaying the narratives of modern developments; it is also one of the technologies through which modernity – and the democratic ideals, social differences and exclusions, and other contradictions which this has produced – is constituted.[9]

Consequent particularly to the French Revolution, many previously private collections were claimed for the public, and numerous new museums – national and provincial – were established. It was during this period, as nation-states themselves emerged and sought to define their populations as citizens, that museums came to be conceived as symbols of national identity and progress, and as sites of civic education for the masses.[10] Not only was the previously private made public, 'exhibiting' also moved beyond the confines of museums with the remarkable flourishing of 'universal' exhibitions, of which the Great International Exposition held at Crystal Palace in London in 1851 was the first.[11] At these the competitive dimension of 'national exhibitionism' was often made explicit, nations being awarded medals and ranked in ceremonies modelled on the Olympic Games (Lindqvist 1993; Harvey, Chapter 8 this volume; J. Bennett, Chapter 10 this volume).

While univeral exhibitions, which were largely concerned with industry and technology, and most museums established in this period, with the exception of art galleries, could be seen as broadly scientific (Forgan 1996: 47), the nineteenth century is also characterized by the development of more specialized public museums of science. Many of the earliest of these, some of which were established in the late eighteenth century, were devoted to natural history, as was the Musée d'Histoire Naturelle, which opened in Paris in 1793 or Charles Willson Peale's Museum in Philadelphia (1784), though this also included some scientific and technological artefacts (Bedini 1965: 22).[12] So too were many of the first 'scientific' museums to open in the New World (Sheets-Pyenson 1989). Anthropology collections were sometimes incorporated in the natural history museums, as in the case of the Smithsonian's Museum of Natural History, the Chicago Field Museum or the Dutch Museum of Natural History, or as part of national self-representations as in the case of the National Museum of Denmark (1916), though from the 1830s they also began to assume distinct identities in some cases, such as the ethnographic museum of the Academy of Sciences in Petrograd (1836), the National Museum of Ethnology, Leiden (1837) and the Pitt-Rivers Museum, Oxford (1885).[13] Museums specializing in machines and technical and scientific instruments also became a distinct type in the nineteenth century, beginning with France's Conservatoire National des Arts et Métiers, established in 1794. More specialist science museums often developed out of more general collections, as did Britain's Museum of Natural History (from the British Museum collections) and the Museum of the History of Science, Oxford (from the Ashmolean collection) (Hackman 1992); or, as in the case of the Science Museum (established 1857) or the Industrial Museum of Scotland (1855), they were based on exhibits originally shown at international exhibitions (Butler 1992). By the early decades of the twentieth century, most of the first wave of nation-states, and many which were established later, could boast not simply *a* national museum, but national museums of both natural history and of science and technology, as well, perhaps, as national museums of art and other subjects.[14]

This flourishing of museums and exhibitions is bound up with the development of distinctive modern ways of seeing the world. For modern cosmopolitan Europeans, Timothy Mitchell argues, representation – particularly 'rendering things up to be viewed' (Mitchell 1991: 2) – became a key means of apprehending and 'colonizing' reality. The world was to be experienced as though it were a picture – a form of apprehending that he calls, in a phrase borrowed from Heidegger, the 'world-as-exhibition' (ibid.: 13). This entailed both a detachment of the viewer – '[t]he person was now thought of as something set apart from the world, like the visitor to an exhibition' (ibid.: 19) – and a depiction of the world as 'ordered and organised' (ibid.) Even where Europeans were keen also to experience 'reality' as directly as possible, as in their ventures into unknown places or, in a rather different way through the development of highly accurate replicas (such as the 'Cairo street' at the universal exhibition in Paris in 1889), the idea of detached representation remained important. This is reflected in the desire of European travellers to photograph or paint the places they visited (preferably from a height which would set the site out as a panorama (ibid.: 24)); and in the proliferation of texts about exhibitions – 'catalogues, plans, sign-posts, guidebooks, instructions, educational talks and compilations of statistics' (ibid.: 20) – and the viewing platforms that were often built as part of them (T. Bennett 1995: 69). This capacity of exhibitionary representation to render the world as visible and ordered was part of the instantiation of wider senses of scientific and political certainty. As Mitchell emphasizes:

> Exhibitions, museums and other spectacles were not just reflections of this certainty, however, but the means of its production, by their technique of rendering history, progress, culture and empire in 'objective' form. They were occasions for making sure of such objective truths, in a world where truth had become a question of what Heidegger calls 'the certainty of representation'.
>
> (Mitchell 1991: 7)

Museums and exhibitions were thus sites in which political power could 'operate . . . so as to appear set apart from the real world' (ibid.: 160); they were a means of casting the newly realized nations, and cultural, racial and class differences, as fact. In this, as later chapters suggest, museums and exhibitions were perhaps particularly effective in that they not only provided a 'picture' but also objects and other tangible 'evidences'.

The emphasis on gaining privileged vantage points from which order and objective truths might be discerned, as well as the disciplinary specialization of museums that occurred in the nineteenth century, can be seen as part of a broader epistemological development that the historian of science, John Pickstone, has called 'analytical', 'museological' or 'diagnostic' (Pickstone 1994). He is careful to emphasize that these new forms of knowing had earlier precursors and that some classical or savant forms of science, technology and medicine continue today. Nevertheless, he argues, it is useful to try to characterize a development which became much more widespread in the nineteenth century. Classical science, he suggests, tended to identify objects in terms of surface characteristics and to explain deductively according to particular natural philosophies (e.g. vitalism, mechanism) which in practice were 'rarely articulated with' the project of a general grammar of nature which the savants espoused (ibid.: 113, 117). Characteristic of the new 'analytical' or 'museological' sciences is 'that they presented their objects as *compounds*, analysable into *elements*', and that 'these elements were *domain specific*' (ibid.: 117; emphases in original). The aim was to be able, within specific types of science, to produce analytical classifications and to diagnose surface characteristics or the workings of compounds in terms of underlying *process*. This was different from the earlier idea of reading and cataloguing the 'book of nature', in that it sought to 'produce deeper, more specialized knowledge' (ibid.) – to delve beneath the surface – and thus to provide a means, ideally, of grasping 'deep structure' and process, which in turn would enable *explanation* and *prediction*. Museums, according to Pickstone, were a key site in which this new form of knowledge was articulated; and to this end universities often established museums or sought to associate themselves with existing museums (Forgan 1994, 1996), though at the same time it should be stressed that not all nineteenth-century exhibitions were 'museological' in Pickstone's sense (Pickstone 1994: 123). Nevertheless, museum collections were an important research source in the nineteenth century and displays were increasingly conceptualized as a manifestation of the analysis of objects into elements, and thus as a kind of diagnosis of an underlying reality. The attempt was to arrange objects and displays in ways which would reveal profound principles. Such profound principles might be evolutionary, though there were other possibilities too, such as the analysis into chemical elements and principles. As Sophie Forgan has described, this was a matter of a good deal of consideration in the planning of the layout of many nineteenth-century museums, including the Natural History Museum, London, and Jermyn Street Geological Museum (Forgan 1994; see also T. Bennett, Chapter 2).[15] Such exhibitions were conceptualized not just as containers of scientific facts, but as themselves integral to the scientific message. This had implications for, among other things, the expertise demanded of curators, links with universities, and museum visitors.

The layout of nineteenth-century museums also differed from earlier museums in that it was expected to speak not only to fellow savants and nobles, but to a general public, many members of which could not be expected to have much prior knowledge. It was often recognized, as Tony Bennett describes in the next chapter, that the kind of deep specialist knowledge that these classifications might divulge to scientists was not necessarily that which would be of most educative value and practical use for the lay person. Considerable effort, therefore, was directed towards making exhibitions educative for, and *legible* to, the new mass public. As Bennett argues, this was also bound up with ideas about transforming the public, and producing citizens who would themselves take on the task of self-education and improving themselves.

Ideas of improvement and progress were integral to most nineteenth-century museums and exhibitions of science. These ideas operated at a number of levels, each of which provided mutual support for the others. At the most expansive level were evolutionary narratives about the progress of humankind and of scientific knowledge; at the national level, each country sought to represent its own story of self-betterment and of civilizing influence upon the rest of the world; and at the level of individual citizens, members of the public were invited to undertake their own personal journey towards greater knowledge and mastery. Museums were sites in which these parallel narratives could converge. Exhibitions could physically knit together the universal and national or racial, and visitors could embody the progressive narratives as they moved through the orderly museum space.

Much of the nineteenth-century museum achievement is still part of our physical and symbolic landscape. However, during the course of the nineteenth century museums were to become less important as sites of scientific activity, and 'museological science', while remaining central to many areas of scientific endeavour, was to become less prestigious and authoritative than 'experimental science', which entails '*control* over phenomena in laboratories' (Pickstone 1994: 132, 113; emphasis in original). While museums have continued to have an important role in validating science for the public, the legitimization of research evidence itself has increasingly become a matter of specialized expert procedures and review, carried out largely in less public spaces. Moreover, with a continued specialization of scientific knowledge, with the increased use of sophisticated technologies and with scientific attention often turned to the infinitely small or large, science has developed a greater mystique of being beyond lay under-standing. Yet, while this may signal a decline in the role of the museum as a site of scientific expertise and legitimization, it also heralds a renewed significance in its role in 'the public understanding of science'. Museums of science in the twentieth century have built on their earlier emphasis on public education to present themselves as experts in the *mediation* between the esoteric world of science and that of the public. This self-perception differs somewhat, I suggest, from that predominant in the nineteenth century, in that it seeks not so much to make science legible through making evident its underlying principles, as to represent science: not simply to *show* or *tell* but to *interpret* it. Moreover, such interpretations are increasingly framed primarily in terms of the public – e.g. through categories such as 'Your Body' or 'Shopping' – rather than science.

The distinction between nineteenth- and twentieth-century exhibitions should not be exaggerated, however, for as we have noted, nineteenth-century displays were often very much concerned with public education and with finding ways of displaying science that would appeal to a lay audience. Nevertheless, I suggest that what we see in the twentieth century are moves away from the dominant nineteenth-century institutional analogy of the museum as a library (Forgan 1994), and with this a greater sense that it is only possible to display fairly limited and partial accounts of science; and a growing conviction that science needs to be embedded in other kinds of stories – and in media which were not typically part of the museum-as-library – to make it attractive to a general public. The orderly visualism of reading – inherent in the library and book analogies, the desire to make *legible*, and the obsession with labelling exhibits (see T. Bennett, Chapter 2) – gives way to less directed and more multi-sensory approaches. Alongside these changes we also see further transformations in the conception of the public.

Recent museum transformations: contexts, interactivity and consumers

In the late twentieth century, many of the nineteenth-century triumphs – the nation-state, empire, racial and social hierarchies, progress and 'deep truth' –

have come to seem much less inevitable. Particularly since the 1960s, we have seen challenges to all of these in the form of ethno-nationalist, liberationist and environmentalist movements, and the growth of interest in 'traditional' culture and heritage, 'minority', 'alternative' and 'New Age' beliefs and lifestyles. The acceleration of globalization and the transformations in capitalist production to more transnational, flexible, disorganized and consumer-led forms are also often seen both as a threat to the relevance of the nation-state and as factors involved in enabling new forms of identity and subjectivity.[16] While there has undoubtedly been a proliferation of different, particularly minority, 'voices' speaking in the public arena, the old political and cultural high ground has not simply been relinquished. On the contrary, what we have seen is an escalation of intellectual battles over the legitimacy of different kinds of representation. The 'Culture Wars' have focused especially on issues of 'political correctness' and 'intrinsic value' in relation to the literary and artistic canon;[17] the 'History Wars' on similar issues in relation to history, multiculturalism and national identity, focused partly on the *Enola Gay* episode;[18] and the 'Science Wars' have seen fierce debate over the epistemological status of science.[19]

It is in this same period that we see some marked changes in museums of science. Not only do existing museums of science come to adopt new technologies of display, new interpretive experiments and new concerns with their visitors and communities, there is also a massive expansion of two particular forms which could broadly be classified under the 'museum of science' label: industrial heritage and science centres. While there has been debate about whether these *should* be regarded as museums of science (e.g. Durant 1992), it is clear that they have posed challenges for more traditional science museums and that these have sometimes sought to borrow the strategies (and personnel) of industrial heritage developments and science centres. Intriguingly, some of the approaches that industrial heritage and science centres take to science are almost the inverse of one another. The former seek to present science entirely contextualized in a 'slice of history' in a specific community, whereas science centres are more concerned with universal laws and principles which transcend particular times and places.

Industrial heritage sites have a number of precursors, such as Skansen, a Swedish open-air museum which opened in 1891, and Henry Ford's Greenfield Village (1929).[20] Nevertheless, since the 1960s the number of these has vastly increased in an expansion which equals that of traditional museums of science and industry in the nineteenth century. In Britain, the Blists Hill development at Ironbridge Gorge (opened to the public in 1973) and the North of England Open Air Museum at Beamish (1972) are generally seen as particularly influential examples.[21] Unlike traditional science museums, these attempt to provide a 'total environment': artefacts are presented embedded in the worlds of which they were part and visitors are invited to enter, or at least get close to, those worlds and lives. In some cases, especially in France and Scandinavia, industrial heritage developments also go under the name of 'eco-museums' and are associated with community regeneration – linking past with present – and a much greater involvement of local populations in the development of displays than is typical of most museums.[22] The development of industrial heritage, as part of a more widespread discussion of what is sometimes called the 'heritage industry' (Hewison 1988), has already been subject to a good deal of debate about its political implications.[23] Questions have been asked about how far such representations provide accounts which are emancipatory for visitors and communities. Is the movement analagous to, and part of, a claiming of history by 'the people'? Or is it simply a way of commoditizing a past in the face of a lack of alternative sources of manufacturing? As with examples we discuss here, the answers are likely to be less clear cut when it comes to dealing with specific cases and the complexities of processes and different participants than the sometimes stark terms of the debate might imply. Nevertheless, these general arguments about the politics of industrial heritage and the extent to which presenting science as part of particular places, times and social relations may enable the public to better understand the importance and/or the dangers of science have clear links with debates taking place within many museums of science; and arguments in some of the chapters here help take this debate further.

The very different strategies of science centres and the specialized hands-on galleries which have sprung up in many science museums also have pre-1960s precedents; in this case interactive exhibits in international exhibitions and museums of science (e.g. the Children's Gallery, established in the 1930s in the Science Museum, London). However, where the latter were often devoted to showing particular applications of science, the new science centres (especially the first to be developed) have concentrated more on relatively abstract scientific principles. The earliest example of a centre devoted to representing scientific principles through hands-on exhibits is the Exploratorium in San Francisco, which opened in 1969. In contrast to industrial heritage sites, science centres and their in-museum equivalents have been subject to rather scant commentary on their political motivations and effects. In many ways this is not surprising, given that such exhibits attempt to deal with 'pure' scientific principles which transcend cultural and social contexts. Yet, from the perspective of social and cultural disciplines, the emergence and rapid spread of this mode of representing science is surely also deserving of comment.

While we must certainly not assume that all science centres necessarily share identical motivations (as Andrew Barry warns in Chapter 6), the Exploratorium is an interesting and prescient case to consider, both because it has been so influential and because its founder, Frank Oppenheimer, provided very clear statements of his intentions (Hein 1990). In the document which set out the rationale for establishing the Exploratorium, Oppenheimer expressed particular concern over the fact that 'For many people science is incomprehensible and technology frightening' (ibid.: 218). The aim of the Exploratorium, as the rationale concluded, was to 'convey the understanding that science and technology have a role which is deeply rooted in human values and aspirations' (ibid.: 221). In a century in which broadly triumphalist popular perspectives on science seemed, especially after the Second World War, increasingly to be discoloured by perceptions of the dangers of technology, there was a task, as scientists such as Oppenheimer saw it, to present positive visions of scientific potential and achievement. Indeed, the phrase which has been adopted by many science museums to describe their central activity in the late twentieth century – 'public understanding of science' – is often conceptualized in terms of 'public appreciation of science' (Lewenstein 1992; see also Irwin and Wynne 1996). It was to this, in part at least, that the Exploratorium was dedicated.

Oppenheimer had personal reasons for wanting to reclaim science as a worthy and positive endeavour, for, together with his brother Robert, he had worked on the production of the atomic bomb. He had, therefore, very direct involvement in the technology which, more than any this century, has created a sense of public fear of the potential of science.[24] Oppenheimer's attempt in the Exploratorium was to represent 'pure' scientific principles unsullied by the context of their production or of their applications. While, on the one hand, he claimed that an understanding of scientific principles was important for everyday life, he also fiercely resisted any suggestion that the Exploratorium should deal with areas of science that might readily be perceived as political (such as the environment) or even that it might include any directly 'how to' exhibits (Hein 1990). Instead, the Exploratorium was to represent scientific laws as transcendent, and scientific process as a formal art. Indeed, as Barry emphasizes in Chapter 6, Oppenheimer was keen to draw analogies with art – the subtitle of the Exploratorium being 'Museum of Science, Art and Human Perception' – so pointing to the individual creative element of science rather than its social or political contexts.

If science centres may have proved attractive partly because of their potential to provide positive and relatively politically 'safe' images of science, another source of their appeal clearly lies in their hands-on interactivity – a mode of display which is becoming increasingly common in contemporary exhibitions. This is sometimes embraced by those involved as a democratizing attempt to, as Oppenheimer put it, 'bridge the gap between the experts and the laymen' (in ibid.: 17; cf. Barry, Chapter 6). Whether this is how the 'hands-on' experience is seen by visitors remains, however, an underresearched question, though several chapters in this book suggest that democratization is not *necessarily* an effect of such representations, and that, in analysing interactive and electronic technologies of display, we need also to consider the politics of the way in which the visitor is imagined.

As Andrew Barry's comparison of the use of French and English use of interactivity in national museums of science illustrates, we cannot simply infer the meanings of particular technologies of display without consideration of national cultural semantics. In Britain in the late twentieth century, for example, visitors may be conceptualized more as individualized choice-making consumers and active learners than they are in France, where the notion of citizenship and the celebration of human–machine interrelations appear more central. At the same time, however, there are also shared – though not universal – transnational conceptions of the meanings of new technologies of display, as Penelope Harvey (Chapter 8 this volume) discusses in relation to Expo '92. Here, clever reflexive use of such technologies in itself signals the capacity of nations and corporations to participate in serious world games such as trade.

In addition to the past-focused industrial heritage and the forward-looking interactive and multimedia display technologies, the late twentieth century has also seen an increased number of exhibitions in museums of science which attempt to relativize or question scientific authority, or to reflect upon the process of exhibiting itself. This may be seen as part of a growing questioning of previous certainties and an increased willingness of cultural institutions and academic disciplines to look reflexively at their own practices. Chapters in the final part of this book describe a number of such attempts in museums of science.[25] What is clear from these accounts is that such 'experiments' can certainly produce interesting and thought-provoking displays.[26] They may, however, also provoke confusion and anger. That they do so is testament, in part at least, to the authority to sanctify science with which museums are still widely invested.

THE CHAPTERS

Chapters in this book are presented roughly chronologically. Tony Bennett and Nélia Dias focus on the nineteenth century. They describe museums of science in this critical period as they sought to open themselves up to wider publics and to inscribe social differences. Both emphasize the growing centrality of 'visibility' and 'legibility' in museum display; Bennett focusing particularly upon this in relation to museums' relationship with the public, and Dias analysing its relation to changing conceptions of science and the definition of racial difference. One important point that both make is that, despite the social divisions that exhibitions in this period might encode, those involved in the creation of museum displays were often liberal in political inclination, and the task is, therefore, to understand techniques of display not simply as attempts to sustain an existing social order. This entails, as other chapters also highlight, consideration of the alternative and contradictory political potentials of museums.

The next two chapters, by Tracy Teslow on the Field Museum of Natural History, Chicago and Steve Allison-Bunnell on the Smithsonian Museum of Natural History, both consider twentieth-century exhibitions struggling with changing scientific and social ideas. The *Races of Mankind* exhibition described by Teslow was originally created in the 1930s and entails an inscription of racial hierarchy similar to that described by Dias. By the 1960s, however, such ideas about race were scientifically and socially discredited, and Teslow describes the awkward attempt by the museum to redisplay the same exhibits in a new framework. Allison-Bunnell likewise describes a science museum finding aspects of its practice – in this case its scientific research – being defined as 'outdated' and documents the museum's struggle to justify what it does as 'relevant'. Both of these chapters, like others in the book, highlight the importance of 'textual' features of museum representations – their rhetorical and poetic strategies and their articulations of time and space – in enabling and constraining particular kinds of 'readings'. In these two chapters what is especially at issue are 'realism' and 'nature', and the mediation of art, craft and types of science.

The remaining chapters in the book examine developments since the late 1960s, focusing particularly on exhibitions created in the past 10 years. Andrew Barry analyses the development of interactivity in science museums, highlighting the alternative possible political and cultural potentials these may entail in different national contexts. I take up the related theme of visitors as 'consumers' in relation to 'public understanding of science' (and the place of interactivity within this), exploring this through a case study of an exhibition in the Science Museum, London, which opened in 1989. Penelope Harvey's analysis of Expo '92 highlights the way in which interactive and multimedia technologies of display have also become part of a transnational competitive exhibitionary arena. Together, these chapters suggest that what we are seeing in these new exhibitionary developments are not just new ways of 'packaging' older projects, but also reconfigurations of 'the public', of 'culture' and of knowledge/power, though the chapters also suggest that there is no single 'meaning' or 'politics' encoded in such reconfigurations.

One aspect of these reconfigurations is an increasing trend towards innovative juxtaposition of styles and towards reflexivity. In the chapters by Mary Bouquet and Jim Bennett we see this trend turned to 'science' and to representation itself. Both describe exhibitions that they played a major role in creating which sought to raise questions about artefacts displayed by highlighting something of the culturally specific relations in which they were embedded. Rather than presenting science as fact, these exhibitions presented culturally and historically relativized accounts. In that both of these exhibitions also reflected on earlier, particularly nineteenth-century, exhibitionary strategies, they can also be read in relation to chapters in the first half of the book. Bouquet's exhibition, which dealt with physical anthropological remains, was intended in part as a commentary on the kind of exhibitions that Dias describes; and the exhibitions at the Whipple Museum for the History of Science, Cambridge, in which Jim Bennett was involved, sought in part to highlight the close interdependencies in the late nineteenth and early twentieth century between techniques of science, exhibition and public management, as described particularly by Tony Bennett.

Such experiments are, however, not always received as their makers hoped: Mary Bouquet found that her ideas were considered an 'insult' to science, and Jim Bennett notes that visitors did not always appreciate the intentions of *Empires of Physics* and *1900: The New Age*. This problem is explored further by Ken Arnold in his discussion of an exhibition on the history of birth control which he mounted in 1993/4 at the Wellcome Institute for the History of

Medicine. As he saw it, in displaying historical material, including propaganda, concerning birth control, he was highlighting the political technologies that had been mobilized by various groups in pursuit of persuading the public to certain understandings. However, as his analysis of visitor reactions shows, visitors' expectations of 'science', of an institution such as the Wellcome Institute and of 'politics' were not always as he had predicted.

Arnold's account raises questions about the framing of debates about science representation in museums. This is pursued further by Thomas Gieryn in his analysis of the controversies over the display of the *Enola Gay* and the exhibition, *Science in American Life*. In both cases, questions over the nature of history, science and the public were at stake. As Gieryn shows, however, it would be a mistake to see such debates as a neat polarization of two sides each trying to justify their case in terms of 'the facts of the matter' or, as he puts it, 'Big Truth'. Instead, claims by both 'sides' were characterized by epistemological modesty and a rhetoric of balance, trust and public interest. The disappearance of authoritative narratives of 'Truth' might be seen as just what the cultural critics and sociologists of science ordered. However, as Gieryn suggests, there may be little comfort for them in the alternative legitimizations mobilized by those authoring science for the public.

As the studies in this book illustrate, museums are thoroughly part of society, culture and politics. As such, they are sites in which we can see wider social, cultural and political battles played out. They are not, however, simply sites, battlegrounds, terrains, zones or spaces. Museum displays are also agencies for defining scientific knowledge for the public, and for harnessing science and technology to tell culturally authoritative stories about race, nation, progress and modernity. It is to the further understanding of such stories, their authorship, techniques, and implications that this book is dedicated.

ACKNOWLEDGMENTS

Special thanks are due to Mike Beaney for saving me from a number of errors here and to Nélia Dias and Sophie Forgan for some helpful suggestions.

NOTES

1   The use of the term 'black box' in the sociology of science was introduced by Bruno Latour in *Science in Action* to refer to 'a well-established fact or an unproblematic object' (Latour 1987: 131) or more specifically as 'an automaton . . . [involving] a large number of elements . . . made to act as one' (ibid.).

2   As is nicely implied in the title of Nick Merriman's analysis of museum visiting, *Beyond the Glass Case* (1991).

3   The sociology and anthropology of science in general, and particularly the social study of scientific knowledge and feminist analysis, have been concerned with such questions. For some overviews see Franklin (1995); Harding (1986); Law (1991); Nader (1996a); Star (1988); Traweek (1993); Woolgar (1988a).

4 A distinction is sometimes made in science studies and in the social sciences more generally between knowledge and practice. My characterization of knowledge here, however, is intended to incorporate both.

5 Foucault makes this point in a different context in *The History of Sexuality* (1979). This is not the same as saying that the State is not involved in the regulation of individuals and populations.

6 The 'encoding'/'decoding' vocabulary is from Hall's classic account of a textual approach to media (Hall 1980). For an account of a range of textual approaches to material culture see Tilley (1990); and for a brief discussion in relation to museums see Macdonald (1996).

7 See Bedini (1965); Findlen (1994); Impey and MacGregor (1985).

8 See Findlen (1994: 134–46), for a fascinating discussion of visitors to these museums, particularly that of Aldrovandi.

9 For an insightful theoretical account and illustration of museums 'rid[ing] the juggernaut of modernity's contradictions' see Fyfe (1996).

10 For discussion see Bennett (1995, especially ch. 3); Duncan (1995); Hooper-Greenhill (1992: ch. 7); Kaplan (1994).

11 For discussion of the Great Exhibition see Altick (1978); Bennett (1995 *passim.*); Greenhalgh (1988); and for more general discussions of universal exhibitions see Benedict (1983), Coombes (1994), Harvey (1996) and Chapter 8 this volume, and Rydell (1993).

12 It should be noted that dates of 'establishment' are not always clear cut and these should, therefore, be taken as approximations.

13 Anthropological collections during this period generally covered both cultural ('ethnological') and physical aspects of anthropology, though some collections focused more on one aspect than the other. For discussion of anthropological museums see Ames (1992), Clifford (1997), Haraway (1989), Jenkins (1994), Jones (1992), Jordanova (1989) Stocking (1985).

14 There are, however, national differences here which deserve further research. For example, neither Spain nor Italy established national museums of scientific or technological history (Begeron 1993).

15 For other discussion of the architecture of museums and related spaces in this period see Markus (1993); Outram (1996).

16 There is a large sociological literature discussing such transformations. See, for example, Giddens (1990), Lash and Urry (1994), Waters (1995).

17 For discussion see Bolton (1992), Hunter (1991), and McGuigan (1996, ch. 1).

18 See Linenthal and Engelhardt (1996).

19 Here the book by Gross and Levitt (1994) has been central in the 'backlash' against social perspectives on science. See Gieryn (Chapter 12), Nader (1996a) and Social Text (1996) for discussion.

20 For an analysis of Greenfield Village see Staudenmaier (1993).

21 For discussion of industrial heritage see, for example, Alfrey and Putnam (1992); Bennett (1995: ch. 4); Butler (1992: ch. 4); Fowler (1992); Walsh (1992).

22 For discussion of the ecomuseum movement see Alfrey and Putnam (1992); Begeron (1993); Hoyau (1988); Poulot (1994).

23 For overviews see McGuigan (1996: ch. 6); Urry (1996); Walsh (1992).

24 He also knew first hand how political definitions could affect the course of a scientific career, having been made an outcast during the McCarthy era on account of a brief period of Communist Party membership.

25 For other examples see Ross (1995), and various examples in Karp, Kreamer and Lavine (1992), Karp and Lavine (1991) and Pearce (1996).

26 The term 'experiment' here is used to indicate the parallel with developments within

anthropology to 'write culture' or present ethnographic research in new ways (for discussion see for example Clifford and Marcus (1986); James, Hockey and Dawson (1997); Rosaldo (1993)). There has also been analogous critique in other disciplines, including the sociology of science (see for example Law (1993); Woolgar (1988b)).

REFERENCES

Alfrey, J. and T. Putnam (1992) *The Industrial Heritage*, London: Routledge.

Altick, R. (1978) *The Shows of London*, Cambridge, MA and London: The Belknap Press of Harvard University Press.

Ames, M. (1992) *Cannibal Tours and Glass Boxes: The Anthropology of Museums* (2nd edition), Vancouver: University of British Columbia Press.

Anderson, B. (1983) *Imagined Communities: Reflections on the Origin and Spread of Nationalism*, London: Verso.

Bedini, S. (1965) 'The evolution of science museums', *Technology and Culture*, 6, pp. 1–29.

Begeron, L. (1993) 'The new generation of museums: technical, industrial and "eco-museums"', in B. Schroeder-Gudehus (ed.) *Industrial Society and its Museums, 1880–1990: Social Aspirations and Cultural Politics*, pp. 91–5, Chur, Switzerland: Harwood Academic/Paris: Cité des sciences et de l'industrie.

Benedict, B. (1983) *The Anthropology of World's Fairs*, London: Scolar Press.

Bennett, T. (1995) *The Birth of the Museum*, London: Routledge.

Bolton, R. (ed.) (1992) *Culture Wars: Documents from the Recent Controversies in the Arts*, New York: New Press.

Butler, S. (1992) *Science and Technology Museums*, Leicester, London and New York: Leicester University Press.

Clifford, J. (1997) *Routes*, Cambridge MA: Harvard University Press.

Clifford, J. and G. Marcus (eds) (1986) *Writing Culture: The Poetics and Politics of Ethnography*, Berkeley, CA: University of California Press.

Coombes, A. E. (1994) *Reinventing Africa: Material Culture and Popular Imagination in Late Victorian and Edwardian England*, New Haven, CT: Yale University Press.

Duncan, C. (1995) *Civilizing Rituals*, London: Routledge.

Durant, J. (1992) 'Introduction', in J. Durant (ed.) *Museums and the Public Understanding of Science*, pp. 7–11, London: Science Museum in association with the Committee on the Public Understanding of Science.

Findlen, P. (1994) *Possessing Nature: Museums, Collecting, and Scientific Culture in Early Modern Italy*, Berkeley and Los Angeles, CA: California University Press.

Forgan, S. (1994) 'The architecture of display: museums, universities and objects in nineteenth-century Britain', *History of Science*, 32 (2), pp. 139–62.

—— (1996) '"A nightmare of incomprehensible machines": science and technology museums in the 19th and 20th centuries', in M. Pointon (ed.) *Museums and Late Twentieth Century Culture*, pp. 46–68, Manchester: Manchester University Press.

Foucault, M. (1970) *The Order of Things: An Archaeology of the Human Sciences* (trans. A. Sheridan), London: Tavistock.

—— (1977) *Discipline and Punish: The Birth of the Prison* (trans. A. Sheridan), London: Allen Lane.

—— (1979) *The History of Sexuality, Volume 1: An Introduction* (trans. R. Hurley), London: Allen Lane.

—— (1991) 'Governmentality', in G. Burchill, C. Gordon and P. Miller (eds) *The Foucault Effect: Studies in Governmentality*, Hemel Hempstead: Harvester Wheatsheaf.

Fowler, P. J. (1992) *The Past in Contemporary Society: Then, Now*, London: Routledge.

Franklin, S. (1995) 'Science as culture, cultures of science', *Annual Review of Anthropology*, 24, pp. 163–84.

Fyfe, G. (1996) 'A Trojan Horse at the Tate: theorizing the museum as agency and structure', in S. Macdonald and G. Fyfe (eds) *Theorizing Museums*, pp. 203–28, Oxford: Blackwell.

Giddens, A. (1990) *The Consequences of Modernity*, Cambridge: Polity.

Greenhalgh, P. (1988) *Ephemeral Vistas: The Expositions Universelles, Great Exhibitions and World's Fairs, 1851–1939*, Manchester: Manchester University Press.

Gross, P. R. and N. Levitt (1994) *Higher Superstition: The Academic Left and its Quarrel with Science*, Baltimore, MD: Johns Hopkins University Press.

Hackman, W. (1992) '"Wonders in one closet shut": the educational potential of history of science museums', in J. Durant (ed.) *Museums and the Public Understanding of Science*, pp. 65–9, London: Science Museum in association with the Committee on the Public Understanding of Science.

Hall, S. (1980) 'Encoding/decoding', in S. Hall, D. Hobson, A. Lowe and P. Willis (eds) *Culture, Media, Language*, pp. 128–38, London: Hutchinson.

Haraway, D. (1989) *Private Visions*, London: Routledge.

Harding, S. (1986) *The Science Question in Feminism*, Milton Keynes: Open University Press.

Harvey, P. (1996) *Hybrids of Modernity: Anthropology, the Nation-state and the Universal Exhibition*, London: Routledge.

Hein, H. (1990) *The Exploratorium: The Museum as Laboratory*, Washington, DC: Smithsonian Institution.

Hewison, R. (1988) *The Heritage Industry*, London: Methuen.

Hooper-Greenhill, E. (1992) *Museums and the Shaping of Knowledge*, London: Routledge.

Hoyau, P. (1988) 'Heritage and "the conserver society": the French case' (trans. C. Turner), in R. Lumley (ed.) *The Museum Time-machine*, pp. 27–35, London: Comedia/Routledge.

Hunter, J. D. (1991) *Culture Wars: The Struggle to Define America*, New York: Basic Books.

Impey, O. R. and A. G. MacGregor (eds) (1985) *The Origins of Museums*, Oxford: Clarendon Press.

Irwin, A. and B. Wynne (1996) 'Introduction', in A. Irwin and B. Wynne (eds) *Misunderstanding Science? The Public Reconstruction of Science and Technology*, pp. 1–17, Cambridge: Cambridge University Press.

James, A., J. Hockey and A. Dawson (eds) (1997) *After Writing Culture*, London: Routledge.

Jenkins, D. (1994) 'Object lessons and ethnographic displays: museum exhibitions and the making of American anthropology', *Comparative Studies in Society and History*, 36 (2), pp. 242–70.

Jones, D. (1992) 'Dealing with the past', *Museums Journal* (January), pp. 24–7.

Jordanova, L. (1989) 'Objects of knowledge: a historical perspective on museums,' in P. Vergo (ed.) *The New Museology*, pp. 22–40, London: Reaktion Books.

Kaplan, F. E. S. (ed.) (1994) *Museums and the Making of "Ourselves": The Role of Objects in National Identity*, Leicester and London: Leicester University Press.

Karp, I. and S. Lavine (eds) (1991) *Exhibiting Cultures: The Poetics and Politics of Museum Display*, Washington, DC: Smithsonian Institution.

Karp, I., C. M. Kreamer and S. Lavine (eds) (1992) *Museums and Communities: The Politics of Public Culture*, Washington, DC: Smithsonian Institution.

Lash, S. and J. Urry (1994) *Economies of Signs and Space*, London: Sage.

Latour, B. (1987) *Science in Action*, Cambridge, MA: Harvard University Press.

Law, J. (1991) 'Introduction: monsters, machines and sociotechnical relations', in J. Law (ed.) *A Sociology of Monsters: Essays on Power, Technology and Domination* (*Sociological Review* monograph), pp. 1–23, London: Routledge.

—— (1993) *Organizing Modernity: Social Ordering and Social Theory*, Oxford: Blackwell.

Lewenstein, B.V. (1992) 'The meaning of "public understanding of science" in the United States after World War II', *Public Understanding of Science*, 1, pp. 45–68.

Lindqvist, T. (1993) 'An Olympic stadium of technology: Deutsches Museum and Sweden's Tekniska Museet', in B. Schroeder-Gudehus (ed.) *Industrial Society and its Museums, 1880–1990: Social Aspirations and Cultural Politics*, pp. 37–54, Chur, Switzerland: Harwood Academic/Paris: Cité des sciences et de l'industrie.

Linenthal, E. T. and T. Engelhardt (eds) (1996) *History Wars: The Enola Gay and Other Battles for the American Past*, New York: Metropolitan Books/Holt.

Macdonald, S. (1996) 'Theorizing museums: an introduction', in S. Macdonald and G. Fyfe (eds) *Theorizing Museums: Representing Identity and Diversity in a Changing World* (*Sociological Review* monograph), pp. 1–18, Oxford: Blackwell.

McGuigan, J. (1996) *Culture and the Public Sphere*, London: Routledge.

Markus, T. (1993) *Buildings and Power: Freedom and Control in the Origin of Modern Building Types*, London: Routledge.

Merriman, N (1991) *Beyond the Glass Case: The Past, the Heritage and the Public in Britain*, Leicester and London: Leicester University Press.

Mitchell, T. (1991) *Colonizing Egypt*, Berkeley and Los Angeles, CA: California University Press.

Nader, L. (ed.) (1996a) *Naked Science: Anthropological Inquiry into Boundaries, Power, and Knowledge*, London: Routledge.

—— (1996b) 'Preface', in L. Nader (ed.) *Naked Science: Anthropological Inquiry into Boundaries, Power, and Knowledge*, pp. xi–xv, London: Routledge.

Outram, D. (1996) 'New spaces in natural history', in N. Jardine, J. A. Secord and E. C. Spary (eds) *Cultures of Natural History*, pp. 249–65, Cambridge: Cambridge University Press.

Pearce, S. (ed.) (1996) *Exploring Science in Museums*, London and Atlantic Highlands, NJ: Athlone.

Pickstone, J. (1994) 'Museological science? The place of the analytical/comparative in nineteenth-century science, technology and medicine', *History of Science*, 32 (2), pp. 111–38.

Poulot, D. (1994) 'Identity as self-discovery: the ecomuseum in France', in D. Sherman and I. Rogoff (eds) *Museum Culture*, pp. 66–84, London: Routledge.

Prösler, M. (1996) 'Museums and globalization', in S. Macdonald and G. Fyfe (eds) *Theorizing Museums* (*Sociological Review* monograph), pp. 21–44, Oxford: Blackwell.

Rosaldo, R. (1993) *Culture and Truth: The Remaking of Social Analysis*, London: Routledge.

Ross, M. (1995) '"Passive smoking": controversy at the Science Museum?', *Science as Culture*, 5 (1), no. 22, pp. 147–51.

Rydell, R. W. (1984) *All the World's a Fair: Visions of Empire at American International Expositions, 1876–1916*, Chicago: Chicago University Press.

—— (1993) *World of Fairs: The Century-of-Progress Expositions*, Chicago: University of Chicago Press.

Shapin, S. (1994) *A Social History of Truth: Civility and Science in Seventeenth-century England*, Chicago: Chicago University Press.

Sheets-Pyenson, S. (1989) *Cathedrals of Science: The Development of Colonial Natural History Museums during the Late Nineteenth Century*, Montreal: McGill University Press.

Silverstone, R. (1989) 'Heritage as media: some implications for research', in D. Uzzell (ed.) *Heritage Interpretation, Volume 2: The Visitor Experience*, pp. 138–48, London: Frances Pinter.

—— (1992) 'The medium is the museum: on objects and logics in times and spaces', in J. Durant (ed.) *Museums and the Public Understanding of Science*, pp. 34–42, London: Science Museum in association with the Committee on the Public Understanding of Science.

Social Text (1996) (special issue on 'The Science Wars', ed. A. Ross), (Spring/Summer), 46–7.

Star, S. L. (1988) 'Introduction: the sociology of science and technology', *Social Problems*, 35, pp. 197–205.

Staudenmaier, J. M. (1993) 'Clean exhibits, messy exhibits: Henry Ford's technological aesthetic', in B. Schroeder-Gudehus (ed.) *Industrial Society and its Museums, 1880–1990: Social Aspirations and Cultural Politics*, pp. 55–65, Chur, Switzerland: Harwood Academic/Paris: Cité des sciences et de l'industrie.

Stocking, G. W. (ed.) (1985) *Objects and Others: Essays on Museums and Material Culture*, Madison, WI: Wisconsin University Press.

Tilley, C. (ed.) (1990) *Reading Material Culture*, Oxford: Blackwell.

Traweek, S. (1993) 'An introduction to cultural, gender, and social studies of science and technology', *Journal of Culture, Medicine and Psychiatry*, 17, pp. 3–25.

Urry, J. (1996) 'How societies remember the past', in S. Macdonald and G. Fyfe (eds) *Theorizing Museums*, pp. 45–65, Oxford: Blackwell.

Walsh, K. (1992) *The Representation of the Past: Museums and Heritage in the Post-modern world*, London: Routledge.

Waters, M. (1995) *Globalization*, London: Routledge.

Woolgar, S. (1988a) *Science: The Very Idea*, Chichester: Ellis Horwood/London: Tavistock.

—— (ed.) (1988b) *Knowledge and Reflexivity: New Frontiers in the Sociology of Knowledge*, London: Sage.

Wynne, B. (1996) 'Misunderstood misunderstandings: social identities and the public uptake of science', in A. Irwin and B. Wynne (eds) *Misunderstanding Science? The Public Reconstruction of Science and Technology*, pp. 19–46, Cambridge: Cambridge University Press.

Chapter 2

Speaking to the eyes
Museums, legibility and the social order

Tony Bennett

In 1885 an anonymous report from the Mineralogical and Geological Department to the Trustees of the Australian Museum recommended the adoption of a 'comprehensive system of exhibition' for the museum's geological collections. The virtue of the system, it was claimed, was that it would enhance the usefulness of those collections (it would help the public to 'understand better the usefulness and attraction of Lithology, Mineralogy, Geology and Palaeontology') by increasing their legibility ('the visitor will be enabled to *rapidly understand by sight what would require pages or books*') (Australian Museum: 5; emphasis in original). Intended 'to correlate the ideas of the visitor or student, by showing him plainly the natural connections between things', this comprehensive system of exhibition was designed with the needs of miners most clearly in mind. Here is how those needs were identified:

> Miners indeed visit the Museum in great numbers in order to obtain the information of which they feel themselves in want, but although they are a very intelligent class of people, they generally want instruction in elementary things which are quite necessary to their purpose, they often entertain wrong theories of their own, sometimes original enough, and they are used to point out at once the knot of any question in their own craft.
>
> They will soon get used to practically distinguish the most common kinds of minerals and rocks, they will, by natural disposition point out physical and regional differences which might have escaped the observation of scientific men, but they want science to be put before them in a popular light, which speaking to their eyes, spares their time, and remains deeply impressed on their memory.

In the Museum's existing displays, the report argued, the stress placed on purely mineralogical principles of classification entailed that 'the only connecting links between specimens' they made visible were those based on 'analogies in their chemical composition, and mode of crystallisation'. Useful though this may be to the specialist, the report admonishes that, 'of the very pith of the subject "*How minerals are formed*" it teaches nothing'. Contrasting this with the situation of the practical miner working 'in a disturbed country where rocks of dissimilar nature are exposed' and who will see in the 'nature of the vegetation or in the colours of the mountains' the '"indications" of the minerals of which he is in search', the report urges instead the automatic legibility of a system that would classify geological exhibits in terms of the modes of their occurrence:

> However, if the same miner had visited a collection in which *the modes of occurrence* of each valuable mineral are clearly exposed by a classification made according to the characters which distinguish each class of mineral deposit and each mode of occurrence, and if the minerals which generally occurred [*sic*] the outcrops are distinguished from those which generally occurred [*sic*] deeper levels; and the nature of the accompanying rocks, sedimentary or eruptive, is shown in connection with the ores and vein stuff which are found with them in each different class of deposit, then, *the miner will, at a glance, understand something of the science of mining.*
>
> If thence, the same miner is transported to the same disturbed country above alluded to he will find, in what such a classification has brought him, some points of comparison which will help him to unfold that problematical book of the earth, to find the boundaries of the different kinds of rocks, read the ways in which sedimentary or metamorphised rocks have been penetrated by eruptive rocks and mineral solutions, and seize some probable indications of the subsequent filling or impregnation of veins, cavities or strata by the rich mineral matter for which he is seeking.

The views are very similar to those of Archibald Livingstone, so much so that he may well have been their author. In his capacity as the Professor of Geology and Mineralogy at the University of Sydney, Livingstone submitted a lengthy report to the Australian Museum in 1880 outlining how the proposed development of a new Technological and Industrial Museum in Sydney might benefit from the experience of a range of European museums, including London's Museum of Practical Geology, the South Kensington Museum and its outpost in London's working-class East End, the Bethnal Green Museum. Throughout his report, Livingstone stressed the need for the organizing principles of displays in technological and industrial museums to be luminously transparent if they were to succeed in imparting useful knowledge to the working classes. Citing the view of a Professor Rankine that 'too much must not be expected from those who can only find time for study after a fatiguing day's work' (cited in Livingstone 1880: xxvi), Livingstone urged the need for the clear and detailed labelling of exhibits if the working man were not to be wearied by his visit and sent away dissatisfied.

My interest, however, lies less in the authorship of the 1885 report than in the general currency of the proposition that museums should 'speak to the eyes' and the arguments on which it drew. Indeed, from this point of view, the anonymity of the report is a part of its historical value in view of the way in which it simply takes for granted a view of the museum as an automated learning environment – that is, as a collection of objects whose meaning is to be rendered auto-intelligible through a combination of transparent principles of display and clear labelling – which, although in fact quite new, had become, by the 1880s, an accepted new *doxa* for museum practice. One of its most influential advocates was Henry Pitt Rivers, whose typological method aspired to order the arrangement of ethnological objects in a manner that would allow the direction and significance of human evolution to be taken in at a glance. Pitt Rivers's aim was to arrange his collections 'in such a manner that those who run may read' (Pitt Rivers 1891: 115–16). By 'those who run', Pitt Rivers meant the working classes. 'The more intelligent portion of the working classes', he says, 'though they have but little book learning, are extremely quick in appreciating all mechanical matters, more so even than highly educated men, because they are trained up to them; and this is another why the importance of the object lessons that museums are capable of teaching should be well considered' (ibid.: 116).

Although the cultural resonances underlying the phrase 'those who run' are now somewhat obscure, we may be sure that its significance was not lost on Pitt Rivers's contemporaries. It served both as a coded reference to the earlier tradition of civic humanism in English painting and art theory and as a challenge to the exclusions of that tradition in which mention of 'those who run' functioned as a shorthand expression for mechanics: that is, for members of the artisan classes whose occupation excluded them from any claim to be included in the public for art. This view was most influentially argued by Sir Joshua Reynolds, who contended that the occupational demands placed on mechanics – routine mechanical work with little free time for mentally improving forms of leisure – inhibited their capacity to acquire those generalizing intellectual abilities which, according to Reynolds, alone made it possible for the individual to acquire civic virtue through exposure to art. John Barry, a mid-century painter who sought to break with the restrictions that characterized Reynolds's conception of the public in arguing for a democratic public of taste that would include all men and women, retained a similar view of the mechanic and of the tensions that would result from his inclusion within the world of art. For this would entail the development of both new forms of painting and new ways of contextualizing art's display that would aspire to make the meaning of art – and hence, also, its capacity to transmit civic virtue – immediately communicable to 'the ignorant'. Yet, while recommending this course of action, Barry simultaneously warned of the dangers inherent in taking it too far, suggesting that when the content of a painting is 'so brought down to the understanding of the vulgar, that they who run may read', the result will be exhibitions of art which lack interest for 'intelligent' visitors as well as any capacity to develop the taste of the vulgar, since 'there will be nothing to improve or reward the attention even of the ignorant themselves, upon a second or third view' (cited in Barrell 1986: 188).

In arguing that museums should arrange their displays so that 'those who run may read', then, Pitt Rivers was signalling the importance he attached to the need for museums to reach working-class constituencies whose occupation had previously been grounds for their exclusion from the world of culture and knowledge. Yet the inclusion of such constituencies is not accompanied by any revaluation of the occupational limitations of those who labour for a living. Although, like the author of the Australian Museum report, Pitt Rivers stresses the lively practical intelligence of the working classes (they are 'extremely quick in appreciating all mechanical matters'), he points out that their capacity for abstract and theoretical thought is limited ('they have but little book learning'). The working-class visitor comes with an inherent deficiency which the museum must compensate for and overcome by the use of unambiguous classificatory principles, rational layout and use of space, and clear and descriptive labelling. These are mandatory changes if – in a new usage of the concept of public which itself signals the end of Reynolds's conception of the restricted liberal public for art – museums are to become effective instruments of public education. We accordingly find similar arguments repeated wherever the educational role of museums comes under discussion in the closing decades of the nineteenth century. The need for clear labels and display principles was endlessly debated at the annual conferences of the Museums Association (see Lewis 1989) and these practices found an influential national champion at the British Museum (Natural History) during the period of Sir William Henry Flower's directorship, when Flower's advocacy of the need for a pristine clarity in museum displays was widely circulated (see Flower 1898). When the British Association for the Advancement of Science (BAAS) conducted an inquiry into the conditions of provincial museums, it too stressed the need for the museum to present itself to its visitors as a readable text. 'A museum without labels', the report arising from the inquiry advises, 'is like an index torn out of a book; it may be amusing, but it teaches very little' (BAAS 1887: 127).

Similar arguments were found in the United States. They were perhaps most succinctly and most influentially expressed by George Brown Goode in his contention that, in order to serve as a means for increasing the knowledge, culture and enlightenment of the people, museums should regard their task as one of arranging a well-planned collection of instructive labels illustrated by well-selected specimens (Goode 1895). The question of public legibility was also very much to the fore in the advice the American Museum of Natural History received from Baron Osten Sacken:

If you present too many objects to an unscientific public the danger is that they will see nothing. If you place before a man, ignorant of natural history, an eagle and a hawk, he will easily observe the structural differences between them. But if you show him one hundred eagles and hawks of different size, shape and color, collected in all the different countries of the world, your man will glare at them, but see nothing and remember nothing. And such is the effect produced on the public generally by larger collections, as those of the British Museum, of the Berlin Museum, etc. Instead of displaying the specimens in the most advantageous light, in the most striking position, such collections, from the multiplicity of objects and the consequent want of space, are obliged to crowd them as much as possible. Hundreds of specimens are crowded in a comparatively narrow space, without sufficient indication of the division in species, genera and families. A walk through a long suit of halls, thus filled, affords more fatigue than amusement, or instruction.

(cited in Gratacap n.d.: chapter 2, p. 63)

Assuming that 'what is needed now, is a collection for the instruction and amusement of the public at large', the good Baron goes on to propose that such a collection should consist solely of representatives of the most common North American mammals and birds. If such a collection is to 'be presented to the eye of the public in the most instructive and attractive manner', then, the Baron argues, 'let the names be distinctly written, the scientific divisions in families and orders clearly indicated; the specimens not too crowded'.

Wherever we might care to look, then, we find, throughout the last quarter of the nineteenth century, a new and distinctive emphasis being placed on the need to arrange and label museum displays in ways calculated to enhance their public legibility by making their meaning instantly readable for the new mass public which the museum increasingly saw as its most important target audience. 'It may be insisted, indeed', argued L. P. Gratacap, natural history curator at the American Museum of Natural History, 'that the careful luminous exhibition and exposition of its collections, so that the public may fully understand them, and learn their lessons, is the chief purpose of the Museum. This work sedulously followed involves not simply a display of labelled objects, but a sequence and order that may teach a lesson' (ibid.: 88). As Baron Osten Sacken's formulations suggest, however, this is not just a matter of new labelling practices. It involves a fundamental reconception of the status and role of the museum object which now forms part of a rationalized exhibition space in which both objects and the relations between them have been thorough-goingly bureaucratized in order that they might serve as the instruments of the museum's commitment to a new form of public didacticism (see Bennett 1995a: 39–44).

Why should this have been so? The stress in most available accounts of this *fin de siècle* development has typically been placed on the importance that was accorded the museum as an instrument for the maintenance of social order (see, for example, Coombes 1988, 1994; van Keuren 1989). In the context of the labour unrest of the period from the 1870s on and the increasing influence of mass-based socialist organizations, the museum, such accounts suggest, was increasingly enlisted in the cause of public education in view of the role it was believed it could play in translating a conservative reading of the implications of evolutionary thought into a physically sensuous and readily comprehensible form with wide appeal. There is much to recommend this line of reasoning, and not just as a retrospective theoretical explanation: there is ample evidence that this is precisely what some contemporary museum administrators and educators thought they were doing. When Albert Bickmore, the founder of the public education programmes at the American Museum of Natural History (AMNH), met Sir William Flower in 1893/4 he thus recorded his impression that 'the great minds which are moulding the destinies of the British nation' were in agreement with the AMNH's assessment 'that that individual and that community and that nation, which is the best educated will be the one which will survive in the great contest of which the labour troubles in our country and in England during that summer were but the distant mutterings of a coming tempest which will sooner or later burst upon the civilised world' (Bickmore n.d.: 121), and outlined the steps being taken in both countries to help museums contribute to this task.

There are, however, a number of shortcomings with such accounts. This is not to suggest that questions of social order were not centrally at issue in the changing museum debates and practices which characterized this period. They were, and with a degree of insistence and urgency that has rarely been rivalled since. Rather, my point concerns how we should understand the role that museums were called on to play in relation to the social order and the part that the new principles of public legibility were expected to perform in enabling museums to fulfil that role. There are three issues at stake here, and although it would be interesting to continue exploring these comparatively across national boundaries, I shall henceforth limit my attention to the British context in identifying these issues and examining their implications.

The first concerns the need to revalue the extent to which museums over this period functioned as instruments of a conservative hegemony in helping to maintain the existing social order. I shall suggest that this neglects the degree to which many of the leading museum administrators and theorists of the period were liberal reformers who, far from espousing a commitment to the *status quo*, valued museums for the contributions they might make in facilitating an ordered and regulated transformation of the existing social order. This helps, to come to the second issue, to account for the stress that was placed on the need for museum displays to be publicly legible. This is difficult to explain if our attention focuses solely on how museums were viewed in the context of contemporary social and political events. The influence of discursive events must also be taken into account. If the question of legibility was to the fore in museum debates and practices, this was centrally because a succession of discursive events – the revolutions in geology and in natural history – entailed that the script of the museum had to be modified in order to represent a new discursive order. Viewed in this light, the museum's task was not so much to shore up the existing social order as to provide the script for a new one, and to provide its visitors with new discursive positions within that order. If it was so important that the museum be read, this was because it offered both a new way of writing the social order and new social inscriptions for social actors; new ways of inserting persons discursively within social and historical relations and of defining their tasks within those relations. The third issue I want to focus on is closely related. It concerns the emphasis that was placed on incorporating principles of auto-intelligibility into museum displays, so that their meaning might be understood directly and without assistance. I shall suggest that this derived primarily from the principles of liberal government and the need for the production of persons who would be increasingly self-directing and self-managing.

Let's look more closely at the first of these issues. In doing so, it is, of course, important to be discriminating, for it was as true then as it is now that museums vary significantly with regard to their philosophies and practices. It is clear, however, that those museums which could most intelligibly be described as conservative were *not* those most involved in arguing the need for new forms of transparency in the organization of museum displays. The British Museum, as it had throughout most of the century, conspicuously dragged its feet, resisting the need for any thoroughgoing revision of its practices. Those who pressed the pace of reform – William Henry Flower at the British Museum (Natural History), Edward Forbes at the Museum of Economic Geology, Henry Pitt Rivers – represented varying shades of liberal opinion in both its Anglican and Dissenting versions. Nor was it any accident that the need for museums to 'speak to all eyes' was pursued most energetically in geological, ethnological and natural history museums. For these were at the forefront of the contest between traditional Tory and Anglican conceptions of the social order – most forcefully, if ambiguously, championed by Richard Owen at the British Museum – and the new liberal social scripts which, at least in the British context, comprised the most immediately influential interpretation of the implications of Darwin's evolutionary categories. In these ways, the advocacy of new forms of public legibility in museums was closely associated with those organizations – the British Association for the Advancement of Science, the Ethnological Society, the 'X-Club' – concerned to identify how the new evolutionary paradigms derived from the natural and historical sciences might contribute to the development of new forms of liberalism in which norms for conduct were to be derived, in some measure, from the laws of evolution. Huxley is a crucial mediating figure here in view of his general advocacy of a species of liberalism based on evolutionary principles; of the support he offered Flower in restructuring the British Museum (Natural History) along Darwinian lines; and of the influence of his public lectures at the Government School of Mines, at the London Institution and, later, in the Sunday Evenings for the People he conducted for the Sunday League, in developing a public didactics which converted the lessons of nature into a morality directed at the working man.

In writing to Frederick Dyster in 1855 outlining the purpose of his London Institution lectures, Huxley indicated that he aimed to show the working classes 'that physical virtue is the base of all other, and that they are to be clean & temperate & all the rest, not because fellows in black with white ties tell them so, but because these are plain and patent laws of nature' (cited in Desmond 1994: 210). In glossing this passage, Adrian Desmond suggests that, by viewing nature as the new source of moral sanction, Huxley aimed to effect a shift in the basis of social authority from the priesthood to a new class of scientific professionals committed to the development of a competitive and technocratic society. Some aspects of the argument were to change. By the 1890s, Huxley, adopting a position similar to that advocated by Mill in his famous essay on nature, denied that nature could furnish a template for morality just as he also denied that the laws of natural evolution could provide any guarantee for the continued furtherance of social evolution. If morality consisted precisely in opposing the influence of socially derived ethical codes to the unmitigated effects of the natural law of the survival of the fittest, Huxley argued in *Evolution and Ethics* (1894), it was equally true that natural processes of competition stood in need of a cultural supplement if they were to serve as a template for social development. What did not change, however, either for Huxley or for his contemporaries, was the urgent need to render nature readable in new ways in view of its potential to serve as the source of new social scripts.

Although those scripts were, in varied ways, evolutionary in character, it is doubtful whether their use in museums is adequately accounted for if seen solely or even mainly as part of a conservative ruling-class response to an increasingly socialistic working class. The main difficulty with this view is its lack of an appropriately specific understanding of the discursive context and of the challenges this presented liberal and reforming opinion which, by and large, remained the driving force behind the new directions in museum policies and practices. On the one hand, there was the need to render nature readable in such a way that its message would undermine the natural underpinnings of both traditional forms of Anglican and Tory social authority and the Lamarckian tradition of evolutionary thought which had nurtured the development of working-class radicalism. On the other hand, there was the need to replace such conceptions with a new reading of nature which, in representing social evolution as the outcome of a multitude of minor and accumulative adaptations to changing circumstances resulting from competitive struggle, aimed to hitch evolutionary thought to the task of the continuing reformation of society in accordance with meritocratic principles by stimulating a 'regulated restlessness' that both encouraged progress as a moral imperative while simultaneously curbing it within limits consistent with the principles of gradual social evolution (see Bennett 1997). The importance of making nature readable, of speaking to the eyes so that all might see, of coding nature's messages into the artefactual environment of the museum as a place where new social scripts and their requirements might be learned and rehearsed, is more readily intelligible when it is clear that what was at issue in this process was the mounting of a challenge to other social scripts, the forms of authority on which they rested and the forms of conduct they implied. The distinctions were fine ones and if 'those who run' were to appreciate them and their significance, the provision of an artefactual regime whose organizing principles would be luminously transparent to all was a pressing necessity.

This was especially so if visitors were to learn and absorb the museum's messages alone and unaided except for the assistance of the rationalized exhibits and their clear and distinct – but solely descriptive – labels. For in a way which marks this period as distinctive, the relationship of the visitor to the museum was envisaged as an autodidactic one. While didactic props such as labels and descriptive catalogues were provided, the visitor's route through the museum was typically unguided. The personalized forms of tour which had characterized institutions like the British Museum prior to the period of mid-century reform were no longer available. Similarly, the older forms of group tour led by unqualified guides associated with institutions like the Tower of London had been roundly criticized and deemed inadequate for the civilizing tasks of the public museum in view of their tendency to substitute an imposed collective reading in lieu of the individualized forms of response which liberal theories of pedagogy required (see Bennett 1995b). And the trained museum guide – or, in American usage, docent – was still a thing of the future. Spurred on by Lord Sudley's influential advocacy, a number of leading museums appointed trained educational guides towards the end of the first decade of the twentieth century, and the resulting 'guide movement' was a major topic of debate at the annual conferences of the Museums Association in the immediately pre-war period (see Kavanagh 1994: 18–21). At the 1913 conference, for example, both Cecil Hallett and J. H. Leonard – the first holding a Bachelor of Arts degree and the second a Bachelor of Science – presented papers summarizing their experiences as, respectively, the Official Guides at the British Museum and the British Museum (Natural History), and suggesting how guides might best perform their function of imparting knowledge to a general public with varying levels of education. The change this entailed in the museum's organization of the visitor's sensorium was clearly summarized by the terms in which Hallett concluded his address:

> The public, as a rule, are not given to the study of guide books, nor to the reading of labels – excellent though these may be, and indeed are in the Bloomsbury galleries; and if there is one thing more clearly shown than another by the experience of the past two years and a half, it is that nothing can bring the general public and a museum into a right relation with each other so well as the living voice of a human expositor.
>
> (Hallett 1913: 200)

This is, of course, only a glimpse of a new technology of visitor management, one in which the museum was to speak to the ears as well as the eyes. For the greater part of the later nineteenth century, however, the visitor was treated solely as an individualized source of sight while the museum itself was envisaged largely as a sphere of visibility. This was not new. In the course of the French Revolution, the revolutionary requirement for transparency in the organization of public life and the insistence that the meaning of civic rituals and institutions should be rendered publicly legible to and for all citizens had led Alexandre

Lenoir, in establishing the Musée des monuments français, to borrow a principle of eighteenth-century architectural discourse, which had required that the exteriors of buildings should convey a transparent meaning that would enable them to serve as 'speaking monuments', in suggesting that the museum should aim to 'speak to all eyes' (*parler à tous les yeux*) (cited in Vidler 1986: 141). What had started off as an element of Enlightenment architectural discourse and had subsequently been transformed into an aspiration of revolutionary cultural and civic policy had, by the end of the nineteenth century, been again transformed into a governmentally organized form of public legibility through which citizens, in being equipped to read the new social scripts proposed by liberal and reforming versions of evolutionary theory, were to learn both their new places and what was required of them if they were to be effectively inscribed into and conscripted for the new competitive and progressive ways of being in time which liberal versions of evolutionary thought proposed.

REFERENCES

Australian Museum, Series 24: Curators' Reports to the Trustees, Box 1: 1881–1887.

Barrell, J. (1986) *The Political Theory of Painting From Reynolds to Hazlitt: 'The Body of the Public'*, New Haven, CN and London: Yale University Press.

Bennett, T. (1995a) *The Birth of the Museum: History, Theory, Policy*, London: Routledge.

—— (1995b) 'The multiplication of culture's utility', *Critical Inquiry*, 24 (1).

—— (1997) 'Regulated restlessness: museums, liberal government and the historical sciences', *Economy and Society* 26 (2).

Bickmore, A. S. (n.d.) 'Autobiography with a historical sketch of the founding and early development of the American Museum of Natural History', unpublished manuscript, American Museum of Natural History.

British Association for the Advancement of Science (1887) *Report of the Committee of the Provincial Museums of the UK.*

Coombes, A. E. (1988) 'Museums and the formation of national and cultural identities', *Oxford Art Journal*, 11 (2).

—— (1994) *Reinventing Africa: Museums, Material Culture and Popular Imagination*, New Haven, CN and London: Harvard University Press.

Desmond, A. (1994) *Huxley: The Devil's Disciple*, London: Michael Joseph.

Flower, Sir W. H. (1898) *Essays on Museums and Other Subjects Connected with Natural History*, London: Macmillan & Co.

Goode, G. B. (1895) *The Principles of Museum Administration*, York: Coultas & Volans.

Gratacap, L. P. (n.d.) 'History of the American Museum of Natural History', (manuscript held at the American Museum of Natural History).

Hallett, Cecil (1913) 'The work of a guide demonstrator', *Museums Journal*, 13.

Huxley, T. H. (1894) *Evolution and Ethics* in J. Paradis and G. C. Williams (1989) *Evolution and Ethics: T. H. Huxley's* Evolution and Ethics *with New Essays on its Victorian and Sociobiological Context*, Princeton, NJ: Princeton University Press.

Kavanagh, G. (1994) *Museums and the First World War: A Social History*, London and New York: Leicester University Press

van Keuren, D. K. (1989) 'Museums and ideology: Augustus Pitt Rivers, anthropology museums, and social change in later Victorian Britain', in P. Brantlinger (ed.) (1989) *Energy and Entropy: Science and Culture in Victorian Britain*, Bloomington and Indianapolis, IN: Indiana University Press.

Leonard, J. H. (1913) 'A museum guide and his work', *Museums Journal*, 13.

Lewis, G. (1989) *For Instruction and Recreation: A Century History of the Museums Association*, London: Quiller Press.

Livingstone, A. (1880) *Report upon certain Museums for Technology, Science, and Art, also upon Scientific, Professional, and Technical Instruction and Systems of Evening Classes in Great Britain and on the Continent of Europe*, Sydney: Government Printer.

Pitt Rivers, H. (1891) 'Typological museums, as exemplified by the Pitt-Rivers Museum at Oxford, and his Provincial Museum at Farnham', *Journal of the Society of Arts*, 40.

Vidler, A. (1986) 'Gregoir, Lenoir et les "monuments parlants"', in J-C. Bornet (ed.) *La Carmagole des Muses*, Paris: Armand Colin.

Chapter 3

The visibility of difference
Nineteenth-century French anthropological collections

Nélia Dias

The study of difference, ethnic as well as cultural, lies at the very roots of anthropological knowledge. The process through which difference comes to be *seen, named and exhibited*, however, is historically and culturally situated, such that one can retrace lines of both continuity and rupture. This chapter examines the visual processes of constituting racial difference, and their theoretical and epistemological presuppositions. When and why does racial difference begin to be represented when previously it had not been? And what was the role of exhibiting difference? Here I examine the close links between the anthropological study of racial difference and the constitution of collections, museums and exhibitions. I also explore the relationships between collections and anthropological knowledge, and the place of both within a broader complex of visual representations.

My account focuses on anthropological collections associated with institutions whose remit was explicitly scientific, namely, the Museum of Natural History (Paris) and the Anthropological Society of Paris. Because my aim is to highlight the assumptions and implications inherent in modes of representation deemed 'scientific' according to the conventions of the day, I exclude from the analysis phrenological collections and those displayed at fairs.

OBJECTS OF ANTHROPOLOGY

Anthropology in France in the second half of the nineteenth century was regarded by its main proponents as a broad science, or natural history, of Man, incorporating physical anthropology, prehistoric archaeology, and ethnography. Following the founding of the Anthropological Society of Paris in 1859 by Paul Broca (1824–1880), French anthropology was rapidly institutionalized through journals, laboratories and collections, and this helped to define its field of investigation and contributed to its growing influence abroad. However, this initial conception of anthropology as a broad complex of sciences soon gave way to a more restricted notion of anthropology as physical anthropology, and the study of cultural facts was subordinated to the biological. In this it differed from the

Anglo-American conception of the discipline, in which anthropology included physical anthropology, linguistics, prehistoric archaeology and ethnology.

Anthropological collections in the nineteenth century seem to have been constituted specifically in order to demonstrate racial differences. Samuel George Morton (1799–1851), who is credited with making one of the first systematic collections of skulls (Meigs 1857), wrote that:

> The principal object in making the following collection has been to compare the character of the skull in the different races of men, and these again with the skulls of the lower animals, and especially with reference to the internal capacity of the cranium as indicative of the size of the brain.
>
> (Morton 1844: Prefatory Note to the second edition)

As he recalled on many occasions, his collection had been created in response to the impossibility of finding materials to 'illustrate' an anatomy course. It was, then, an *a priori* conception of racial difference which guided the development of collections and the founding of craniology, a sub-discipline which lay at the heart of nineteenth century anthropology. On the basis of an assumption of the existence of diverse human races, there followed research into, and the 'discovery' of, differentiating characteristics between them, beginning with those which appeared on the face and the skull, but leading into less visible features. For Broca 'craniology provides not only first order characteristics for distinguishing between and classifying the subdivisions of humankind; it also provides precious data on the intellectual worth of these partial groups' (Broca 1866: 7). While craniometric studies can be said to have begun with Louis Daubenton (1716–1800), the eighteenth-century concern had been only to investigate the distinctions between humans and animals. Differences between human 'races' only became a subject of interest in the nineteenth century. As one commentator remarked of craniology's 'founding father': 'Daubenton did not know how to recognize in even the most typical of these bony heads a single marked character that would distinguish them from those of our nation' (Hamy 1907: 261). During the course of the nineteenth century, however, craniology developed a complete system of measurement employing specific instruments and specific indices capable of making fine comparisons between both races and individuals (Delisle n.d.: 642). At the same time, anthropology increasingly sought to establish itself as a recognized discipline in the eyes of scholars and the general public. Collections of objects were, as we shall see, also bound up with these institutional aspirations. They provided tangible evidence of the classificatory and deductive skills of anthropology and of the racial differences which anthropology identified. In this way they played an important part in the methodological and theoretical consecration of difference.

Methodological and theoretical arguments were invoked by anthropologists to justify the privilege they accorded to the study of physical, rather than linguistic and ethnographic, features. These arguments rested in particular on a deep conviction 'that physical organization, especially craniological characters, governed the development of psychic capacities' (Williams 1994: 259). Broca explained:

> In the first instance, the study of the formation of the head, provides precious data for a parallel anatomy of races; furthermore, the skull contains the brain, which is the organ of thought, and whose appearance influences the phenomena of intelligence as well as the exterior configuration of the head.
>
> (Broca 1861a: 139)

As Nancy Stepan has argued:

> Human variation and difference were not experienced 'as they really are, out there in nature', but by and through a metaphorical system that structured the experience and understanding of difference and that in essence created the objects of difference.
>
> (Stepan 1993: 362)

In their search for differentiating characteristics of the skull and of the face in human groups, anthropological studies focused on the Other – inferior races, women, idiots, criminals. In the process, they confirmed the latter as objects of difference and otherness.

VISUALIZING DIFFERENCE

Anthropologists in the second half of the nineteenth century set about establishing sources of data – collections of skulls and skeletons – by and through which differentiating physical features could be made visible. However, the features which anthropologists attempted to 'reveal' were not simply whatever was *visible* but only those features which were *observable* under a disciplined gaze and with the assistance of instruments of observation and measurement.

Collections, by arranging specimens into series and presenting particular types and exemplars, put observed difference on display. This provided a supplement to and a substitute for verbal descriptions by presenting the results in the form of numbers. In this way, collections played a part in anthropology's quest for a new – visual and numerical – language which would avoid 'subjective impressions' underlying textual descriptions. Along with the development of exhibitionary spaces they also provided a means of making difference visible to the public and inscribing it into the memory of visitors. This was a major reason why the comparative anatomy of human races and the study of physical remains (skeletons, skulls, crania) was privileged over physiology and the study of functions and processes in the living.

The emphasis on anatomical facts – conceived as 'natural' rather than 'cultural' – raised anthropology's status to that of a science of observation; and by implication differences were 'naturalized' by and through collections. Collections were, then, closely associated with a perceived transformation of anthropology from being a speculative endeavour to having proper scientific status. As Broca observed:

Since rich materials of study have accumulated in public museums and particular collections, it [anthropology] has become a true science of observation. The study of material objects, whose description and interest may easily be discussed and inspected, has replaced more or less ingenious conjectures and more or less seductive hypotheses which neither lend themselves to a direct demonstration nor to direct refutation. It is for this reason that we clearly see that in every country anthropological advances follow the development of anthropological collections.

(Broca 1878a: 328)

AUTHENTICATION

Creating collections involved obtaining and identifying skulls and skeletons, and assuring their authenticity. Throughout the nineteenth century the provenance and attribution of specimens received were carefully registered. However, the ways of obtaining materials and the criteria of validation underwent changes. In the 1840s, Samuel Morton was typical in acquiring specimens from 'respectable' donors, such as 'Dr Dournik... A Dutchman of noble family' (Morton 1844: 12). What was deemed important was the aristocratic origin or the gentlemanly status of the donor together with their personal experience. As he wrote of another of his sources:

Mr Gliddon's residence for the greater part of 23 years in Egypt, and his varied official and other avocations, together with his acquaintances with the people, and their language, have given him unusual facilities for collecting the requisite materials; while their authenticity is amply vouched for by one who blends the character of a gentleman with the attainments of a scholar

(Morton 1846: 93)

In the 1860s, as anthropology gained disciplinary autonomy, this changed dramatically. For the first time, the good faith of donors of noble origin was considered insufficient as evidence of authenticity. In part this was because materials were increasingly received from a much wider range of sources, such as graveyards, archaeological excavations, anatomy rooms and morgues. What authenticated these specimens in the eyes of the expanding anthropological community was not their *origins* but the scientific procedures to which they were subject. Through the practice of dissection, conducted in a specific place – the laboratory – in the presence of an audience made up of colleagues, cadavers were transformed into scientifically dismembered bodies. The laboratory was thus a veritable ante-chamber of the museum. It was the space in which scientifically authenticated artefacts, and in effect scientific 'facts', were produced.

FACTS

The whole nineteenth-century French school of anthropology was marked by a cult of facts, in which there was a constant preoccupation with distinguishing facts from interpretations and the objective from the subjective. Despite this, as has been well shown by Stephen Jay Gould: 'Broca and his school used facts as illustrations, not as constraining documents. They began with conclusions, peered through their facts, and came back in a circle to the same conclusions' (Gould 1981: 74). What is at issue, then, is their conceptions of scientificity, truth and objectivity.

In its quest for scientific legitimization, anthropology took medicine as its model. According to Broca 'In order to give anthropology a solid foundation, it must follow the example of medicine in grouping all findings around the most certain facts, that is to say anatomical facts' (Broca 1878b: 174). Broca's claim of a common scientific method was the beginning of a rhetorical argument about the scientific status of anthropology modelled on an already established discipline. Broca's anthropology emphasized the links between the brain and intellectual and mental capacities in order to disassociate itself from vitalist and ethical perspectives (Williams 1994). As Elizabeth Williams has argued, the separation of the intellectual and the moral 'relieved anthropology of the burden of moral fatalism and, perhaps more important given its embrace of neutral scientism, of the very appearance of involvement in moral concerns' (ibid.: 263).

Disciples of facts, nineteenth-century anthropologists repeatedly proclaimed their distrust of theory. As one of Broca's own disciples, Paul Topinard, wrote of his master: 'Repudiating all theory, relying completely on work, he patiently amassed numbers, let them speak for themselves and made craniometry a mathematical science' (Topinard 1891: 132–3). However, the 'discovery' of facts was, of course, dependent on methodological procedures, especially rules of observation. The human body was not directly legible but only offered itself up to the gaze of the scholars by means of rigorous instruments of observation and measurement. However, if facts were regarded as objective and theory-free they should not be contested, as Broca emphasized in his controversy with Louis-Pierre Gratiolet; the disagreement 'centred on the interpretation of facts far more than on the facts themselves' (Broca 1861a: 301). 'Interpretation' was regarded as separate from the facts themselves, which were regarded as not properly disputable. Facts, obtained through systematic study, were interpretation-free 'reflections of nature'.

As anthropological facts were seen as 'objective realities', the way was open for their display and exhibition. Exposing facts to the scrutiny of a community of scholars, and to the general public, provided anthropologists with a means of demonstrating the objective status of their knowledge and, moreover, doing so in a public arena in which it could be seen to be openly available for inspection and verification. 'The entire collection is deposited in the Academy of Natural

Sciences of Philadelphia, where it is open to inspection on the afternoon of Tuesday and Saturday throughout the year', wrote Morton (1844: Prefatory Note to the second edition). Broca likewise deposited his collection of thirteenth-century Parisian skulls at the Anthropological Society of Paris. Displayed artefacts were thus subject to witnessing, and this endowed them with 'truth' and the capacity to serve as instruments of knowledge.

In 1872 an anthropological museum was set up at the Laboratory of Anthropology in parallel with the museum of the Anthropological Society of Paris. The Laboratory of Anthropology, which had been set up in 1867, had been conceived from its beginnings as an educational laboratory with sessions in practical work. It was here, through the practice of dissection, that fragments of bodies were attributed with particular – physical, physiological and pathological – characteristics:

> Casts are taken of their exterior forms; all anatomical particularities present are described in detail and drawn; brains are conserved in alcohol and, as these fragile organs may not be put, without inconvenience, into the hands of students, a plaster cast is made by a special professor who engages both in modelling and sculpture, and, finally, once the anatomical study is completed, the skeletons are prepared and mounted for the museum.
>
> (Broca 1875b: 369)

Anthropologists such as de Quatrefages, Hamy and Topinard, came to criticize their predecessors for the limited number of skulls which were observed. They thus assigned Camper to the prehistory of ethnic craniology on account of the fact that his observations were based on eight skulls, unlike Blumenbach who, with his collection of 245 skulls, was said to have inaugurated ethnic craniology (Quatrefages and Hamy 1882: 155). Rather than basing their results on isolated and partial observations, the observational model became one of multiple and varied inspections based on vast collections. The *series*, into which collections were organized, was crucial to the growth of a statistical conception of facts.

Unlike deductions drawn on the basis of a few skulls judged as representative and typical, the series statistically highlighted standard types. The selection of a typical skull became a matter of methodological expertise based on the calculation of averages and not of *a priori* theorizing. This, of course, required a notion of 'sufficient series'. For Broca, a series of 20 skulls was judged sufficient; and he asserted that across such a series significant numerical data could be obtained, even though specimens were taken at random rather than selected (Broca 1861b: 645). Indeed, their randomness was evidence of their 'objectivity': facts were allowed to 'speak for themselves'.

Establishing that the sole certain basis of science 'consists in proceeding from the simple to the compound, from the known to the unknown, from matter and organism to functional phenomena' (Broca 1871/2: 28), entailed privileging tangible data. In the case of craniology, this meant facts were obtained by a specific 'research method', namely, craniometry. As facts were regarded as theory-free, bodily fragments were thought of as 'natural facts', despite their having been subject to the cultural processes of dissection, categorization, classification and exhibition. Nevertheless, reservations had been expressed over the 'reality' of facts which had been obtained through the use of instruments. Léonce Manouvrier, for example, was critical of the fact that some of the craniological features which anthropologists regarded as facts could only be seen with the aid of instruments (Manouvrier n.d.: 778). His implicit suggestion was that these were not facts but artefacts. This questioning on the part of anthropologists of the power of instruments is also posed in other scientific domains, around the 1860s, as has been shown by Ian Hacking (1983).

THE SEARCH FOR A NEW LANGUAGE

Under Broca's influence, measuring and the use of instruments of observation were massively extended; and together with the associated use of quantitative data and the reformulation of the status of the observer, anthropological findings were extensively revised. Thanks to measurement, one could obtain 'precise formulas and figures' (Topinard 1885a: 128) which served to objectify racial difference. Of course, what to measure was not written on the body and anthropologists had to make judgments. What they privileged highlights the scientific conventions of the period.

The search for anthropometric characteristics had its counterpart in anthropologists' suspicion of descriptive physical features which they judged 'vague', 'personal' or shaped by 'preconceived ideas'. These were contrasted with 'precise and scientific' anthropometric characteristics which 'made certain fields of anthropology almost a mathematical science' (ibid.: 852). This opposition between the observable, measurable and numerical anthropological features and the descriptive physical characteristics depicted in words and images was seen as part of a broader dichotomy between facts and value-judgments, or objectivity and subjectivity. Verbal language was increasingly regarded as too contaminated with subjectivity for scientific objectivity, and increasingly scientificity was associated with representing difference in statistics, charts and tables rather than words:

> Science only matured and advanced through measuring; beyond this, all is illusion: impressions and personality replace the brute fact, implacable before which we must kneel. The eternal objective of anthropological science is to replace a word, or a phrase by a numerical figure, a formula. An average feature is sometimes inaccessible to sight, but it can be apprehended by a figure.
>
> (Topinard 1885b: 399)

Effacing the presence of the subject and creating a numerical language were made possible through the use of specific instruments. These were heuristically important in two ways: first, in accessing facts uncontaminated by human intervention, and second – as the senses were regarded as fallible – in disciplining sensory observation. As Broca wrote:

> The aim of these instruments is to replace evaluations which are in some way artistic, dependent on the perspicacity of the observer, of the accuracy of his glance – and sometimes even of his preconceived ideas – by mechanical and uniform procedures, which permit the results of each observation to be expressed in figures, to establish rigorous comparisons, to reduce as far as possible the chances of error.
>
> (Broca 1860–63: 349–50)

Without going into detail here about the various techniques of anthropometrical measurement (craniometry, cephalometry, encephalometry, osteometry) or of the instruments used (callipers, goniometers, cephalographs, craniographs, craniostats, sliding compasses) it is important nevertheless to give some attention to the graphical method, especially craniography.

The craniograph, which provided an automatic reproduction of the contour of the cranial and facial profile, provided greater accuracy and also reduced human presence, since the instrument was supposed to 'work' mechanically, as if autonomous: 'The craniograph plots in the twinkling of an eye all of the contours' (ibid.: 351). Consequently, pictures and graphical reproductions obtained by mechanical procedures were accorded a higher objective status than human productions. This had very important epistemological ramifications, for 'Pictures became more than merely helpful tools; they were the words of nature itself' (Daston and Galison 1992: 116).

This instrumental apparatus needs to be examined in relation to the senses. On the one hand, instruments allowed, in effect, an improvement of perception and an extension of the reach of the senses. With the aid of instruments it was thus possible to see features imperceptible to the eye. On the other hand, instruments improved and disciplined the senses, which were regarded as essentially fallible. Results obtained by just looking were liable to be judged erroneous, incorrect and subjective. The senses were recognized as being at root physiological and hence extremely variable and fallible. However, this recognition meant that, at the same time as there was a focus on instruments that extended the reach of the senses, there was uneasiness expressed by some over the reliance on the senses at all in the establishment of facts. This led to attempts to account for physiological dimensions of seeing and the active role of the subject in constructing sensory reality. Attempting to account for the subjectivity of vision was itself part of process of conceptually reconstructing 'human vision into something measurable and thus exchangeable' (Crary 1991: 16–17). Quantification and the focus on instruments of measurement in anthropology were common to sciences of this period, which were engaged in a struggle to attain 'observation without an observing subject' or, to put it otherwise, 'the objectification of scientific observation' (Switjtink 1987: 268).

'SUPERB SKELETONS AND WITHOUT ODOUR': NATURAL OBJECTS/CULTURAL OBJECTS?

In the eyes of nineteenth-century anthropologists, the dissection of cadavers and the preparation of skeletons – whether in the laboratory or on field trips ('one scrapes bones, puts them in to soak, then exposes them to fresh air, and in a short time they become superb and without odour' – Broca 1865 in 1863–66: 78–9) – detracted nothing from the status of anatomical preparations as facts, as 'natural objects'. The same was the case with bronze busts and casts, which were viewed as having been modelled or sculpted 'after nature'. If there was one criterion which presided at the exhibitionary assembly of such dissimilar elements, it was, it seemed, likeness to reality. For example, the fact that busts and statues of exotic races were produced by artists following geometric procedures in the presence of a model was enough for these objects to be considered useful anthropological data. Thus, bronze busts by Charles Cordier, student of Rude, 'genuine works of art', had a 'value both scientific and artistic' (Verneau 1898: 335). René Verneau, assistant curator of anthropology at the Museum of Natural History, recognized nevertheless that an 'anthropological gallery inevitably presents for the general public a somewhat monotonous appearance. We have tried to arrange the pieces in the least disagreeable manner for the eye, while scrupulously respecting methodical classification' (ibid.). An artistic effect was thus sought at the level of modes of display and of the diversity of materials, which, in the anthropological gallery of the museum, included oil paintings, photographs and bronze busts.

The insistence upon presenting objects in a manner considered 'pleasing to the eye' was part of a system of conventions of the period which guided the ways in which reality was depicted. Thus, French anthropologists, in order to make the contents of exhibitions intelligible, had to use conventions that were familiar to the viewers. Bronze busts were thus considered in the same way as anatomical preparations and skulls. Both were valued for their informational content and consequently the artistic dimension of the production of representations was effaced, and they acquired the quality of 'mirrors of reality'. Without going into details about the notion of realism, and the realisms in nineteenth-century displays, both of which have been explored by Ludmilla Jordanova (1993: 255–6) and Jann Matlock (1995), it is worth noting that while anthropologists accepted that art and reality-nature were distinct entities, they sought nevertheless to identify affinities and overlaps between the two. In other words, although art and anthropology were seen as different enterprises, it was accepted that art could be a form of anthropology (see Teslow, Chapter 4); thus, the busts produced by Cordier and the sculptures of Emmanuel Frémiet, while possessing an artistic quality, were simultaneously considered as anthropological data or 'working objects' (Dias 1997). Moreover, both art and anthropology in the second half of the nineteenth century shared a similar concern with constructing realistic representations.

VISUAL DISPLAYS

Visual documents relating to exhibitions of this period are small in number and the lack of catalogues of the collections of the Museum of Natural History and the Society of Anthropology of Paris makes it difficult to grasp the precise nature of their exhibition techniques and representational strategies. Nevertheless, it appears that two exhibitionary models developed. One, a permanent feature of anthropological museums and galleries, was devoted to research and teaching, and was particularly directed to men of science and a limited public. The other deployed the framework of Universal Exhibitions, and aimed at a large public (see Harvey, Chapter 8 of this volume). These two exhibitionary frameworks, far from contradicting each other, were complementary. The same men were frequently in charge of both, as was the case with Topinard, who was responsible for both the collections at the Broca Museum and the international exhibition of anthropological sciences at the Universal Exhibition of 1878. As he said of the latter:

> the aim of attending is threefold. It concerns: 1) putting illustrative pieces before the eyes of important men . . . 2) showing travellers the most characteristic human types . . . and substantiating for them, in some way, current anthropological *Instructions* with the help of a series of objects or tableaux representing in relief or in colour the gradations and fundamental varieties of each character . . . 3) interesting the mass of the public in the development of specific studies in which man is the object, and bringing the public into contact with results obtained and the truths which follow, with reference to medicine, philosophy, history, law, all the social sciences, arts, etc.
>
> (Topinard 1877: 555–6; emphasis in original)

The demand for 'instruction by the eyes, giving as much of the scientific point of view as possible while remaining attractive for all' (Topinard 1889: 24) was not regarded as antithetical to, but, on the contrary, lay at the very heart of, the nineteenth-century exhibitionary enterprise (cf. T. Bennett, Chapter 2 of this volume). To show meant both to demonstrate and to show off. Thus, to see nineteenth-century museums and exhibitions as instruments of the 'vulgarization' of knowledge is to lose sight of the importance of the visual as a means of simultaneously *displaying*, *demonstrating*, and *illustrating* arguments. These three levels are implicit in Topinard's reference to illustrative pieces (for experts), objects and tableaux designed to show human types and 'substantiate' written texts (for travellers) and, because this is the general public, 'contact with results'. Recourse to the tactile metaphor is revealing of the status assigned to the general public: it was necessary to give the latter 'elementary notions, general ideas'. through materials which would 'speak to the eyes' (ibid.), such as anatomical preparations, skulls, skeletons and brains displayed in such a way that the public could receive the message without difficulty.

At the international exhibition of anthropological sciences in 1878 a series of skeletons and crania was arranged in narrative mode to depict evolution from anthropoid apes to man, and from primitive to civilized races. In going from one room to another, visitors were invited to undertake a journey in space and time, and to be simultaneously spectators of and actors in a *story* which unfurled before their eyes. There were four sections to the exhibition: *Comparative anatomy* – anatomical specimens, dried or conserved in alcohol; series of mummified brains, models of cerebral convolutions, ancient and modern skulls, skeletons, skulls of microcephalics, and artificially deformed skulls; *General external characteristics* – life-size figures and busts, artificial reproductions of racial types in wax and plaster, paintings, drawings, photographs, mummies, models or engravings of ethnic types, 'crude sculptures of savages, likely to throw some light on their origins and their traditions' (Topinard 1877: 556); *Detailed external physical characteristics* – samples of hair, eye colour, skin colour, models, paintings and reproductions of the nose, the eyelid and the ear, series of microscopic preparations of the system of hairs and of the skin; and *Instruments, apparatus and procedures of research.*

Physiological characteristics were excluded in exhibitions such as this, as it was thought that they 'lend themselves badly to an exhibition destined to speak to the eyes and are often only appreciated through their effects' (ibid.: 555). Physical characteristics, 'on the contrary, . . . demonstrate themselves and may be highlighted in an exhibition in a good many ways' (ibid.). They had the advantage of being stable and measurable, with results that could be expressed graphically in figures and charts. The close association between physical characteristics and the notion of demonstration was not arbitrary, and this raises the question of how far the choice of physical rather than physiological characteristics as central elements of anthropological collections was shaped by strategic, rhetorical and exhibitionary demands.

The bodily representations in exhibitions incorporated and blurred the nature/culture boundary: 'crude sculptures of savages' along with life-size figures and models of ethnic types were exhibited as anthropology, and photographs and pictures of costumes were displayed in a separate ethnography section. In the same way, in the anthropology gallery of the Museum of Natural History: 'Each human group is represented by all that which may account for its physical characteristics. Apart from portraits and photographs, display cases contain busts, masks, torsoes, naturally shaped limbs, sometimes even complete individuals' (Verneau 1898: 332). For anthropologists, the important nature–culture boundary lay not in the representational media used to depict the body (casts, busts, sculptures), but in what they referred to – the body naked or clothed.

Dichotomies between nature and culture, and anthropology and ethnography, referred ultimately to a division between body and mind. But this is not to say that there was a strict division between body and mind; on the contrary, cultural features or, more precisely, ethnographic objects designated as 'products of human intelligence', were considered testimony of specific physical organization.

Moreover, cultural modifications of the body were considered appropriate anthropological objects. Thus, artificial deformations of the skull (in America and in Europe, notably at Toulouse) and dental mutilations were exhibited (ibid.) along with such artefacts as engraved bones, skull trophies and a drinking cup made from the dome of a skull. However, these were displayed not in terms of resulting from cultural practice, but as evidence of modifications made to human nature alongside other 'modifications' such as bone lesions caused by illness. Although anthropologists were aware that some skull modifications were the product of 'ethnic habits', their interest was not in these 'habits' in themselves, but only in what they saw as modifications to the intelligence and to the behaviour of individuals and groups.

Exhibitions, with their focus on racial characteristics, inevitably conveyed social and political messages. One of the aims of the Universal Exhibition of 1878 was to bring the public 'into contact with results obtained and the truths which follow, with reference to medicine, philosophy, history, law' (Topinard 1877: 555–6). That so many disciplines exhibited like 'truths' only served better to define the boundaries between man and animal, between occidental man and the Other, and between the *normal* and its alter, the pathological. Although some anthropological exhibits might appear to be interpretable in other ways, it was emphasized that, say, the display of Lamarck's genealogical tree of animals, culminating in Man, was intended, not to degrade humanity but to highlight the distance of Man from the anthropoides (Broca 1878a: 334).

The role of science, then, was to make visible the laws of nature and the hierarchical order. Social laws were conceived as part of this natural order; and, by implication, the breaking of social laws was evidence of natural pathology. Thus, a display of assassins' skulls was intended to demonstrate how the infraction of social laws was 'reasonless' and thus associated with brain function (ibid.: 335). The concept of normality, as implicated here, occupied a central place in various nineteenth-century sciences, from medicine through anthropology to sociology. It is perhaps in this normalizing orientation that the specificity of anthropological and medical collections resides, particularly with regard to morally orientated 'major public' anatomical collections, such as the Spitzner Museum. Anthropologists attempted to establish anthropometric canons specific to different races, something which in effect produced the idea of the 'exception from nature' and 'freak'. As Susan Stewart has pointed out:

> Often referred to as a 'freak of nature', the freak, it must be emphasized, is a freak of culture. His or her anomalous state is articulated by the process of the spectacle as it distances the viewer, and thereby it 'normalizes' the viewer as much as it marks the freak as an aberration . . . . On display, the freak represents the naming of the frontier and the assurance that the wilderness, the outside, is now territory.
>
> (Stewart 1984: 109–10)

Demonstrating an invisible classificatory order governing both mammals and races through the medium of visible things – skulls, brains, anatomical preparations, skeletons – required specific exhibition techniques. At the Museum of Natural History the visitor was presented first with prehistoric human races, followed by materials relating to physiological varieties and pathologies of the skeleton and the body, and finally contemporary human races (classified according to a geographical order). This was intended to provide evidence for the unity of the human species over time – fossil men to contemporary men – and across space (the diverse races being presented as varieties of the same species). In passing through the various rooms and going from one case to another, the visitor was invited to undertake a chronological and geographical journey – 'we began with the Negroes . . . we will conclude with Whites' (Verneau 1898: 334) – a journey which provided visual and conceptual access to the long history of human life on earth. Chronological diversity was mapped onto spatial diversity; and the 'primitive' was relegated to other time and space. While the collections of the museum essentially emphasized the comparison between human races, those of the Anthropological Society of Paris privileged comparison between man and animals (through comparative osteology of mammals and comparative anatomy of their brains) and European, especially French, craniology. Through these it was possible to visualize *difference* at all levels, from the general to the particular, and to *naturalize* socially and culturally constructed differences.

Written text was deemed insufficient to persuade visitors of the existence of 'natural difference'. More conclusive proof – i.e., factors untouched by human intervention, such as graphs and statistics – was thought necessary. 'These questions are touched on here and there in our exhibition not with assertions, but with facts . . . which allow each to choose according to his feelings. For the volume of the brain, evidence is provided by statistics' (Topinard 1889: 26). Certain of the persuasive power of figures, anthropologists of this period knew the benefit of either demonstrating assertions (e.g. the brain volume of diverse races) or, in a much more subtle manner, showing in non-verbal representations that which was not visualizable. Thus, the average skull, being virtual, 'may only be represented through figures or through a drawing carried out on the basis of the figures' (Manouvrier n.d.: 778).

If statistics had persuasive power, it was on account of the fact that they were displayed in institutions, museums, which, as so notably shown by Ludmilla Jordanova, 'are loci of power, they guarantee the validity of what is seen' (Jordanova 1993: 259). The exhibition of material evidence was a visual confirmation and a demonstration which rendered words and text superfluous; moreover, their persuasive power derived from a conviction that to see is to believe. In and through the space of the exhibition the visitor could observe and verify human nature and racial difference. Nevertheless, what visitors were presented with had in the final analysis been seen and judged worthy of being seen by 'experts'. The selections and categorizations of objects that shaped exhibitions were passed over in silence, as if the visitor and expert had identical visual experiences and modes of seeing. In this way 'scientific and medical museums sustain . . . [a] sense of unmediated vision' (ibid.).

VISUAL CULTURE AND THE LEGITIMIZATION OF DIFFERENCE

The nineteenth century is incontestably the century of museums – of spaces designated for the exercise of the gaze. While modernity is now associated with a new visual regime, we still need further work on the ways in which diverse fields of knowledge were used to create both visual languages and spaces for viewing. In geology and paleontology, for example, the search for a visual language capable of revealing depths was expressed in maps and book illustrations (Rudwick 1992). In the domain of physiology, Etienne-Jules Marey's (1830–1904) creation of a graphical language for expressing bodily movements was similar to the tables, charts and other graphical representations used by anthropologists. As 'historically specific ways of knowing the natural world give rise to related modes of writing about it' (Jordanova 1986: 17), we need not assume that the similarity between disciplines was necessarily the result of mutual influence.

Nevertheless, it is significant that the search for a visual language should be at the centre of diverse disciplinary fields and in some cases it is possible to detect a cross-fertilization of ideas. A focused concern with the *visual* is manifest not only in exhibitions and museums of art, archaeology, history, ethnography and natural history, but also in the theoretical preoccupations among physiologists, anthropologists and art historians with the phenomenon of vision. Exhibition organizers' concern to supply visitors with 'sights' reveals their awareness of both the epistemological and aesthetic stakes underlying the act of seeing. In this sense, science as well as scientific collections became part of a cultural field defining both *what* and *how* to see.

We have argued that the process of constituting racial difference is associated with the ways in which it is visualized. That the physical characteristics privileged by anthropology were imperishable and capable of being conserved raised the worthiness of the evidence. As Topinard wrote: 'The skeleton is the only part of Man which is conserved in sepulchres, and the skull is that which is collected most easily . . . The bones alone put us into the presence of disappeared populations, of extinct races' (Topinard 1891: 134). However, this raises the question of the role of material data in the construction of knowledge. The 'discovery' of human and animal remains and, in effect, 'natural facts', is problematic, as is shown by Mary Bouquet (Chapter 9 of this volume; also 1993) with reference to Eugène Dubois' *Pithecanthropus*. It is worth noting that the critique of craniology and of the cephalic index at the end of the nineteenth century was brought about through taking into account physiological features such as height, limb length, hair-type, eye colour, many of which involved soft tissues and thus were difficult to display in an exhibition. Moreover, Boas's critique of the stability of human types led to an invalidation of all racial classifications. However, to understand the visualization of racial difference as a cumulative process in which 'correct interpretations' come to replace socially and culturally biased interpretations would be reductive. If nineteenth-century French anthropologists 'saw' racial and sexual differences in brains and skulls, this was essentially because the ability to interpret requires a training within a cultural tradition.

Anthropological collections, then, had an important role in the way in which racial difference was conceptualized. Besides providing spaces for visualizing difference, museums and exhibitions functioned as systems of evidence and proof, and as institutional mediations between scholarly and public conceptions. It should be noted that this was not simply a naturalizing of social inequalities which the scholars wished to see sustained. On the contrary, the conception of a *physical* difference, that is, of a *natural* inequality between human groups, was developed not by conservative but by committed liberal and democratic anthro-pologists who often simultaneously (though sometimes with difficulty) argued for *social equality* (as, for example, did Broca in relation to the sexes). Never-theless, the fact that these 'natural' differences were proclaimed in large public and *democratic* arenas – museums and exhibitions which all citizens had a right to enter – was undoubtedly highly influential in fostering racial inequalities. Museums and collections, with their devotion to visualization and the display of knowledge, and with their scientific commitment to 'objectivity', were particularly powerful cultural institutions for the production and legitimation of 'natural' differences.

ACKNOWLEDGMENTS

The research for this paper was supported in part by a grant from the Fundação Luso-Americana. I would like to thank Barbara Kirshenblatt-Gimblett and Daniel J. Sherman for their helpful comments in our conversations on some of the issues discussed here. I am also grateful to Sharon Macdonald for her translation and insightful criticism of this paper.

REFERENCES

Bouquet, M. (1993) *Man-ape, ape-Man:* Pithecanthropus *in Het Pesthuis,* Leiden: Nationaal Natuurhistorisch Museum.
Broca, P. (1860–63) 'Mémoire sur le craniographe et sur quelques-unes de ses applications', *Mémoires de la Société d'Anthropologie de Paris,* 1, pp. 349–78.
—— (1861a) 'Sur le volume et la forme du cerveau suivant les individus et suivant les races', *Bulletins de la Société d'Anthropologie de Paris,* II, pp. 139–204, 301–21, 441–6.
—— (1861b) 'Crânes parisiens du Moyen Age. Brachycéphalie et dolicocéphalie', *Bulletins de la Société d'Anthropologie de Paris,* II, pp. 645–51.
—— (1863–66) 'Instructions générales pour les recherches et observations anthro-pologiques (anatomie et physiologie)', *Mémoires de la Société d'Anthropologie de Paris,* 2, pp. 69–203.

—— (1866) 'Anthropologie', in P. Broca *Mémoires d'Anthropologie* (reprinted 1989), Paris: Jean-Michel Place.

—— (1871/2) 'The progress of anthropology in Europe and America, an address before the Anthropological Society of Paris', *Journal of the Anthropological Institute of New York*, 1, pp. 21–42.

—— (1875a) 'Instructions craniologiques et craniométriques', *Mémoires de la Société d'Anthropologie de Paris*, 2, pp. 1–208.

—— (1875b) 'Ecole pratique des hautes études. Laboratoire d'anthropologie. Rapport annuel', *Revue d'Anthropologie*, IV, pp. 368–72.

—— (1878a) 'Discours. Congrès International des Sciences Anthropologiques', *Matériaux pour l'Histoire primitive et naturelle de l'Homme*, pp. 325–35.

—— (1878b) 'Leçon d'ouverture du cours d'anthropologie', *Revue d'Anthropologie*, VII, pp. 172–82.

Crary, J. (1991) *Techniques of the Observer: On Vision and Modernity in the Nineteenth Century*, Cambridge, MA: The MIT Press.

Daston, L. and P. Galison (1992) 'The image of objectivity', *Representations*, 40, pp. 81–128.

Delisle, F. (n.d.) 'Indices', *Dictionnaire des sciences anthropologiques*, Paris: Octave Doin.

Dias, N. (1991) *Le Musée d'Ethnographie du Trocadéro (1878–1908): Anthropologie et Muséologie en France*, Paris: Editions du CNRS.

—— (1994a) 'Photographier et mesurer: les portraits anthropologiques', *Romantisme*, 84, pp. 37–51.

—— (1994b) 'Looking at objects: memory, knowledge in nineteenth century ethnographic displays', in G. Robertson, M. Mash, L. Tickner, J. Bird, B. Curtis and T. Putnam (eds) *Travellers' Tales: Narratives of Home and Displacement*, London: Routledge.

—— (1997) 'Cultural objects/natural objects: on the margins of the categories and the ways of display', *Visual Resources*, XIII, pp. 33–47.

Gould, S. J. (1981) *The Mismeasure of Man*, New York: Norton & Co.

Hacking, I. (1983) *Representing and Intervening: Introductory Topics in the Philosophy of Natural Sciences*, Cambridge: Cambridge University Press.

Hamy, E-T. (1907) 'La collection anthropologique du Muséum national d'histoire naturelle', *L'Anthropologie*, 18, pp. 257–76.

Jordanova, L. (ed.) (1986) *Languages of Nature: Critical Essays on Science and Literature*, London: Free Association Books.

—— (1989) 'Objects of knowledge: a historical perspective on museums', in P. Vergo (ed.) *The New Museology*, London: Reaktion Books, pp. 22–40.

—— (1993) 'Museums: representing the real?', in G. Levine (ed.) *Realism and Representation: Essays on the Problem of Realism in Relation to Science, Literature, and Culture*, Madison, WI: The University of Wisconsin Press.

Levine, G. (ed.) (1987) *One Culture: Essays in Science and Literature*, Madison, WI: The University of Wisconsin Press.

Manouvrier, L. (n.d.) 'Laboratoire d'anthropologie', 'Méthode des Moyennes', *Dictionnaire des sciences anthropologiques*, Paris: Octave Doin.

Matlock, J. (1995) 'Censoring the realist gaze', in M. Cohen and Ch. Prendergast (eds) *Spectacles of Realism: Gender, Body, Genre*, Minneapolis, MN: University of Minnesota Press.

Meigs, J. A. (1857) *Catalogue of Human Crania, in the Collection of the Academy of Natural Sciences of Philadelphia, based upon the third edition of Dr. Morton's 'Catalogue of Skulls'*, Philadelphia, PA: J. B. Lippincott.

Morton, S. G. (1844) *Catalogue of Skulls of Man and the Inferior Animals in the Collection of Samuel George Morton*, Philadelphia, PA: F. Turner.

—— (1846) 'Observations on Egyptian ethnography, derived from anatomy, history, and the monument', *Transactions of the American Philosophical Society*, IX, pp. 93–159.

de Quatrefages, A. and E-T. Hamy (1882) *Crania Ethnica; les crânes des races humaines*, Paris: J. B. Baillière.

Rudwick, M. J. S. (1992) *Scenes from Deep Time: Early Pictorial Representations of the Prehistoric World*, Chicago: The University of Chicago Press.

Stepan, N. L. (1993) 'Race and gender: the role of analogy in science', in S. Harding (ed.) *The 'Racial' Economy of Science*, Bloomington and Indianapolis, IN: Indiana University Press.

Stepan, N. L. and S. Gilman (1993) 'Appropriating the idioms of science: the rejection of scientific racism', in S. Harding (ed.) *The 'Racial' Economy of Science*, Bloomington and Indianapolis, IN: Indiana University Press.

Stewart, S. (1984) *On Longing: Narratives of the Miniature, the Gigantic, the Souvenir, the Collection*, Durham, NC and London: Duke University Press.

Switjtink, Z. J. (1987) 'The objectification of observation: measurement and statistical methods in the nineteenth century', in L. Kruger, G. Gigerenzer and M. Morgan (eds) *The Probabilistic Revolution*, Cambridge, MA: The MIT Press.

Topinard, P. (1873) 'De la méthode en craniométrie', *Bulletins de la Société d'Anthropologie de Paris* VIII, pp. 851–9.

—— (1877) 'Instructions spéciales. Instructions pour l'anthropologie et la craniologie', *Revue d'Anthropologie* V, pp. 555–7.

—— (1885a) *Eléments d'anthropologie générale*, Paris: Delahaye & Lecrosnier.

—— (1885b) 'Instructions anthropométriques pour les voyageurs', *Revue d'Anthropologie*, 3, pp. 397–424.

—— (1889) 'Anthropologie', *Exposition Universelle internationale de 1889: Catalogue. Exposition rétrospective du travail et des sciences anthropologiques*, Lille: Imprimerie Nationale.

—— (1891) *L'Homme dans la Nature* (reprinted 1989), Paris: Jean-Michel Place.

Verneau, R. (1898) 'Les nouvelles galeries du Muséum: la galerie d'anthropologie', *L'Anthropologie*, IX, pp. 327–36.

Williams, E. A. (1994) *The Physiological and the Moral: Anthropology, Physiology and Philosophical Medicine in France 1750–1850*, Cambridge: Cambridge University Press.

Chapter 4

Reifying race

Science and art in *Races of Mankind* at the Field Museum of Natural History

Tracy Lang Teslow

In 1933, the Field Museum of Natural History in Chicago mounted an ambitious exhibition entitled *Races of Mankind*, which consisted of 101 life-size bronze sculptures of the 'principal' human racial types. Malvina Hoffman, a renowned sculptor from New York, who had studied under Auguste Rodin, created the figures over a period of several years, in some cases travelling around the world to find her models. The exhibition, mounted to coincide with the Century of Progress World's Fair in Chicago that year, was a huge success initially, attracting millions of visitors and much attention from the press.

Races of Mankind was an explicitly typological exhibition, emphasizing unity and hierarchy through bronze statues that were intended to be both authentic, accurate scientific objects and dramatic expressions of humanity; both examples of general racial types and of particular individuals. Using physical anthropological theories that grew out of a European legacy concerned with categorizing and stratifying humans, the Field Museum and Malvina Hoffman reified Western notions of class, culture and race, placing Europeans and white Americans at the peak of racial evolution.

The *Races of Mankind* statues, and the exhibition they were presented in for more than 30 years, claimed their scientific authority from their location in a science museum and from the anthropologists who sanctioned them as authentic representations of individual humans and general human types. But it was the artistic medium and rendering that gave the statues their expressive power and made the notion of racial typology accessible to the public. Hoffman's realistic art reified a racialist hierarchy more than any set of bones, chart of nose shapes, comparative scales or plaster figures ever did. The museum encouraged visitors to see in the sculptures expressions of ineffable, unmeasurable human qualities, and while they imbibed humanity, they also were instructed in the quantifying and categorizing scheme of physical anthropology.

Hoffman's work was touted by the Field Museum's curators as both scientific and artistic. Berthold Laufer, Curator of Anthropology, claimed the sculptures were 'the result of careful selection of subject and long anthropological study'. He compared the exhibition to a convention of live racial representatives who had been frozen in bronze for the benefit of science and education 'to facilitate study of their characteristic features and preserve them permanently' and praised the bronze sculptures for their 'insight into the mind of the primitive' (Laufer 1931: 3). Sir Arthur Keith, a renowned Scottish physical anthropologist and adviser to the exhibition, echoed Laufer's sentiments. Hoffman, he said, 'was commissioned to proceed to those lands where native races are at their purest and there register in clay and finish in bronze the living lineaments of selected types . . . Her representations of humanity are works of both beauty and truth' (Field 1942: 9).

By the 1960s, when the exhibit was dismantled, the figures themselves and the exhibition as a whole had come under attack as not only inaccurately rendered and categorized, but fundamentally racist in its construction. Activist Leroi Jones, writing on behalf of the Committee for Unified Newark, addressed a scathing letter to the museum condemning a 'Map of Mankind' based on the *Races of Mankind* exhibition and approved by the museum, as full of

> consistent and glaring inaccuracies . . . which can only be the result of ignorant white nationalism and white racism . . . We wish to protest the existence of this map and any other product put out by Hammond and Company which incorpaorates [*sic*] this kind of white racist pseudo anthropology.
>
> (Jones: 1969)

Six months later the museum asked C. S. Hammond & Company to discontinue their *Races of Mankind* leaflet and map, stating that 'We do not wish the Field Museum's name to be associated with it . . . "The Races of Mankind" as it now stands is scientifically indefensible and social [*sic*] objectionable.'[1]

Yet in 1993, Hoffman's sculptures continued to be viewed by some visitors as remarkably evocative and authoritative depictions of humanity, not as monuments to racial hierarchy, nor as despicable totems of institutionalized racism, but as hopeful tributes to human spirit and diversity. A review of the *Races of Mankind* sculptures still on display at the Field Museum argued once again that the 'statues depict not only racial types but also the inner character of the subjects, capturing the human spirit as it's expressed in each individual . . . balanced in a magically arrested moment that's both immediate and timeless' (Conrad and Tillotson 1992: 8, 30).[2] Significantly, these viewers saw in the aesthetic appeal of the sculptures a humanistic counterpoint to scientific claims about human physical diversity which made the message they took away about race more, rather than less, coherent and compelling. They argued that the 'subjectivity of art has the potential to enhance scientific inquiry rather than impede it' and contended that 'The disparate unity captured in these statues, their varied wholeness, is Babel reformed into coherence by artistic vision' (ibid.: 8–9). The continuing acclaim and scorn with which the exhibition and its figures have been met over the last 60 years attests to both the Field Museum's success in constructing provocative statements on race through artistically rendered humans and its failure to control how those figures are perceived by viewers, despite explicit disavowal of their scientific value. Where, in 1933,

Berthold Laufer saw scientific purpose in capturing vanishing primitive races, and where, in 1969, Leroi Jones saw institutionalized racism, in 1993, some modern viewers see Hoffman's sculptures a scientific proof of the 'glorious diversity' of race (ibid.: 30).[3]

DISPLAYING HUMANS: AN OBJECT FOR NATURAL HISTORY

In sending Malvina Hoffman around the world to consult with anthropologists, observe natives, and then return to the West to cast her impressions into bronze for display in a Chicago museum, the Field Museum was participating in a legacy of institutional imperialism in which artefacts, and occasionally people, were appropriated, via trade or conquest, for study and display. In the nineteenth century it was not uncommon for individuals representing 'exotic' peoples to be brought to Europe or America for display at fairs, museums and scientific gatherings to educate and titillate. While the early twentieth century remained an imperial era in which Western depictions of colonial locales often included genuine or improvised natives, such as those at the 1931 French Exposition Coloniale, museums, despite their need for authenticity, eschewed the spectacle of live humans. Display of living humans increasingly became the province of carnival freak-shows and exposition side-shows of the exotic, meant as titillating entertainment, not objective science.

In *Races of Mankind*, the elegance of Hoffman's art and the museum setting removed the side-show aura from the observation of native peoples, by removing the authentic people and the non-scientific carnival atmosphere. Museum patrons could examine exotic people unable to respond or return the look. The exhibition encouraged a kind of voyeurism, sanitized of shame in the culturally approved setting of a museum in which such seeing is given scientific sanction as the pursuit of knowledge and cultural sophistication. The bronzes were exhibited in a setting reminiscent of an art gallery, without their cultural context, save for the few objects Hoffman depicted in her sculptures. While her bronzes might strike viewers as more 'human' than the usual plaster figures, their exposition did not offer the viewer an encounter with other subjective identities. The figures were at once familiar, in their generalized humanity as *homo sapiens*, and strange, in their racialized individuality in which living identities were effaced to be renamed 'Shilluk Warrior' or 'American Man' and their subjective, culturally situated life histories erased.

In their reliance on objects to convey information and authenticate scientific claims, natural history museums also rely on an epistemology of realism in which sight is the privileged sense, the sense through which we receive knowledge about the world. *Races of Mankind* was clearly based on this epistemology, in which the bronze sculptures, as well as the other displays, relied exclusively on the sight of viewers to convey their information, whether textual, schematic or sculptural. Yet visitors could not resist the inherently tactile nature of sculpture. Despite the dual

Figure 4.1 The *Races of Mankind* exhibition hall showing the 'Unity of Man' statue in the middle, at the back, with Laufer's 'avenues of primitives' on either side. On the right side are the Senegalese Drummer, the Shilluk Warrior with his spear, and an Ituri pygmy family, all African peoples. On the left side are an Australian aboriginal woman, a Semang pygmy with his spear, a Solomon Islander climbing a tree, and the Hawaiian Surfer. (neg. no. GN78455, courtesy of the Field Museum, Chicago)

prohibition, as both a natural history exhibition and an art gallery, visitors encountered *Races of Mankind* with their hands as well as their eyes. Assistant Curator Henry Field noted that visitors were particularly taken with the elongated lip of the Ubangi woman and the Afghan man's navel (Field 1953: 227). The museum counteracted this infraction by reapplying the patina as visitors' touching rubbed it off, maintaining both the illusion that the sculptures were untouchable and the integrity of the sculptures as integrated individuals, rather than artificial creations mimicking life.

The museum setting allowed a kind of contact with exotic peoples that was impermissible in exhibitions of living people. Just as visitors could gawk at the statues without shame or fear that the figures would respond, so too could they give in to their desire to touch the exotic. In the ultimate objectification, real people had been transformed into 'durable monuments' to racial hierarchy, arrayed for public consumption and scientific study. It was the perfect anthropological collection: living racial types, culled from all over the world, transported to Chicago and arranged in a single hall, permanently preserved in every detail and available to sight, touch and measurement in a way no genuine living subject ever was. It was a gallery of race, calculated to be the envy of every physical anthropologist.

MALVINA HOFFMAN: ARTIST CUM ZOOLOGIST

The object-centerd logic of natural history museums required that the topic of human race be presented through static displays of artefacts and text. In most museums, actual human bones, teeth and hair were displayed, along with the statistics, charts, and photographic studies that comprised the evidence for racial categories. Occasionally, plaster casts and figures like those used in other anthropological exhibitions were displayed as well.

Staff at the Field Museum wanted to mount a more dramatic exhibition that would attract visitors, enhance the museum's reputation among its peers, and compete favourably with the Century of Progress World's Fair opening in Chicago in 1933. Henry Field sought an artist who could produce representations of humans as racial types in a manner that would provide both the requisite scientific precision and 'be the most popular, not only in the museum, but on the continent' (ibid.: 132). In their quest for an artist that could produce 'realistic portraits with an artistic flair' (ibid.: 189–90), Field Museum staff were led to Malvina Hoffman, on the suggestion of trustee Marshall Field. By the late 1920s Hoffman was highly regarded for her portraiture and realistic sculpture, important qualifications to the staff and trustees, who wanted figures that 'anyone could recognise and feel to be authentic without being repulsive' (Hoffman 1936: 3). When Assistant Curator Henry Field, visiting Hoffman in her New York studio to discuss the project, saw marble busts of African natives she had done after a trip to Africa in 1926, he was convinced she could attain the standard of realism and drama they sought.

Field Museum staff betrayed some understanding that artists, even those working in a realistic naturalistic style, were translators, whose personal and aesthetic vision would shape the sculptures and compromise a strictly authentic presentation of racial types. Originally, Field and Laufer thought they would have to hire four artists because of the size and scope of the project. The scientific and educational intent of the exhibition was to present racial types to the public in a unified manner that would convincingly illustrate natural racial categories of humanity. Field clearly understood that divergent sculptural styles could undermine that picture of reality. He did not take the impossibility of various artists all creating equally faithful transcriptions of racial reality as evidence that such observation might not be possible nor that such neatly defined racial types did not in fact exist in nature. Field and the museum staff understood that the sculptures were not in fact the same as the individuals they portrayed, but nevertheless they believed that racial types existed in nature – bronze sculptures were a pragmatic and dramatic substitute for the real thing.

In Malvina Hoffman, Field Museum staff hoped they had found a sculptor whose artistic sensibility coincided with their scientific and dramatic needs, one who could skilfully produce elegant and mimetic figures without also introducing a subjective vision. Realists like Hoffman saw their artistic project as the expression of natural forms through detailed life-like renderings, catching their subject in a moment which revealed something essential, and evoking it through the artistic blending of meticulous detail and classical form. Reflecting on her role in the *Races of Mankind* project, Hoffman described herself as a technician or conduit. 'I had to efface my own personality completely', she wrote, 'and let the image flow through me directly from the model to the clay, without impediment of any subjective mood, or conscious art mannerism on my part' (ibid.: 12; see also Hoffman 1939 and 1965). In the context of the Field Museum sculptures, this kind of realism was the artistic counterpart of empiricism and scientific method in its faith in and reliance on observation of presumably stable natural entities. Realist art implied a belief that the world could be sensibly reduced to essentials, accurately reproduced and ordered. Hoffman's bronze sculptures were intended to be permanent, accurate reproductions of human individuals that Field and Laufer could arrange in a museum gallery to represent the natural order of mankind. Hoffman's realistic style suited scientific exhibition because it did not challenge the existence or form of the scientists' natural order or the Western social order, as some forms of modernism sought to do through distorted shapes and spaces, but rather replicated them by working within Western traditions of form and aesthetics to evoke 'natural' beauty. Hoffman's bronzes implied an acceptance and reinforcement of prevailing paradigms of natural and social order that was conveyed to the viewer through life-like detail, frozen in metal, catalogued and arrayed in the space of a science museum.

To ensure the utmost authenticity in the figures, Hoffman was instructed to travel across the globe to discover some of her subjects *in situ*. Characterizing her travels as a scientific expedition to find and bring nature to the public, museum literature never failed to highlight the lengths to which the staff and Hoffman had gone to bring representatives of the world's people to the museum for public edification. Her quest was cast as if she were a zoologist, travelling across the world to find her subjects in the wild and to appropriate their lives (in bronze, rather than through taxidermy) for display in a museum setting. Her travels had the aura of scientific authenticity and authority, of directly observing the truth of naturally occurring racial types in their habitats. Rather than shooting, stuffing and mounting her subjects in dioramas, Hoffman copied them in clay, to be transformed into a 'skin' of bronze, mounted on pedestals in a gallery of humanity. Like Carl Akeley's lions and gorillas, Hoffman's figures were promoted to the public as authentic. Realistic display styles were not presented as harbouring a point of view, as a collection of objects tainted with purposive intervention, but as a peephole into reality (Haraway 1989: 38). That Hoffman actually modelled many of her figures from photographs and workers at the Exposition Coloniaie in Paris, expediently selected friends and acquaintances for models, and manipulated her subjects' clothing and accoutrements to present more 'primitive' types, were facts hidden from visitors to the museum, who were offered a narrative of empirical, objective science cast in bronze.

WHY BRONZE? REIFYING A RACIAL HIERARCHY

The use of bronze for a natural history museum exhibition was in many ways surprising. Bronze is expensive and producing figures in it requires expertise that natural history museums do not possess. Moreover, bronze fails to convey colour and texture as accurately as more traditional representational forms. In its choice of bronze, it seems that the museum exchanged degrees of accuracy and authenticity for dramatic impact and the unique qualities of bronze sculpture.

Earlier exhibition plans for physical anthropology presumed the use of more traditional figures. Laufer's original 1916 plans called for standard painted plaster figures, while the original plans for the *Races of Mankind* hall included newly developed flesh-coloured wax-and-plaster figures, decked out with real hair and glass eyes – what Henry Field called 'true realism' (Field 1953: 197). When Malvina Hoffman refused to work in anything but bronze,[4] Field was amenable – his conception of the exhibition had been inspired in part by his impressions of Herbert Ward's dramatic bronzes of Africans at the Smithsonian – but he, President Stanley Field, adviser Arthur Keith and Laufer still had to be convinced.[5] Substantial additional funds had to be raised (ultimately from Marshall Field) and the number of figures had to be reduced from 164 to 100. This was a pivotal decision by the Field Museum, because the entire character of the exhibition changed, and it raises the question of why Field Museum staff preferred bronze, and what the bronze sculptures and their 'artistic flair' were meant to convey.

Bronze was not the ideal medium to convey racial characters through sculpture. While the *Races of Mankind* bronzes may be more compelling, more lively and life-like in their active poses and carefully detailed features than inanimate plaster figures ever were, they remain patently artificial. Strikingly, bronze fails to convey many physical features crucial to racial comparison, including skin colour. To partially remedy that deficiency Hoffman had the figures coated in chemical patinas to suggest variation in skin tone: the native Americans are reddish, the African figures are nearly black, and the east Indian and Asian figures are shades of tan (Hoffman 1936: 12).

The museum also compensated for the deficiencies of bronze by devoting approximately a quarter of the exhibition space to quantitative and comparative displays designed to describe characteristics which Hoffman's sculptures failed to convey adequately, including examples of actual hair types, charts on eye colour, skeletal displays and photographic transparencies depicting racial types in colour. This portion of the exhibition, which reflected more typical anthropological display practices, utilizing glass cases to house data on human physical characteristics, indicated the extent to which the curators themselves found

Hoffman's realistic figures insufficiently informative. Race was defined in these displays through morphological features, including skull and skeletal form, as well as through behaviour. A series of skulls was exhibited to demonstrate differences between the races, as was a series of charts on hair, eye and skin colour, and nose, mouth and ear shape. In addition to these, physical anthropologists in 1933 were prepared to find racial typology in a morphology of behaviour. One case presented casts of hand and feet in various poses, taken from some of Hoffman's subjects, including sets of Chinese hands holding chopsticks and a paintbrush, and hands of Balinese dancers. The technical exhibitions reinforced the idea of hierarchy through racial typology, particularly in comparative displays. For example, one glass case presented a 'comparative series of skeletons of the principal races' (Laufer 1931: 3). The range of races was presented as a linear series, with an implied hierarchy from primitive to civilized, starting with an Australian aborigine and culminating in a 'Caucasian'. Included in the range were a 'Negro' and two 'mongoloids', including a Native American. Another case offered a comparison of human and ape skeletons, in a series that ranged from a gibbon, to an orang-utan, a chimpanzee and a gorilla, finally culminating in a European. The combined effect of these two displays was production of an evolutionary *scala naturae*, in which the Australian aborigine, mongoloids and Negroes provided an evolutionary link between the apes and civilized man, epitomized by the European (Field 1942: 44, 47).[6] The displays were not exhibited in an evolutionary context, however. The entire exhibition was devoid of any information on or speculation about the evolution of human races, instead focusing on contemporary geographical distribution, delineation of racial features and variation, and exposition of modern scientific anthropological methods.

While bronze appealed to Hoffman for aesthetic and artistic reasons, it seems to have appealed to the Field Museum's staff for practical and metaphorical reasons, both of which addressed issues of decay. Bronze is an elegant and low-maintenance medium, which plaster is not. In addition, no science museum had ever mounted an entire exhibition in bronze. But the most salient reason for their acceptance of bronze figures was the real and metaphorical permanence of the material. Field, Laufer and museum literature repeatedly stressed the value of Hoffman's statues as a permanent representation of the world's races, making them forever available for study, and in particular as a way to preserve vanishing primitive races. Indeed, Laufer claimed that due to 'the rapid extinction of primitive man due to white man's expansion over the globe many a vanishing race will continue to live only in the sculptures displayed in this hall' (Laufer 1931: 3). According to Henry Field, in *Races of Mankind* 'modern man met with his own image . . . portrayed in imperishable bronze' (Field 1953: 226). Laufer and Field believed their exhibition was more than a compendium of current anthropological theory, a neutral exposition on race. Rather, they intended it to address social instability by emphasizing the rationally ordered and determined nature of life, in which vanishing primitive races could be preserved and better understood, despite their inevitable demise at the hands of more civilized and progressive human races. Under the heading of 'Social Anthropology', in the technical portion of the exhibition, displays were devoted to delineating racial problems in the United States, immigration issues and anti-miscegenation laws, promoting the efficacious application of racial science to national and world problems. In contrast to a threatening perception of society imperilled by decay and degeneration, the Field Museum offered a stable and familiar world order, frozen in bronze, at once humanitarian in its theme of unity and its preservation of endangered primitives, and reassuring in its reinforcement of the natural place of Europeans and Americans at the top of the evolutionary heap.

Hoffman's bronze sculptures, *Races of Mankind* as a whole, indeed the entire physical anthropological project of the Field Museum, were intimately tied to the reinforcement of order in an increasingly chaotic world. The pervasive faith in American scientific, commercial and social progress characteristic of the late nineteenth and early twentieth century had been severely shaken in the 1910s and 1920s. The horror and scale of the First World War fundamentally undermined belief that civilization was marching ever forward. The subsequent failure of the League of Nations did nothing to improve Americans' sense of security in a contentious world. At home, fear for the fate of society took ugly forms: nativism, red scares, race riots. Widespread union strikes, particularly in the coal and steel industries, convulsed communities and heightened growing fear of communism. The years between the Great War and the Great Depression were marked by virulent anti-radicalism and efforts to hunt down radicals thought to endanger civil society, particularly communists and anarchists. Fear of moral and intellectual decline spurred eugenic theories and culminated in the nativist anti-immigration National Origins Act, 1924. The Prohibition Amendment of 1919 was a boon to organized crime; in Chicago, Al Capone created a $60 million empire in the 1920s, through sale of liquor and drugs, gambling and prostitution. In the South, the Ku Klux Klan hit its peak membership of 5 million in 1925. By 1929, when Field first contacted Hoffman, the world economy was falling apart; in 1933, when the exhibition opened, the country was entrenched in the Depression (Leighton 1949; Tuttle 1970).

One response of American science and business to domestic and foreign threats was to reinvigorate Americans' faith in progress, hence the theme of the 1933 World's Fair – 'The Century of Progress'. At the fair 'scientific idealism' – 'a deification of the scientific method and glorification of anticipated scientific solutions to social problems' – was promoted to 32 million visitors in Chicago through a wide range of industrial and scientific exhibits, including a fountain of a man, a woman and a robot entitled *Science Advancing Mankind*, and a Harvard University-sponsored physical anthropology laboratory at which fair-goers could be measured (Rydell 1985: 529, 533). Henry Field and Berthold Laufer planned the opening of their anthropological exhibitions to coincide with the 'Century of Progress' fair, hoping to attract some of the fair's enormous attendance and, more crucially, to participate in the reinforcement and preservation of Western social order by demonstrating to museum-goers that man had travelled an illustrious and progressive path.

Since 1916 Laufer had planned a physical anthropological exhibit to present man's 'place in nature' (Laufer 1916). In 1927, Henry Field, fresh from his Oxford University tutelage under Henry Balfour, L. H. Dudley Buxton and Sir Arthur Keith, transformed Laufer's plan with his own 'dream' of two physical anthropological exhibitions telling the 'Story of Man' in adjoining halls. One became the Hall of the Stone Age of the Old World, a series of dioramas depicting prehistoric man in Europe, from 250,000–6,000 BC, and the other became the Hall of the Races of Mankind. These two exhibitions would portray the 'complex history of mankind . . . exactly as it developed, link by link' (Field 1953: 131).

The ostensible goal of these exhibitions was educational and humanitarian, implicitly exhorting museum-goers to accept the reassuring vision of a progressive, unified path of humanity. In his Preface to the Field Museum *Races of Mankind* leaflet, Curator Laufer articulated this hope:

> Anthropology is essentially a science of human understanding and conciliation based on profound human sympathies that extend alike to all 'Races of Mankind' . . . If the visitors to the hall will receive the impression that race prejudice is merely the outcome of ignorance and will leave it with their sympathy for mankind deepened and strengthened and with their interest in the study of mankind stimulated and intensified, our efforts will not have been futile and will have fulfilled their purpose.

Laufer also carefully tried to limit the scope of the exhibit, criticizing 'the general confusion of the terms race, nationality, language, and culture' in the study of race and reminding visitors that race was an exclusively biological concept. It 'means breed and refers to the physical traits acquired by heredity' and not 'the total complex of habits and thoughts acquired from the group to which we belong . . . the social heritage called culture'. Laufer applied this distinction between biological and cultural origins to the behaviour of nations as well as individuals. It is cultural traditions, he argued, not the biological origins of its members, that determine national behaviour (Field 1942: 8).

Henry Field was not as careful in relating his progressive vision. According to Field, visitors to the Hall of the Stone Age viewed an iconography of human progress: weapons and fire as 'the first step toward supremacy over the beasts'; two men, a woman and child as the 'first family'; the development of art, agriculture, domesticated animals, pottery, tools, homes and ritual burial (Field 1953: 212–14).[7] The allegory of prehistoric man provided visitors not just with facts about the development of humanity but a moral for modern existence:

> Prehistoric man shows the fluctuating history of man. He shows us that there is hope – there is always hope – for the future of mankind . . . Man's struggles and victories began several million years ago – and those struggles were against

greater odds, those victories more inspiring, than any man has known since the time that records were first inscribed on pictographic tablets.

(Field 1953: 215–16)

Lurking in Field's morality tale and behind the construction of the exhibit was a vision of race that offered the non-European races a decidedly marginal role in history. In contrast to Laufer's hopeful vision, Field's views echoed those of his tutor and exhibit adviser Sir Arthur Keith, who propounded a divisive view of race as the source and result of evolutionary competition. In his view, vanishing races were not merely a tragic result of cultural conflict; they were evidence of the evolutionary struggle among races for survival of the fittest.

In one of his major works, *The Antiquity of Man*, Keith argued that 'When we look at the world of men as it exists now, we see that certain races are becoming dominant; others are disappearing. The competition is world-wide and lies between varieties of the same species of man' (Keith 1929: 724–33). The source of competition, he argued was a 'tribal spirit', a race prejudice that causes people to remain with their own kind and to be antagonistic towards others who look different, a condition that leads to competition, with some groups dominating and exterminating others. Physical isolation allowed emerging characteristics to be preserved and augmented within groups. For Keith, race prejudice was the key to human cultural and evolutionary progress:

The human heart, with its prejudices, its instinctive tendencies, its likes and dislikes, its passions and desires, its spiritual aspirations and its idealism, is an essential part of the great scheme of human evolution – the scheme whereby Nature, through the eons of the past, has sought to bring into the world ever better and higher races of mankind.

(Keith 1973: 26)

The pacifist goals of the League of Nations and others who sought to bring all humanity together into 'a single harmonious united tribe' would be achieved only by sacrificing everyone's 'racial birthright' through a common pooling of blood, each race distributing to a common progeny the inherited traits that their ancestors had struggled to preserve and enhance. For Keith this price was too high. Conversely, the cost of continued race prejudice was one he justified; competition is the price of continued progress. '[R]ace prejudice and, what is the same thing, national antagonism, have to be purchased, not with gold, but with life . . . Nature keeps her human orchard healthy by pruning; war is her pruning-hook' (ibid.: 45, 47, 48–9).

Following Berthold Laufer's call for unity and sympathy in the Preface to the Field Museum guide to *Races of Mankind*, in his introduction Keith instead called on the visitor to attend to human difference. Keith argued that all people are amateur anthropologists by virtue of their ability from birth to discern subtle and gross differences in the appearance of people they encounter, from family members to our community to 'stray people from distant lands'. So unerring is this instinctive racial prejudice that 'scientific measurement can never rival the accuracy and completeness of the rule of thumb method practised by the man in the street'. In particular, 'true artists', like Hoffman, have a highly developed intuition for racial qualities. For Keith, race prejudice was not the outcome of ignorance, as it was for Laufer, rather it was the source of insight. Confronted with the 'Unity of Mankind' group, Keith noted not the links between races, but rather highlighted differences among humans. 'It is right that this group should hold a central position in the hall, for no one can look at those three figures without asking the question, Why this diversity of racial type?' (Field 1942: 10–11).

CULTURE, READ IN AND OUT

The racial reality that Field Museum staff were interested in portraying was not only that of physical features, but also one of behaviour and culture. The sculptures' active poses and cultural trappings encouraged viewers to believe that they were encountering actual individuals caught in an authentic moment of life, a series of voyeuristic snapshots. Undoubtedly, culturally augmented figures contributed to the identification of variation among similar racial types for museum visitors who were untutored in the minute distinctions used by anthropologists, particularly given the stereotypical nature of the types (for example, a Hawaiian surfing, an African warrior with a spear, a Chinese man pulling a rickshaw). The ubiquity of artefacts in the sculptures also speaks to the conflation of culture, behaviour and morphology in the definition of racial types. All the life-size figures (with one significant exception) were clothed and most were accompanied by representations of cultural artefacts such as drums, weapons and food. For example, a Tamil man from India, described by Hoffman as climbing a palm tree to collect toddy for wine, is wrapped in textured cloth, is climbing with the aid of ropes around his feet and chest, and carries a basket slung around his waist. Another basket and scythe sit at the base of the tree. Most of the busts and heads were also dressed in some fashion. Often, poses, such as tribal dances, hunting stances and praying postures, were presented as racially characteristic, implying a biological basis for culturally specific behaviours. Hoffman remarked that she 'watched the natives in their daily life' and then selected for her figure's pose 'the moment at which I felt each one represented something characteristic of his race, and of no other' (Hoffman 1936: 12). Curator Laufer claimed the figures were shown in active poses to 'permit the study of the physical functions which are more important for evaluation of a race than bodily measurements' (Laufer 1931: 3).

Indeed, so crucial were the cultural accoutrements and behaviours in identifying race, they had to be improvised when particular models were insufficiently accessorized or animated. For example, Hoffman expediently acquired an Indonesian model from the French Exposition Coloniale. Whisked from the service entrance of a Balinese restaurant to her studio in Paris, the boy was put

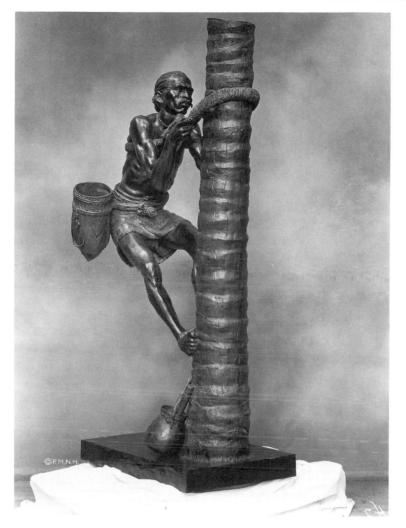

Figure 4.2 Tamil Climber, *Races of Mankind* exhibition. Like nearly all the other figures in the exhibit, he is clothed and caught in a moment with the artefacts of his life, here a tree, a rope and a basket slung on his hip. The figure and his artefacts are highly detailed. Hoffman used her technical skills to simulate the intricate weaving on the basket, the patterned cloth of his loin-cloth, the rough hemp of the rope, the tree bark, and her subject's protruding ribs. (neg. no. MH43, courtesy of the Field Museum, Chicago)

in a batik loin-cloth and directed to strike a pre-arranged pose (Hoffman 1936: 172, 174). Other models, like the Balinese boy, were posed with artefacts and clothing that did not reflect the reality of the state in which Hoffman found them, but instead served to portray them as primitives. A young Samoan man, for example, was posed holding an ancestral war knife and labelled as a warrior, as if he was still wielding it in 1931, when in fact he was a member of a Mormon colony in Hawaii.

Malvina Hoffman's treatment of her subjects demonstrates how she, and the Field Museum staff who authorized her work, imposed their own culturally contingent definition of beauty on the models and then read it back out of the sculptures as a creation of nature. Berthold Laufer hailed Hoffman's bust of a Mangbetu woman as a 'Negro' type of beauty (Laufer 1931: 3). The Mangbetu figure depicted a young woman from central Africa whose hair has been interwoven with raffia to create a large conical head-dress. She was one of three African women with elaborate head-dresses that Hoffman sculpted in a classical form, shorn of distracting and personalizing detail in favour of formal lines and elegance. In fact, the Mangbetu figure depicts not 'Negro' beauty, but native dress interpreted as 'Western' beauty. If Hoffman and museum staff had intended to represent native forms of beauty rather than selected practices that conformed to Western aesthetics, they also would have displayed busts of a Ubangi woman with a lip disc and a Burmese woman wearing neck rings, rather than exhibiting them as examples of physical deformations. The selection and depiction of subjects for exhibition reflected the aesthetic philosophies of Field Museum staff and Malvina Hoffman, not those of the people represented to the American public.

Hoffman was perfectly open in applying her aesthetic bias to her subjects. Indeed, she regarded it as her job. Of the Tasmanians, who could not be included in the exhibit of living races because they were extinct, Hoffman wrote 'It was a great relief to me, for they were ugly enough to make celibacy an easy task, and sculpture an impossible one' (Hoffman 1936: 13). When she could not avoid modelling an 'ugly' race altogether, such as the Bushmen of Africa, whom the Field Museum insisted be included in the exhibit because they typified primitiveness, she sculpted them in forms that both minimized characters she found ugly and at the same time evoked the requisite primitivism through a highly detailed, heightened naturalism. In her search for Bushman models Hoffman visited the Musée de L'Histoire Naturelle in Paris to see the remains of the 'Hottentot Venus' and was so dismayed by the encounter she 'came very near to abandoning the project' (ibid.: 155). The woman immortalized derisively as the 'Hottentot Venus' was Saartjie Baartman, an African brought to Europe in 1810 as a curiosity. She was considered a convincing and grotesque example of the inferiority of native peoples, and was considered particularly curious because of her protruding buttocks, which were a physical feature common to the Bushmen (Gilman 1985).[8] Hoffman's response to viewing the cast of this poor woman, this 'monster piece of female ugliness', as she called her, was to insist 'that I be given artistic freedom to select at least the best possible representative of a race and not the ugliest, even if every anthropologist in the world preferred the latter' (Hoffman 1936: 155). The resulting sculpture of a Bushman family from the Kalahari Desert in southern Africa is an example of what art historian Linda

Nochlin has referred to as the 'relentless naturalism' of Hoffman's racial sculptures. Nochlin's derogation of Hoffman's 'appalling concentration on surface detail, resulting in a kind of waxworks realism in bronze', unwittingly reveals the technique by which Hoffman complied with museum demands while remaining faithful to her own standards of beauty (Nochlin 1984: 106).[9]

UNITY AND HIERARCHY

The conflation of culture and biology in *Races of Mankind* also reflected the hierarchical nature of the curators' racial typology. Human types were defined by a concept of race that linked skills, character traits and level of 'civilization' to bodily forms and arrayed in a range from the most primitive to the most civilized. In the latter category is 'American, from Brooklyn New York', a white body-builder Hoffman found in Brooklyn. The rationale for labelling him 'American' was ostensibly that most Americans were of his 'white stock', and thus he represented the United States. In the exhibition he was grouped with others from the Americas, all of whom were native peoples. By 1942 the sculpture was re-labelled 'Nordic', representing northern Europe and the United States, and was grouped with the Europeans (Field 1942: 50; Hoffman 1936: 165; Field Museum Anthropology Archives). What is remarkable about this sculpture, apart from the blatant effacing of other equally 'American' and 'European' races, is its contrast to every other full-size figure in the exhibition. He is stripped of any clothing or cultural trappings, implying a transcendence of culture, of class, even of race. He recalls no moment of life, but rather classical statuary. In contrast to the Tamil, who is clearly a worker, and an emaciated one at that, 'American' or 'Nordic' man represents a classless, raceless human pinnacle.

The arrangement of the exhibition also implied hierarchy. It was comprised of 33 full-length sculptures depicting the principal races, combined with life-size heads and busts representing subdivisions within the principal races (Field 1953: 134, 193). In a 1927 diagram, the American races were placed at the far end of a rectangular hall, between the Indonesians and the north Asians, while the Europeans were set in the middle, between Africans and Asians. A monumental 15-foot statue entitled the 'Unity of Mankind', featuring a pillar, surmounted by a terrestrial globe and surrounded by three muscular men representing the main human races – black, white and yellow – stood at one end (Field Museum Anthropology Archives). The arrangement implied no obvious hierarchy. By 1933 the design had changed dramatically. The centre of the exhibition was an octagonal room dominated by European and American races with the 'Unity' statue at its centre (Field 1942; Hoffman 1936: 11; Field Museum Anthropology Archives). The 'Unity' sculpture was intended to emphasize the unity of man as one species, and marked the heart of the exhibit. Rooms on either side displayed racial types from Asia, Africa and Oceania, what Laufer termed 'avenues of primitive man' (Laufer 1931). From 1927 to 1933, Europeans had

Figure 4.3 American/Nordic Man. Hoffman called him 'God's gift to women'. The reference to classical sculpture is explicit in his complete nakedness, in the absence of any artefacts, and in the pose, which does not depict any particular or racially characteristic behaviour. The sculpture is not so much modelled from life as from standard tropes in Western sculpture. (neg. no. MH25, courtesy of the Field Museum, Chicago)

been moved from a relatively egalitarian placement as three races among many, to a central and culminating position, indicated both by the architectural form of the space and the placement of the monumental and thematically dominant 'Unity of Mankind' statue.

THE ELUSIVE ALPINE, OR THE TROUBLE WITH TYPOLOGY

Hoffman's sculptures were presented in the scientific arena of a natural history museum in a way that, rather than problematizing race, presented race as a natural category, objectively discovered and elucidated by the science of physical anthropology. Berthold Laufer promised museum-goers that the exhibition would present 'the most perfect representatives of all living races . . . transformed from life into bronze' (ibid.). The exhibition explicitly, through texts referring to the sculptures, and implicitly, in its conception, arrangement and existence in a natural history museum, promulgated the idea that races are bounded, natural entities which we can objectively and unambiguously record and understand. The exhibition suggests that races are readily distinguished and that individuals embodying traits typical of those races are easily found. The experience of Hoffman, museum officials and anthropological advisers in planning and constructing the exhibition suggests otherwise.

Similar to difficulties biologists encounter in defining species, anthropologists' efforts to categorize human races ran into what proved to be ultimately insurmountable problems in demarcating types because, among humans, the physical characters used to define race are not separable into discrete types. Evident differences between humans represent graded variations that cannot be sorted into sets of characters that each define a single race, or even a distinctive mix of supposed originally pure races. While the distribution of one character, say nose shape, might suggest a particular set of racial groups, another character will sort out differently. Indeed, in 1942 Laufer conceded the difficulty in defining races and racial characteristics, stating that

> in speaking of white, yellow, black, and red men we follow merely a popular terminology and take surface impressions for granted, while as a matter of fact the colour variability of the complexion in individuals is almost infinite, and no one is strictly white or yellow or black or red.
>
> (Field 1942: 6)

None the less, in 1933 many physical anthropologists believed that science would eventually solve these racial puzzles and that humans could be categorized discretely. The *Races of Mankind* exhibition presented human racial typology as it was understood in 1933, organized around 'Negro', 'White' and 'Mongoloid Stocks'.

The essential tension in constructing typologies is the balance between generalized archetypes and specific instantiations. Tension between the ideal and the instance is evident in the anthropological wrangling over the accuracy of Hoffman's sculptures as racial representatives and the occasional insistence that particular features be modified away from accurate rendition of an individual's features and toward some typological mean. Hoffman's transcontinental quest for racial types, which received so much publicity, was predicated on the ease with which she or a local expert might find unambiguously typical individuals. In fact, Hoffman found wide disagreement among the experts about what constituted a suitably typical individual. Hoffman encountered 'endless contradictory opinions' about the Kalahari Bushmen and found it difficult to 'satisfy all the experts', particularly regarding the appropriate size of her female figure's buttocks. She resolved the controversy by relying on the authority of anthropologists at the Cape Town Museum in South Africa, who sanctioned her figure as an 'average medium example' (Hoffman 1936: 155). She ran into the same problem with 'the facts' about 'Alpine' northern Europeans: 'The number of experts consulted on the subject of what constituted a pure Alpine type resulted in confusion and contradictions all along the line. Each anthropologist seemed to have his own pet idea about the elusive Alpine' (ibid.: 165).

The tension in typologies between unity and specificity is embodied in the 'Unity of Mankind' statue, the exhibition's 'central and dominating motif' (Field 1953: 192). Representing humanity as 'a well-defined, fundamentally uniform species, which has spread all over the surface of the earth' (Laufer 1931), the 'Unity' figures were intended to represent all members of their type and yet also be minutely accurate in their particular features, just as each of the racial types in the exhibit were supposed to be both precise copies of live individuals and representatives of types that encompassed a degree of variation. Whereas the 101 racial figures emphasized the localization of typical racial characters in individuals, and by implication the existence of racial categories in nature, the 'Unity' figures emphasized archetypal racial generalization as 'idealized' bodies, cobbled together from typologically 'perfect' parts of various individuals to properly represent the entirety of their racial division. (For example, the legs of the white figure were based on those of Davis Cup champion Malcolm Whitman (Field 1953: 198).) As ideal figures, each embodied 'the highest qualities of his race' and was 'worthy of minute study', according to Laufer (1931). In contrast, each racial type, as a member of a hierarchy, was identified with labels indicating the specific type (i.e., 'Ainu Man' or 'American'), the model's country of origin and which of the main racial 'stocks' it represented. While the black 'Unity' figure represented *all* 'Negro' races, the white figure *all* 'Whites', and the yellow figure *all* 'Mongoloid' races, the individual racial types were often categorized as mixtures of the primary stocks: the Ainu of Japan were characterized as a 'White–Mongoloid Mixture' and the Hawaiians and Samoans as a 'White–Mongoloid–Negro Mixture'. The generalized, idealized representation broke down. Field and Laufer confronted the unruly gradation of physical traits; despite their best efforts, tidy categorization eluded them.

The presence of mixed races in the exhibit reveals some of the conceptual confusion underlying the study of race in physical anthropology, though the exhibit never dealt with it explicitly. Faced with the range and mix of human variation, and the extreme difficulty in discerning discrete races, anthropologists in the nineteenth century increasingly retreated to reconstructing a few hypothetical 'pure' original races from the heterogeneity of contemporary variation. To deal with the persistent problem of categorizing living races, anthropologists resorted to variously sorted mixtures of original 'pure' types combined with selected 'racial' characteristics that reflected cultural and linguistic lineages as much as purportedly hereditary ones (Stocking 1968: 58–9, also 42–68, 110–32, 161–94). None of the resultant racial schemes found universal acceptance. Omission in the exhibition of debate over the character and origin of races was consistent with the Field Museum's depiction of science as a powerful tool for organizing the world based on reasoned and quantified observation, and of racial types as unproblematic natural categories. The exhibition left unclear how mixed racial types fit into their three-legged racial scheme. Questions about the evolution of the races, such as how sufficient isolation was maintained to perpetuate racial types or where these types arose and when, were side-stepped in the exhibition. By emphasizing the exhibition as a collection of contemporary racial types and arranging them according to the continents and countries in which they were found in 1933, the implied evolutionary tree of which they were a part, and all the attendant conceptual and definitional problems, could be left unaddressed.

SEEKING IDEAL OTHERS: AN IMPERIALIST LEGACY

Despite Field Museum rhetoric, the individuals depicted in the exhibit were hardly the scientifically selected racial types museum-goers were led to expect. In many cases Hoffman took advantage of her social position to obtain models through the auspices of her hosts, either modelling acquaintances and friends who were her peers or coercing those in less powerful social positions, such as servants or peasants, to pose for her, expediencies that caused Field and Laufer concern about the scientific accuracy of the sculptures but which did not ultimately preclude their inclusion in the exhibit. Among the purportedly representative racial types included in the exhibit were exhibit adviser Sir Arthur Keith ('Nordic, Great Britain'), Hoffman's close friend Eugene Rudier ('Mediterranean, France'), who ran the foundry where most of the sculptures were cast, and prominent Chinese philosopher and social critic Hu Shi ('Chinese, type of scholar, China') (Field 1942: 50; Field 1953: 196; Hoffman 1936: 159–160, 232; Spence 1981: 206; Field Museum Anthropology Archives).

Hoffman approached her foreign subjects with a mixture of class and race prejudice, colonialist superiority and romanticism. Hoffman's gross stereotyping of native people is revealed in her autobiographical account of her Field Museum travels, *Heads and Tales*. In central Africa, Hoffman stayed on the reservation of an English game-hunter where she was afforded access to the pygmies of the Ituri Forest. Hoffman recounted, in a relentlessly patronising tone, her perceptions of these 'little people', comparing them unfavourably to monkeys, whose 'power of observation and natural ingenuity had far surpassed that of the pigmies'. Hoffman observed that 'they are not as deformed as one might suppose', and wondered if their condition might be similar to that of Shetland ponies, which 'never grow up into real ponies', the implication being that these natives were not real humans either. Her description of their hunting and eating practices sounds more like that of monkeys or hyenas than humans:

> When good fortune comes their way, the tribe settle down around the body of a dead elephant, killed by one of their diminutive tribal heroes, and treat themselves to a field-day of overeating until their little tummies swell up, and after a good deal of scratching and chattering the happy families fall asleep.
> (Hoffman 1936: 149)

CONCLUSION

It should come as no surprise that Malvina Hoffman held paternalistic, even what we would consider racist views, nor that these views affected the kinds of models she used and how she portrayed them. Nor, for that matter, is it particularly remarkable that an exhibition on race mounted in 1933 would fall in line with racialist, if not explicitly racist, theories and presuppositions. What we see by examining *Races of Mankind* is the construction of the science of race and its public face. We see a process in which a confluence of art, anthropology, museum conventions and personal as well as professional convictions about race reproduce human racial categories, first as naturalized, scientific knowledge and second as artistic intuitions.

In 1933 museums did not survey visitors to gauge their response to exhibitions, so it is difficult to know what actual responses were to *Races of Mankind*. It garnered a great deal of attention when it opened, receiving two million visitors in the first year, and even years later images of the sculptures were reproduced in printed materials on human races. Perhaps some visitors in 1933, retaining the symbolism of the 'Unity of Mankind', took away Berthold Laufer's message about human unity and sympathy, viewing the array of sculptures in much the same way some visitors do today. No doubt some others hewed to Arthur Keith's view and remembered the exhibit as testimony to essential differences and the role of race in human fate. Perhaps response to the exhibit depended upon whether or not a visitor identified with any in the congeries of race, and if so, which ones.

Whatever visitors have thought about race and *Races of Mankind*, the predominant message of the exhibit was clear: racial groups exist in nature. The natural existence of biologically definable racial groups was implied by the apparently genuine individuality of the bronze sculptures. While the dramatic individuation of the racial sculptures undoubtedly enticed visitors in the 1930s, just as it does today, the context of the sculptures in their original exhibition subsumed individuality and diversity within a hierarchical scheme that relegated 'black' and 'yellow' races to primitive status on the margins of the civilized 'white' races. Visitors to *Races of Mankind* in the 1930s were meant to see that individuals are members of racial groups which fit into a natural hierarchy, and are not merely part of a glorious, egalitarian diversity.

By the 1960s *Races of Mankind* had become an embarrassment to anthropologists at the museum, who viewed it as scientifically inaccurate as well as socially and politically indefensible. In the 1970s, the museum reinstalled the figures outside the exhibition halls as a 'Portrait of Man', intentionally placed to 'disassociate them from the Field Museum's anthropology exhibits' and instead to present them as random 'individuals from here and there about the world' so that 'the viewer will be less apt to take them as a statement on race' (Cole 1984). They are presented by the museum without any order or hierarchy and without any anthropological information – they are merely decorative objects, displaying human physical and cultural diversity, but implicitly not typology. For anthropologists, the artistic power of the bronze sculptures was insufficient to justify their exhibition in a museum of science because the racial hierarchy they embodied was no longer acceptable. In a post-colonial era, when scientific theory views race as no more than a contingent mixture of genes resulting in an indivisible range of characteristics, and when racial and ethnic groups actively protest formerly legitimate race constructions, the Field Museum could no longer display Hoffman's sculptures as artefacts of natural history. Yet, despite their precautions, the staff have been unable to rein in the authority of the science museum setting. Given recent reactions to Hoffman's sculptures, it seems that so long as they sit in the Field Museum hallways, under its purview, visitors will construe them as both inspiring artifice and authoritative scientific objects. The shifting status of the *Races of Mankind* sculptures – from scientific copies of natural racial types to decorative objects to insightful invocations of diversity – is pointed testimony to the plasticity and socially constructed nature of meaning, as well as to the power of scientific authority and institutions to construct truths.

For those concerned to promote understanding rather than division among people, *Races of Mankind* is a troubling legacy, one that we have not wholly escaped. The terrible irony in the genuine concern of Laufer, Field and Keith with world stability and progress, with advancing human understanding to improve the human condition, was its irredeemable basis in a genteel racism, in which Europeans, particularly Nordics, are the central players, both in an exhibition of prehistoric human development confined to the last 250,000 years in Europe and in a racial exhibit literally centred on European types. Today, as societies and individuals search for reassurance and solutions in a world that continues to be marked by injustice and conflict, by heated debates over race and ethnicity, we may find that though the science of race has been rejected, some of the rhetoric is chillingly familiar. The story of *Races of Mankind* is a cautionary tale about the power and limits of science, scientists and scientific institutions.

ACKNOWLEDGMENTS

This paper has benefited from the thoughtful comments of Bob Richards, George Stocking, Gregg Mitman and Linda Kerber, as well as members of the History of the Human Sciences Workshop at the University of Chicago where I presented an early draft. At the Field Museum, Janice Klein, in the Anthropology Department, Ben Williams, in the Library, and Nina Cummings, in the Photography Department, were generous with their time and knowledge. Also, I would like to thank the Morris Fishbein Center for the History of Science and Medicine at the University of Chicago and the Getty Center for the History of Art and Humanities for generous grants which supported my research.

NOTES

1 Draft, to Ashley P. Talbot, Senior Editor, C. S. Hammond & Company, 29 January 1970, Anthropology Archives, Malvina Hoffman collection, Field Museum of Natural History, Chicago.
2 The belief that art and science are compatible representational practices, that art can enhance the ability of scientists to reveal truths about the natural world, harks back to eighteenth-century and earlier representations of the body. See, for example, Daston and Galison (1992), and Stafford (1991).
3 For a similar review see Wolff (1980); for a generally positive but more balanced consideration of Hoffman's work see Decoteau (1989/90).
4 Ironically, Hoffman objected to the hyperrealism of wax and plaster figures desired by Field and Laufer. According to Field she objected to 'an international Madame Tussaud's waxworks with nearly nude figures', the very epithet with which her bronze figures were later dismissed by some critics (Field 1953: 197).
5 There are contradictory accounts of exactly when and how this decision was made. Hoffman contends that she went ahead and cast two of her first five figures in bronze and surprised Stanley Field with them when he came to Paris to see them. She claims he was immediately taken with them, saw the advantages of bronze and promptly consulted with Marshall Field to raise the necessary additional funds. Henry Field, on the other hand, claims that the decision to go with bronze was made some time after Hoffman met Sir Arthur Keith in England. He claims that he and Keith weighed Hoffman's objection and talked over the problem of the sculptural medium 'time and time again', finally being 'won over to the bronzes, with a few stone heads to break the monotony' (Hoffman's precise characterization of the exhibit). Field then supposedly returned to Chicago and consulted with Laufer who agreed, particularly after Hoffman suggested using patina to suggest skin color, and recommended to Stanley Field that the contract be amended (see Field 1953 and Hoffman 1936: 11–12).
6 An archive document indicates the existence of a plan to collapse these displays into one ranging from old-world monkeys, through the orang-utan, chimpanzee and gorilla, to an Australian aborigine, ending with a Nordic type, in a more clearly evolutionary series with the aborigine placed as a 'missing link'.

7 This narrative is reminiscent of nineteenth-century social evolutionary schemes promulgated by anthropologists such as Lewis Henry Morgan in *Ancient Society* (1877), and Edward B. Tylor in *Researches into the Early History of Mankind and the Development of Civilization* (1865).

8 After her death at 25 in 1815, Baartman became a subject for the comparative anatomy of Georges Cuvier and Henri de Blainville. They published monographs in which she was compared as a primitive human to orang-utans. Her genitalia were given special consideration, as an index of primitiveness. According to Stephen J. Gould, her genitalia are among the remains still preserved in Paris. Among the works that consider the role of science in the iconography of race, and in particular the 'Hottentot Venus', is Gilman (1985). See also Gould (1985).

9 Regarding realism see also Nochlin (1970, 1971, 1981).

REFERENCES

Cole, G. (1984) 'Suggested letter re: display of Malvina Hoffman sculptures', December, Anthropology Department, Archives, Malvina Hoffman, Field Museum of Natural History, Chicago.

Conrad, D. C. and K. J. Tillotson (1992) 'The races of man', *Reader, Chicago's Free Weekly*, 22 (28), section 1.

Daston, L. and P. Galison (1992) 'The image of objectivity', *Representations*, 40 (Fall), pp. 108–28.

Decoteau, P. H. (1989/90) 'Malvina Hoffman and the "Races of Mankind"', *Women's Art Journal* (Fall 1989/Winter 1990), pp. 7–12.

Field Museum Anthropology Archives, Anthropology Department, Field Museum of Natural History. Chicago.

Field, H. (1942) *The 'Races of Mankind'*, Preface by Berthold Laufer, Introduction by Sir Arthur Keith, (4th edition), Popular series, Anthropology Leaflet 30, Chicago: Field Museum of Natural History.

—— (1953) *The Track of Man, Adventures of an Anthropologist*, New York: Doubleday & Company, Inc.

Gilman, S. L. (1985) 'Black bodies, white bodies: toward an iconography of female sexuality in late nineteenth-century art, medicine, and literature', *Critical Inquiry*, 12 (Autumn), pp. 204–42.

Gould, S. J. (1985) *The Flamingo's Smile: Reflections in Natural History*, New York: W. W. Norton & Co.

Haraway, D. (1989) *Primate Visions*, New York: Routledge.

Hoffman, M. (1936) *Heads and Tales*, New York: Charles Scribner & Sons.

—— (1939) *Sculpture Inside and Out*, New York: Bonanza Books.

—— (1965) *Yesterday is Tomorrow: A Personal History*, New York: Crown Publishers, Inc.

Jones, L. to E. Leland Webber, Director, and L. Siroto, Assistant Curator of African Ethnology, 7 August 1969, Anthropology Department Archives, Malvina Hoffman collection, Field Museum of Natural History, Chicago.

Keith, Sir A. (1929) *The Antiquity of Man* (7th impression), London: Williams & Norgate Ltd.

—— (1931) *The Place of Prejudice in Modern Civilization* (reprinted 1973), QUEST.

Laufer, B. to F. J. V. Skiff, 18 April 1916, Malvina Hoffman, History of the Hall of Races of Mankind 1930–1934, Anthropology Department Archives, Field Museum of Natural History, Chicago.

—— (1931) 'The projected hall of the Races of Mankind (Chauncey Keep Memorial Hall)', *Field Museum News*, December, 2 (12).

Leighton, I. (1949) *The Aspirin Age, 1919–1941*, New York: Simon & Schuster.
Morgan, L. H. (1877) *Ancient Society* (1878 edition reprinted 1985) Tucson, AZ: University of Arizona Press.
Nochlin, L. (1970) 'The ugly American', *Art News* (September), pp. 55–70.
—— (1971) *Realism*, New York: Penguin.
—— (1981) 'Return to order', *Art in America* (September).
—— (1984) 'Malvina Hoffman: a life in sculpture', *Arts Magazine* (November), pp. 106–10.
Rydell, R. (1985) 'The fan dance of science, America's world's fairs in the Great Depression', *Isis*, 76, pp. 525–42.
Spence, J. D. (1981) *The Gate of Heavenly Peace: The Chinese and Their Revolution 1895–1980*, New York: Penguin.
Stafford, B. M. (1991) *Body Criticism: Imaging the Unseen in Enlightenment Art and Medicine*, Cambridge, MA: The MIT Press.
Stocking, G. (ed.) (1968) *Race, Culture, and Evolution*, Chicago: University of Chicago Press.
Tuttle, W. (1970) *Race Riot: Chicago in the Red Summer of 1919*, New York: Athenum.
Tylor, E. B. (1865) *Researches into the Early History of Mankind and the Development of Civilization*, London.
Wolff, T. (1980) 'Old-fashioned art you would love to hold', *Christian Science Monitor* (30 April), p. 19.

Chapter 5

Making nature 'real' again
Natural history exhibits and public rhetorics of science at the Smithsonian Institution in the early 1960s

Steven W. Allison-Bunnell

One finds few working painters or sculptors in the back rooms of an art museum, busily supplying the galleries with new works. There are no physicists in the basements of science centres generating new laws of the universe for public exhibition. These scenarios sound absurd because we have long taken it for granted that museums exhibit objects or bodies of knowledge that have been produced at other times and sites in the intellectual economy of our culture. Whatever interpretive work the museum does to give the object or knowledge meaning, if it is recognized at all, is of a different sort than that involved in its production. Public representation relies on technical research only for factual authority; the actual process of creating public exhibitions bears no resemblance to the process of generating the knowledge they portray.

Take, for example, natural history museums: even though a considerable amount of research is still conducted in natural history museums, technical research is almost entirely divided from public exhibition at many institutions. But there was a time when the private spaces of natural history museums housed scientists whose work *combined* research and public exhibition. The great comparative anatomy collections of the nineteenth century, such as Louis Agassiz's Museum of Comparative Zoology at Harvard were both formed by and instantiated a technical research programme in classification (Winsor 1991). Furthermore, combining knowledge production with its representation was not simply convenient, serving merely to shorten the distance information had to travel in its route from point of origin to public exhibition; exhibition also influenced research. Henry Fairfield Osborn's desire for public exhibitions at the American Museum of Natural History that would prove his theories of social Darwinism required new research in vertebrate paleontology at the turn of the century (Rainger 1991). In these historical cases, the boundary between research and exhibition blurred both in epistemology and practice.

In fact, until the 1960s, the naturalist's cognitive skills involved in observing nature and epistemological goals of description and replication shared a close kinship with those of the artistically trained exhibits personnel. Much as the sociology of scientific knowledge has shown that, in the laboratory, tacit or 'craft' knowledge plays a crucial role in generating experimental data, the museum is another place where it is difficult to create an *a priori* definition of science that relies on a privileged system of completely formal knowledge (Collins 1985: 51–78). The fact that science cannot easily be formalized has implications not only for how we view science – its activities become more ordinary-looking – but also for how we conceptualize the process of popularizing science. This insight joins a critique of the dominant model of science communication that treats science communication as a process of packaging and transmitting fully formed knowledge, and that measures success by the degree to which the hard core of technical knowledge remains free from distortion (Hilgartner 1990; Myers 1990; Shinn and Whitley 1985).

To explore the proposition that knowledge production and representation are not easily disengaged, I will present an analysis of an educational film made at the Smithsonian Institution in 1964 that created a visual and narrative rhetoric of the overlap of research and exhibition. Produced by the Smithsonian Museum Service, which operated public outreach programs and responded to public enquiries, *The Leaf Thieves* is a 28-minute colour film that tells the story of plans for a tropical rainforest life group in the proposed Hall of Plant Life at the National Museum of Natural History (Burnham 1964a; Allison 1995).

As a piece of historical evidence, *The Leaf Thieves* is both useful and problematic. It is useful because, having been made at the Smithsonian for television and school distribution, it is a consciously constructed public projection of the museum's mission, methods and identity (Cowan 1963, 1992; Burnham 1964b). But of course such a projection can only answer questions about how the institution *wished* to be seen; it only indirectly conveys internal practices and attitudes. However, archival materials and recent interviews illuminate the same internal concerns and activities surrounding research and exhibition that *The Leaf Thieves* portrays. Therefore an examination of the film simultaneously serves two functions. First, the film provides a point of entry into the larger story of the rainforest exhibit's project to replicate nature at the Smithsonian and the questions it raises about the relationship between research and exhibition. Second, dissecting an instance of popularized science by drawing upon background materials explaining its creation illuminates the interests, authority and institutional logics behind the popular images we consume (Silverstone 1985).

My analysis will articulate the rhetorical strategies *The Leaf Thieves* deploys as it talks about research and exhibition. This presumes that the form of a text or image does not simply contain content passively, but that specific forms of representation and discourse do real, indispensable work in structuring the uses of the knowledge represented (Dear 1985; Gilbert and Mulkay 1984; Myers 1990). The film's rhetorical strategies are both visual and verbal, and I will examine aspects of the overall narrative structure (the logic or inference suggested by the order of scenes or images); specific visual images and actions, staged or 'actual'; word choice and syntax in the narration.

As no evidence of viewer reaction to the film survives, assessing the effect of the film's rhetorical strategies on its target audience is impossible. It certainly joins the ranks of natural history films made by and about scientists and explorers such as William Douglas Burden, who created narratives simultaneously interweaving stories about his expeditions for the American Museum of Natural History in the 1920s and 1930s with stories about the animals he observed (Mitman 1993). The curator who first proposed producing the film wanted it broadcast on the nature and outdoor television programmes of the time (Cowan 1961b).

However, film producer Sophy Burnham's lack of technical training and her outsider status as a woman, though informed by the curators, constituted her institutional role as Assistant Curator of the Museum Service to be a stand-in for the projected audience. As Macdonald points out, for women exhibit-makers at the Science Museum in London, the significance of this role is not that the actual audience maps directly onto the suppositions of the authors, but that their designation as audience-surrogates is the means by which the institution accounts for the audience in formulating the story (Macdonald 1996). In recounting her visits with the curators, Burnham herself tied her role as naïve observer of their world to her gender, saying, 'All of these men were so kind to this little girl coming in' to ask them about their work (Burnham 1992). In a traditional world of museum science, where the only women scientists were curators' wives who had escaped amateur status by sheer seniority, a self-described 'schoolgirl' represented the ultimate layman.

The first four minutes of the film define contemporary museum science in terms of laboratory equipment and procedures. This section sets up the core problematic of the rest of the story: how to relate traditional museum practice to 'modern science'. Next, the film's central segment, running for 18 minutes, recounts the Museum of Natural History's 1962 'Botany Exhibits Expedition' to Kaieteur Falls in then-British Guiana. Here, science and exhibition begin to merge, for both the botanists and the exhibits staff are given the identity of explorers and field scientists instead of laboratory scientists. The final six-minute section quite surprisingly depicts the botanists more as clerks than explorers. Paradoxically, the exhibits staff at work back in the model shop appear active and creative, forging a link back to the earlier definition of modern science based on laboratory apparatus.

THE INSTITUTIONAL JUSTIFICATION

This complicated and indeed contradictory narrative logic can be better understood in light of the institutional concerns motivating the film's production. In a memorandum to the Secretary of the Smithsonian requesting funds to produce the film, Botany Curator Richard Cowan, who headed the botany hall project and the expedition to British Guiana, argued that the film footage of museum staff at work in the rainforest could stand as an exemplar for museum science in general:

Using the expedition as the unifying mechanism, and the rain forest as an example, this film would illustrate a few of the biological problems and principles that scientists seek to unravel, such as the inter-relationships of plants and animals. It would aim to indicate the kinds of problems that remain to be solved and the importance attached to a solution of some of them. The film would also show the work of artists and illustrators in the biological sciences, depicting specimens and building models for scientific or exhibit use.

(Cowan 1963: 2)

The juxtaposition of 'problems that remain to be solved' and the 'work of artists and illustrators' implies that the artists and illustrators actively contribute to the knowledge production process. It is from this brief that the film's images of exhibit-making practices link to the practices of technical research.

This project is best seen in the wider context of the post-war promotion of science that created a new iconography of modern science. Advocates of higher-quality science communication in the 1960s emphasized scientific literacy in order to enable enlightened public decision-making, preserve democracy and share a grand 'adventure of the human spirit' (Krieghbaum 1967: 4–13). But Cowan's comments 30 years later reveal a more instrumental attitude toward public outreach:

[V]ery often people get the impression that there isn't much left to discover, there isn't much of a frontier in science and biology specifically, because they know so little about it. So the idea there was to give some idea of the excitement of discovery in various areas of the natural history sciences. Also something about how people *do* research. That was important because, again, we always had the problem, . . . as long as you have to keep trying to convince legislators . . . to let a little money out, you have to continue to do this sort of thing: educating people generally, educating the legislators, the Congressmen in particular.

(Cowan 1992)

Conveying 'the excitement of discovery' is not some abstract entertainment for a civilized citizenry, but the very basic and unapologetic recognition that, if science is to be funded, the public must be convinced of its value and interest.

Cowan's desire to remind the public that there are exciting *frontiers* in biology must also be seen against the backdrop of the American manned space pro-gramme after Sputnik, which, Michael Smith argues, was conceived within the government as a means of regaining national competitiveness and re-inventing America's pioneer explorer identity (Smith 1983: 191–8). Furthermore, if biology was to maintain its share of public funding, it had to compete against the highly charged images of high-tech aerospace engineering and physics. One means of doing so involved directly expropriating or tapping into the potent rhetoric of the post-Sputnik space race. *The Leaf Thieves* connects the natural history museum to the space race by including in its imagery of the museum's work a technician polishing a slab of meteorite and an animated graphic of drifting stars and a comet.

Along with attracting funding in the post-Sputnik era, Cowan also wanted to make biological science careers attractive to young people at a time when making new recruits to science was a pressing national concern in the United States:

> In the forty-one years from 1920 to 1961 only some 12,000 Ph. D.'s were earned in botany, zoology, and miscellaneous biological subjects. . . . Not even these figures, however, adequately show the dearth in the biological sciences of scientists, scientific illustrators, artists, plastics technicians, technical assistants, and other biologically oriented personnel. One reason for this shortage is that many young people who might naturally be attracted to biology as a career are never acquainted with the breadth of opportunity and wide range of skills utilized in the profession.
>
> (Cowan 1963: 1)

It is striking that Cowan lumps all levels of expertise and practices into a single, unified 'profession' consisting of 'biologically oriented personnel'. The public discourse of scientists in debates over scientific authority often involves boundary work that narrows what counts as doing science, whereas Cowan's effort at recruitment expands the category (Hilgartner 1990).

NARRATIVE LOGICS PROMOTING MUSEUM RESEARCH

Glossing museum science as lab science

The first step in *The Leaf Thieves*' narrative logic expands the publicly perceived definition of the museum to include research along with exhibition. The Smithsonian scientists had long viewed research as more central to its identity and reputation than its exhibits (Taylor 1974: 74–5). Though genuinely committed to the exhibits programme, Cowan expressed a residue of this sentiment in his brief for the film: 'such a film would also serve to show the work of the Smithsonian. Few people have any idea of the size and scope of the Institution, and few realize the extent of its research function' (Cowan 1963: 3). Cowan seemed unconvinced that the exhibits by themselves sufficiently telegraphed the activity behind the scenes.

The film opens with a sequence that carries out Cowan's directive, but in a purposefully ironic, playful mode. Burnham first addresses the stereotypes of natural history museums:

> [Smithsonian Castle] The ordinary person has a preconceived image of a natural history museum.

[man walking through dark hall with ethnographic specimens] Sometimes he sees this.

[Figure 5.1: mad scientist with bubbling glassware] And sometimes this.

[alcohol-preserved zoology specimens in storage area; slow music – clarinets] He also has an image of collections, and of what happens there.

(Burnham 1964a)

An instantly recognizable popular image of science, the mad scientist was important enough to Burnham's iconography to use an architect friend of hers who 'had a rich, crazy face . . . to play the part of the mad scientist and to put some dry ice into a glass of water and have it bubble up all blue' (Burnham 1992). This is Burnham's playfulness and irrepressible sense of humour at work. In interview, she says, 'I made fun of the film, and I made fun of the idea of museums' (ibid.).

Figure 5.1 The staged Mad Scientist with dry ice and glassware; from *The Leaf Thieves* (1964) (courtesy of the Smithsonian Institution Office of Telecommunications)

Following Cowan's brief, Burnham then goes on to expand the category of museum science specifically to include lab-based experimental science whose visual signs are high-tech machinery and procedures:

[Figure 5.2: man in tie pouring liquid nitrogen out of Dewar flask into radiation counter; plinky 'industrial' music] But this is out of date. A new time has come with new techniques and new fields to explore.

[close-up of sample bottle; sketch reconstructing archaeological site; man setting 'pressure' dial on radiation counter] Now charcoal from the cook-fire of an ancient Indian village is studied, and its age calculated by Carbon-14 dating.

(Burnham 1964a)

Figure 5.2 The 'Real Scientist' pouring liquid nitrogen into a Carbon-14 counter; from *The Leaf Thieves* (1964) (courtesy of the Smithsonian Institution Office of Telecommunications)

After the clearly staged, jokey mad scientist of the stereotype, with his bubbling beakers, we are immediately given the image of the real, serious scientist, with his steaming flask and blinking machinery. Though the narrator deconstructs the stereotype, its iconographic resemblance to modern science is clear and crucial – if what goes on in the museum is to be classified as modern science, then it must look like what everybody knows science looks like. In the American popular press, that iconography most frequently involved high-tech equipment and chemistry laboratories (LaFollette 1990: 112–16). Specimens in jars are too inert, sadly representing an anachronistic nineteenth-century form of knowledge based on collection and enumeration instead of experiment and theory. As a substitute for specimens, the Carbon-14 counter proves that the museum has made the transition to space-age laboratory science, and this portrait of active, experimental, manipulative research is the image with which the botany expedition and exhibits work must interact.

As one of the largest museum systems in the world dependent on public funds, the Smithsonian clearly had a crucial interest in not being viewed as scientifically moribund. Prior to the film's production, Burnham's boss at the Museum Service, historian G. Carroll Lindsay, worried that

> a great deal of research in natural history can go forward independent of natural history museums. Modern trends toward a concentration on research in ecology and social relationships make good progress through field work and theoretical studies which are only indirectly related to taxonomy, systematics, and object-oriented anthropology.
>
> (Lindsay 1962: 237)

Lindsay goes on to remind critics that taxonomists retain an abiding interest in the legacy of the greatest of biology's theorists, Darwin, and to call for the Institution's renewed competitiveness (ibid.: 238).

A sequence in the last section of the film tries to reconnect museum research to laboratory biology by suggesting that cancer researchers would turn to the museum's mouse collections to identify the strains of lab animals they used. When I asked Burnham about the mice, she volunteered,

> [A]t that time, people were very concerned about whether there was anything important about basic research and comparative taxonomy . . . And you had to be able to defend the work that you were doing to Congress in order to get more money. So we were constantly being aware of educating the public to the importance of this kind of – it wasn't research, but study, I guess you would call it.
>
> (Burnham 1992)

In Burnham's telling, non-museum scientists stigmatized collections as haphazard, idiosyncratic, and amateur. She attributed her awareness of this image to the curators themselves: 'they were aware also that they were on the fringes of the "Real" work – real in capitals and quotation marks' (ibid.). As their public advocate, it was her job to legitimize their work and, sharing Cowan's target, to raise its standing where it mattered – with Congress. Crucially, Burnham herself remained ambivalent about the nature of the museum's research, admitting, 'I always felt that we were very defensive about it, but that it was extremely difficult to defend' (ibid.). So although she was charged to portray the traditional work of the museum as having modern relevance, she found it difficult ultimately to do so.

Merging museum research and exhibition

Burnham's ambivalence can be seen as leading to the film's second rhetorical turn, which portrays the practices and technologies of exhibit-making as scientific in their own right, indeed eventually appearing even more 'scientific' than the activities of the real scientists themselves. Burnham links research and exhibition in a counter-intuitive set of steps that serve to remedy the difficulties in establishing a direct connection between museum and laboratory research. In the first move, following Cowan's brief, the museum's research mission is articulated in terms of the rainforest exhibit expedition. The field footage, filmed before *The Leaf Thieves* was scripted, casts the expedition team in another familiar and powerful role compared to the laboratory scientist: the field naturalist and explorer. These scenes connect the collecting activities of the botanist-explorers to the artistic practices of the exhibit-builders, which in turn are the images which are finally linked favourably to the images of modern science. This connection is essential to the film's narrative logic, because, once back at the museum and in a setting analogous to the laboratory, the botanists' own research practices in the museum end up appearing lacklustre and without an obvious relationship to modern science as defined at the beginning of the film. The irony of this strategy lies in the fact that natural history is made scientific by what might appear as an anachronistic detour through exhibit-making.

The botanist as explorer

In the field sequence, Burnham's ambivalence about collections fades, for we see the botanists as proper explorers, and their identity is both familiar and robust (LaFollette 1990: 55). They are khaki-clad and booted; their anonymous native helpers chop through the jungle with machetes. The viewer's expectations of what white explorers should look like and how they should behave are fulfilled in the narrative created with the footage which botanist Thomas Soderstrom originally took snap-shot style:

> [Brink of Falls and downstream; rainbow, gorge] They had two months to hunt and explore the forest. What grows at the base of the Fall, for example, eight hundred feet below and masked in mist and moss? . . .
> [Falls; group on rocks from above; cliffs and mist, rushing water] Tons of water throwing itself eight hundred feet in a thunderous cascade to the rocks below. . . Beneath them raced the rapids. The scientists could neither carry cameras and equipment, nor easily collect many plants.
>
> (Burnham 1964a)

Penetrating the impenetrable, awesome natural forces thwarting their search for knowledge – these are the themes running through this sequence. They echo the popular writings earlier in the century about explorer-taxidermist Carl Akely's collecting expeditions in Africa earlier this century (Haraway 1989). The evocative music and the narrator's forceful, masculine delivery give the already dramatic pictures of the botanists dwarfed in the gorge an unmistakable excitement and sense of adventure. This frontier is just as uncharted as Outer Space and as familiar an icon as an African safari.

It is here in the field that research and exhibition naturally merge under the definition of natural history as exploration. By reverting to a definition of science as natural history and conflating it with experimentation and space exploration, collecting for the exhibit becomes scientific. The rainforest exhibit is warranted as scientific because there is no visible division of labour between the botanists and the artists:

> [Cowan bundling specimens; Cowan gathering plant from canoe with pruning clippers; Sayre with sketchbook wrapped in foil, guide carries rope and machete; flowering plants] This is rain forest, and the scientists came, drawn by curiosity, to discover its forms of life . . . This expedition had two goals. Like most, it was formed to find what lived in the forest, how it lived, and where.

[Soderstrom setting up slide camera] But unlike others, this expedition was to reproduce in a three dimensional museum exhibit, the rain forest of Kaieteur Fall.

(ibid.)

The narration reinforces the image of exhibition as science by explaining the drive to collect and reproduce the rainforest in terms of the scientist's curiosity and desire to make new discoveries.

Nowhere in this sequence is the expedition and the rainforest reproduction within the museum justified on educational grounds with relation to the visitor. Collecting specimens and reproducing the field site are woven into the very fabric of scientific practice and knowledge claims. Although these scenes include exhibit preparator Reginald Sayre and the team's local guides (a skilled botanist, Rufus Boyan, among them), the narrator says only that 'the scientists came'. And though we see Cowan putting plants in a herbarium press as well as packaging exhibit specimens, there are few cues, visual or verbal, that differentiate distinctly the practices of technical collecting from the practices of exhibit collecting.

The model-maker as scientist

Furthermore, the most tangible signs of the exhibit's authenticity and scientific credibility are images of the painstaking collecting process. We see Sayre and Cowan removing a rubber mould of the bark of a fluted tree. Sayre is shown removing moulds of patches of soil, rolling them up like a carpet (Figure 5.3). This technology of replication is identical to Latour's notion of an 'inscription device' as a laboratory technology that transcribes a natural process, such as a solution running through a chromatography column, into an 'inscription', such as a peak on a paper chart (Latour 1979: 51). The 'portable nature' created by impressions of rocks and tree trunks which may be rolled up and carried away is a literal, macroscopic version of the processes of inscription and translation at work in the laboratory which domesticate unseen natural phenomena and make them available for the scientist's manipulation and interpretation (Latour 1979; Allison 1995).

The means by which the model-makers carry out this translation further aligns the interests of the model-makers' and the botanists' way of seeing. Figure 5.4 shows master model-maker Paul Marchand constructing a model bromeliad at the expedition's camp in British Guiana. Sayre describes Marchand's method and expertise in this way:

First he collected the plant and disassembled it and would determine how to make the parts in wax to assemble and to make it look real again. He made molds for each part and assembled the wax models back to reality and then painted them identically to the original.

(Sayre 1992b)

Marchand's craftsmanship inscribes nature into wax and paint, and in doing so

Figure 5.3 'Capturing nature': Reginald Sayre removing a latex mould of rainforest soil; from *The Leaf Thieves* (1964) (courtesy of the Smithsonian Institution Office of Telecommunications)

constitutes the real as much as it discovers it. Sayre's phrases 'real *again*' and '*back* to reality' suggest that the plant is itself treated as a model, subject to disassembly and re-assembly. The model has become as real as the original, and in fact reconstitutes the original in all relevant respects.

Figure 5.4 'Back to reality': model-maker Paul Marchand modelling a bromeliad from beeswax in British Gurana, 1962 (photograph by Thomas R. Soderstrom; courtesy of the Smithsonian Institution Department of Botany, National Museum of Natural History)

Furthermore, making the model 'look real again' involves a dialogue with the real rather than a simple imprint. Sayre added that 'sometimes, if you had a smaller leaf, you'd make it shorter just by cutting it off and [smoothing out] the wax' (Sayre 1992b). 'And then after [Marchand] finished and he found out he wanted another leaf in there he might do something with the same mold and shape it the size he wanted' (Sayre 1992a). Exact duplication and judgment about what the thing *ought* to look like intermingle. On one hand, Marchand's standard of accuracy demanded a separate mould for each leaf in acknowledgment of its uniqueness. But he also might decide that the real thing was not real enough and needed more leaves to look right. Suddenly, the passive technician who slavishly duplicates nature without insight or understanding has become an active artisan (with the Aristotelian connotations of agency the term implies), interpreting how things are to look and reshaping nature according to a conception of ideal type or internal aesthetic. The plant parts go from unique individuals to representatives of 'leaf-ness' which can be amplified in multiple copies and then altered to take on the appearance of uniqueness. Embedded in the modelling process is a tension between uniqueness as a raw material and as a created artefact. This tension closely resembles the process of seeing and creating similarity and difference which Mary Winsor attributes to Louis Agassiz's approach to classification in the nineteenth century and which remains today at the core of traditional morphological taxonomy (Winsor 1991).

Exhibition as modern science

The narrative logic of Act 3 of *The Leaf Thieves* poses the problem that although the botanists looked properly scientific in the field as nineteenth-century explorer-naturalists, back in the museum their identity is disaggregated from that of the exhibit-makers and, startlingly, the exhibit-makers end up looking more scientific than the botanists. This set of moves originates in Burnham's ambivalence about the scientific usefulness of museum collections.

The curator as file clerk

The scenes staged after the expedition of the botanists working in the museum depict them as white-collar workers in ties, sitting at desks in rather tidy offices or paging through stacks of herbarium sheets (Figure 5.5). Cowan talks into a dictation machine, but is given a potted plant for his desk, along with an enormous nineteenth-century floristic monograph conspicuously opened to an illustration of some exotic tropical flower. Without these props and the hand-lenses hanging around their necks, the botanists might be accountants or managers, given the contrast of these visually sparse scenes to the visual definitions of science earlier in the film. As dramatizations, the botanists' actions are stylized and rather inscrutable – what do they see when they look through their hand-lenses? What do they do with their knowledge? The narrator

Figure 5.5 Botany curators David Lellinger and John Wurdack examining herbarium specimens in the US National Herbarium (housed in the Smithsonian Castle); from *The Leaf Thieves* (1964) (courtesy of the Smithsonian Institution Office of Telecommunications)

interprets what we see, certifying, 'All plants are catalogued and preserved in the national collections, so that any scientist can find and study them again. Each new species, each new plant collected becomes a fact, a tangible point of reference on which to base a conclusion' (Burnham 1964a). But the announcer's authority to name the curators as scientists because their collections embody 'facts' is undermined by the lack of visual signs that would prove them to be scientists more convincingly than simply saying so.

This image of the botanists as scientific file clerks is not merely an accidental result of low-budget film-making. For though Burnham was fascinated with the individual psychology of the Smithsonian's curators, the drama of their field exploits and the beauty of the treasures in their collections, she personally viewed taxonomy as being more than vaguely bureaucratic. In a popular magazine article written shortly after Burnham left the Smithsonian, she called it 'at least an open question' whether the 'cataloguing' done by the museum (the term also used in the film) was real research at all (Burnham 1966: 46). When speaking her own mind, Burnham turns Lindsay's lament that modern biology no longer needs museum collections into a full-on assault on taxonomists:

> Every day he takes a tiny shell from a tray, puts it under a microscope, and compares it with a master specimen. He writes out a tag in careful calligraphy, spelling out its name, date, catalogue number, and other relevant information. He puts it in another tray . . . and this he does with the patience of Penelope, day after day, year after year.
>
> (ibid.)

Burnham's words fairly drip with disdain for the repetitive, meticulous record-keeping and the minute and therefore meaningless detail of the practice of classification. Just as Penelope wove and unravelled her winding-sheet as a stalling tactic, so, according to Burnham, the curator contributes nothing to the actual growth of knowledge. Burnham claims that these academically trained curators 'fled' from academia, where the 'really exciting work, that material that is forming the foundation of new research' is done (ibid.). Given such an indictment of the curator's practice and lack of scientific vision, Burnham had to turn elsewhere for an image compelling enough to sell museum science to the public.

Into the exhibits laboratory

Ironically, Burnham finds what she is looking for in the traditional but visually rich and active practices of the exhibit-makers, which she links to modern science. This link was foreshadowed by the fact that, although the botanists did not consider the exhibits work to be strictly identical to their research, they naturalized it into their own sphere by using modern scientific terminology for their exhibit activities. Cowan's script for a small in-house display about the botany hall explains, 'The purpose of this exhibit is to represent graphically some of the steps involved in gathering and organizing data in the field for subsequent use in the laboratory for constructing a life group' (Cowan 1962b). The key words here are 'data', used to describe material destined for the hall, 'laboratory', which refers to the exhibits shop, and 'the field', being the locale to be reproduced. Internal correspondence throughout the period consistently refers to collecting for the exhibit as 'obtaining' or 'gathering' new 'data' and the field locations are 'study sites' (Cowan 1961a, 1962a, 1964). This conception of exhibit-making as 'study' directly contradicts the received view of science communication as passive transmission, and establishes the habitat group's status as a new piece of knowledge. At the same time that the habitat group is intended as a transparent window onto nature, the 'study' that embeds 'data' into the representation via the model-makers' inscription devices is at root an interpretive, and therefore, a knowledge generating process.

The Leaf Thieves similarly naturalizes exhibits into research by recognizing that, although the exhibits are part and parcel of the old-fashioned knowledge embodied by the specimen collections, the *activities* involved in generating the exhibits bear a resemblance to the experimental science of the laboratory. Admittedly, part of the problem with the portrayal of the botanists is a filmic artefact, since the botanists' scenes were staged, while the exhibit-makers' appear less so. The botanists were of course not professional actors, and they are not to blame if their efforts to recreate their daily activities are a bit self-conscious. Furthermore, the spaces and props of their profession are by nature undramatic, their dress is white-collar and their cognitive processes remain entirely internal and invisible to the viewer.

On the other hand, the exhibit-makers were filmed as they went about their daily work. Their work is visual, concrete and *generative*. The tasks of making moulds, assembling and painting model plants and sculpting taxidermy mannequins look more documentary, as if these activities did not require rehearsal. Moreover, the space of the model shop is crowded with every sort of artefact in varying degrees of construction: stuffed animals, mounted and painted fish, life-sized replicas of cacti, sculptures of aboriginal humans and dinosaurs. Like the blinking Carbon-14 counter or the mad scientist's bubbling beakers, the exhibit shop denotes the doing of science: the products of their science surround the workers literally, tangibly, in a way that the botanist's offices and file drawers cannot. Because films can portray vividly physical activity while mental activity must be implied, the physicality of the exhibits shop forms an indirect linkage between natural history and modern science, which, for the same reason, is itself not illustrated by theorists, but experimentalists.

The exhibit-makers' attire also serves to construct their film identity as thoroughly modern scientists. We see Sayre dressed in a tie and lab coat while he wires plastic leaves to a shrub. What single item of clothing besides the lab coat has the power to signify that its wearer is doing science? But the botanists do not wear lab coats, and although it would clearly have been dishonest to dress them in lab coats if they had no need to wear them, the fact that they did not need them implies that their activities are not hands-on or experimental.

However, *The Leaf Thieves* does portray the process of building an exhibit as hands-on, requiring sophisticated equipment and techniques. The narrator describes Sayre's work: 'The specialist welds a group of copper molds together into a gang mold, sprays colored plastisol on the gang mold, cooks it in an oven for three minutes at three hundred and fifty degrees, and removes the plastic leaves' (Burnham 1964a). Both the level of detail with which Burnham describes the process of making a plastic leaf and the complicated materials and techniques shown on screen evoke an experimental protocol, complete with steps and exact numbers to be followed.

This notion that the exhibit-makers work with scientific precision is in fact an integral part of their professional identity. Though trained as an artist, and ultimately deferential to the scientific authority of the curators, Sayre did not simply blindly follow their specifications, content with a strict division of intellectual labour. Instead, he developed his own understanding of the things he was assigned to work on. When a new project began,

> we'd really make time to do a little research if we weren't sure what we had to do. I spent a lot of time in the library down there, and I got to know the librarian so well, because I had never done anything in natural history until I came to the American Museum [of Natural History]. *There* I learned that you've got to be precise about certain things. Most people, they go to work and they do their job every day, but in the museum you can't do it that way.
>
> (Sayre 1992a; emphasis in original)

Sayre clearly did not see himself as a mere technician or routine worker, but brought considerable independent thinking and a strong sense of vocation to his model-making.

Interpretive skill was crucial to the model-maker's success. An article by Sayre's boss at the American Museum gives detailed instructions for making artificial plant leaves and parts, but ends with this firm admonition:

> No techniques or methods, no matter how highly developed or skillfully carried out, can succeed in giving life to artificial plants unless the preparator is himself completely familiar with all aspects of the plant in its growing state. He must have observed nature itself with such care that he will recognize, not only by his artistic instinct, but also by his highly trained eye, any fold or permutation of an artificial plant that is not consistent with its appearance in nature.
>
> (Peterson 1958: 34)

Sayre's attitudes were not simply to do with one man's pride in his workmanship, but a part of a larger corporate ethos. Furthermore, Peterson's distinction between the preparator's 'highly trained eye' and his 'artistic instinct' comes after more than 20 pages of step-by-step instructions on leaf moulding and fabrication. He would not have made such a claim, even as an afterthought, if he had hoped, by formalizing a largely craft-based process, to de-skill the job and recruit less professional practitioners. Rather, he cuts against the enormous rhetorical weight of his instructions to maintain the scientific nature of the enterprise in order to ensure that the model is 'consistent with its appearance in nature'.

CONCLUSION

This analysis of the narrative structure and iconography of *The Leaf Thieves* reveals both the genesis and function of a piece of scientific popularization as a promotion of institutional interests in the public arena, and the identities of knowledge producers in natural history museums. The Smithsonian's public portrayal of museum science as properly modern and relevant by the standards of the mid-1960s relied on images of laboratory science, the romance of field study and the creation of a family resemblance between the anachronistic scientific qualities of exhibition-making and laboratory science. This narrative structure certified museum research as properly scientific, both to attract new recruits to the field and to secure funding from Congress, during a period in which 'Big Science', and the space programme in particular, stood in the public imagination as the quintessence of modern science in general. The desire to raise public awareness of the value of traditional museum science required translating the knowledge and practice of natural history as represented by the Smithsonian botanists through exhibit-making. This was necessary because, by the visual standards of documentary film-making, the images of pure taxonomy alone were deemed too sterile to be able to build sufficient public interest in the field to ensure its continued support (Silverstone 1985).

Partnership in knowledge production

Just what were the resources available to the film to convert the scientist's cognitive taxonomical practices into the model-maker's more recognizable artistic practices? Natural history research and exhibition are historically rooted in the same forms of knowledge and practice. At the height of their influence in the late nineteenth and early twentieth centuries, scientific taxidermists sought to establish themselves as skilled partners to technically trained naturalists in generating and representing descriptive knowledge (Star 1992). These attempts failed as university-based laboratory research programmes solidified a definition of biology as experimental and mechanism-orientated, to the exclusion of the naturalist's descriptive view of objects *as* knowledge (ibid.; Hagen 1984). This definition finally caught up with the Smithsonian in the late 1960s, when its Secretary, S. Dillon Ripley, championed state-of-the-art theoretical types of biology, such as ecology, and exhibits that were 'increasingly directed toward the presentation of *ideas* rather than *objects*' (Ripley 1968; emphases in original). If the descriptive epistemology of the naturalist no longer looks today like legitimate scientific knowledge, it is not that it never counted as such, but that the hegemony of knowledge based on the intervention of the laboratory is now complete, and the knowledge of representation in and of itself, to use Ian Hacking's dyad, has been successfully trivialized (Hacking 1983).

Several suggestive questions arise concerning the nature of the knowledge embedded in natural history habitat groups. First, if the rubber and plaster moulds are Latourian inscription devices that domesticate natural phenomena, what do they transform nature into as it is translated from the field site into the habitat group in the exhibit hall? As its name implies, natural *history* narrativizes nature, and natural history museum habitat groups represent a highly developed story-telling technology (Wonders 1993). Turning the hurly-burly of nature into a coherent, logical story not only requires the artist's ability to create verisimilitude, but also the discernment to select which particular details encode the chosen story into the habitat group. Unlike most habitat groups, which featured animals at the centre of their tableaux, the story the rainforest was meant to tell was strictly about the intrinsic beauty and scientific interest of plants. In order to ensure that plants would receive proper attention, animals were to be excluded from the habitat group entirely (Killip 1948). The rubber moulds, in the service of realism, translate nature through the botanists' interests in promoting their field to the public.

The title to the film, *The Leaf Thieves*, offers another clue about the habitat group's construction of the natural. Intended or not, it creates the following equation: stealing = preciousness = desire to possess. Theft removes an object from its rightful place and therefore both expropriates it and renders it valuable. The mass of leaves in the British Guiana jungle were not valuable until their plaster moulds were spirited away from the Tropics; while still there, they were only a few examples among many possible specimens, whereas once installed in the museum's collections, the moulds are crucial inscriptions that enable trans-lation. Museum collecting has been so profoundly tied up with Western colonialism that, even when the collecting was itself not an act of domination, the popular representation still almost subliminally framed it as such (Haraway 1989).

This equation for the technology to capture, transport and sequester bits of nature inside the museum's walls also highlights the paradox of the overlap between exhibition and research. In looking for differences between popular and technical scientific texts, Greg Myers distinguishes between popular 'narratives of nature' that omit the presence of the scientist and technical 'narratives of science' that bring scientific practice and reasoning into the foreground (Myers 1990: 142). But habitat groups do their work precisely through a tension between these two narratives. At the same time that the habitat group-maker's art submerges his craft (the narrative of nature), the viewer's awareness of the *illusion* of reality continually draws attention to the artistic finesse of its making (the narrative of science). Combining these two narratives, the habitat group becomes more real than real, a phenomenon which Umberto Eco calls 'hyper-reality' (Eco 1986). The exhibit team 'leaf thieves' did not steal the rain forest *per se*, they stole its essence.

A moral for science communication

Finally, the story of *The Leaf Thieves* helps to contextualize the present division of labour between exhibition and research, where the expertise of educators is privileged and scientists play an advisory role in the exhibit-making process. *The Leaf Thieves* depicts the end of the age of scientists as exhibit-makers for, by the end of the 1960s, it was increasingly common for the Smithsonian to employ outside exhibit-developers whose interests stemmed from wider societal concerns and definitions of science which did not align well with the curators' internal agendas. By the end of the 1960s, under the direction of professional exhibit-makers influenced by the growing ecology movement, the rainforest exhibit as it was finally built had been transformed from a narrative taken from the book of nature into an icon of 'the interdependency of life' imperilled by human exploitation (Mahoney 1973: 2). Objecting to the activist motives of the exhibit, the curators withdrew to the sidelines of the exhibit-making process (Kier 1973).

That episode marked the bifurcation of the educational and research missions of the museum, so that today, the two enterprises, while carried out under the same roof, are no longer intimately connected either by practice or by shared knowledges and contexts (Allison 1995). The division between exhibition and research has served to dissolve the unique characteristic of natural history museums as places where scientific research and public representation interlock. Having severed the fundamental linkage between the production and public representation of knowledge, there is indeed no particular reason why either science or exhibition must continue to coexist under the same roof, and the identity and mission of natural history museums will be decided by struggles between these two programmes, rather than the negotiation of a symbiosis.

Hilgartner describes how scientists deploy the dominant conception of science communication as the transmission of the hard core of scientific research in order to blame the communication process for errors and bias (Hilgartner 1990). However, in professionalizing the communication process, science writers and educators have also relied on the dominant definition to frame a symmetrical claim, articulated by John Burnham, that scientists' esoteric overspecialization caused them to cease to be interested in or capable of popularization (Burnham 1987: 248). But, as long as both scientists and science communicators hold on to the flawed model of neutral transmission, science communication will remain unable to accurately portray the blurry intersection between creating and representing scientific knowledge.

REFERENCES

Allison, S. W. (1995) 'Transplanting a rain forest: natural history research and public exhibition at the Smithsonian Institution, 1960–1975', Ph.D. dissertation, Cornell University.

Burnham, J. (1987) *How Superstition Won and Science Lost: Popularization of Science and Health in America*, New Brunswick, NJ: Rutgers University Press.

Burnham, S. (1964a) *The Leaf Thieves*, 16mm sound motion picture film. Smithsonian Institution Archives Accession No. 93–085, Box 8.

—— (1964b) 'Smithsonian scientific expedition film to be premiered here on October 22'. Smithsonian Institution Archives Record Unit 276, Box 53.

—— (1966) 'The Smithsonian faces forward', *The Washingtonian Magazine* (November), pp. 33–40, 46.

—— (1992) 'Oral history interview'. Tropical Rain Forest Interviews, Smithsonian Institution Archives Record Unit 9565.

Collins, H. M. (1985) *Changing Order: Replication and Induction in Scientific Practice*, London: Sage.

Cowan, R.S. (1961a) to A. C. Smith, 11 August. Smithsonian Institution Archives Record Unit 155, Box 15.

—— (1961b) to Thomas R. Soderstrom, 21 November. Smithsonian Institution Archives Record Unit 155, Box 12.

—— (1962a) to A. C. Smith, 3 March. Smithsonian Institution Archives Record Unit 155, Box 12.

—— (1962b) to J. Ewers, 19 November. Smithsonian Institution Archives Record Unit 155, Box 12.

—— (1963) 'Copy of memo which Dr. Cowan would send to Dr. Carmichael'. Smithsonian Institution Archives Accession No. 91–087, Box 5.

—— (1964) to L. Swallen, 2 June. Smithsonian Institution Archives Record Unit 155, Box 15.

—— (1992) 'Oral History Interview'. Tropical Rain Forest Interviews, Smithsonian Institution Archives Record Unit 9565.

Dear, P. (1985) '*Totius in verba*: rhetoric and authority in the early Royal Society', *Isis*, 76, 1, pp. 145–61.

Eco, U. (1986) *Travels in Hyperreality*, New York: Harcourt Brace Jovanovich.

Gilbert, N. and M. Mulkay (1984) *Opening Pandora's Box: A Sociological Analysis of Scientists' Discourse*, Cambridge: Cambridge University Press.

Hacking, I. (1983) *Representing and Intervening: Introductory Topics in the Philosophy of Natural Science*, Cambridge: Cambridge University Press.

Hagen, J. (1984) 'Experimentalists and naturalists in twentieth-century botany: experimental taxonomy 1920–1950', *Journal of the History of Biology*, 17, 2, pp. 249–70.

Haraway, D. (1989) 'Teddy bear patriarchy: taxidermy in the Garden of Eden, New York City, 1908–36', in D. Haraway *Primate Visions: Gender, Race, and Nature in the World of Modern Science*, pp. 26–58, New York: Routledge, Chapman & Hall.

Hilgartner, S. (1990) 'The dominant view of popularization: conceptual problems, political uses', *Social Studies of Science*, 20, 3, pp. 519–41.

Kier, P. (1973) to S. D. Ripley, 2 February. Smithsonian Institution Archives Record Unit 257, Box 8.

Killip, E. P. (1948) 'Department of Botany: future exhibitions'. Smithsonian Institution Archives Record Unit 155, Box 15.

Krieghbaum, H. (1967) *Science and the Mass Media*, New York: New York University Press.

LaFollette, M. (1990) *Making Science Our Own: Public Images of Science 1910–1955*, Chicago: University of Chicago Press.

Latour, B. (1979) *Laboratory Life: The Social Construction of Scientific Facts*, Beverly Hills, CA: Sage.

Lindsay, G. C. (1962) 'Museums and research in history and technology', *Curator*, 5, 3, pp. 236–44.

Macdonald, S. (1996) 'Authorizing science: public understanding of science in museums', in A. Irwin and B. Wynne (eds) *Misunderstanding Science? The Public Reconstruction of Science and Technology*, pp. 152–71, New York: Cambridge University Press.

Mahoney, J. (1973) 'It all depends: an exhibit on ecology'. Smithsonian Institution Archives Record Unit 342, Box 91.

Mitman, G. (1993) 'Cinematic nature: Hollywood technology, popular culture, and the American Museum of Natural History', *Isis*, 84, 4, pp. 637–61.

Myers, G. (1990) *Writing Biology: Texts in the Construction of Scientific Knowledge*, Madison, WI: The University of Wisconsin Press.

Peterson, G. (1958) 'Artificial plants', *Curator*, 1, 3, pp. 12–35.

Rainger, R. (1991) *An Agenda for Antiquity: Henry Fairfield Osborn and Vertebrate Paleontology at the American Museum of Natural History, 1890–1935*, Tuscaloosa, AL: University of Alabama Press.

Ripley, S. D. (1968) to J. P. Hammerschmidt, 12 December. Smithsonian Institution Archives Record Unit 155, Box 14.

Sayre, R. (1992a) 'Oral history interview'. Tropical Rain Forest Interviews, Smithsonian Institution Archives Record Unit 9565.

—— (1992b) 'Video history interview'. Tropical Rain Forest Interviews, Smithsonian Institution Archives Record Unit 9565.

Shinn, T. and R. Whitley (eds) (1985) *Expository Science: Forms and Functions of Popularization*, Boston, MA: D. Reidel.

Silverstone, R. (1985) *Framing Science: The Making of a BBC Documentary*, London: British Film Institute.

Smith, M. L. (1983) 'Selling the Moon: the U. S. manned space program and the triumph of commodity scientism', in R. W. Fox and T. J. Jackson Lears (eds) *The Culture of Consumption: Critical Essays in American History, 1880–1980*, New York: Pantheon Books.

Star, S. L. (1992) 'Craft vs. commodity, mess vs. transcendence: how the right tool became the wrong one in the case of taxidermy and natural history', in A. Clarke and J. Fujimura (eds) *The Right Tools for the Job: At Work in Twentieth-century Life Sciences*, Princeton, NJ: Princeton University Press.

Taylor, F. (1974) 'Oral history interviews'. Smithsonian Institution Archives Record Unit 9512.

Winsor, M. (1991) *Reading the Shape of Nature: Comparative Zoology at the Agassiz Museum*, Chicago: University of Chicago Press.

Wonders, K. (1993) *Habitat Dioramas: Illusions of Wilderness in Museums of Natural History*, Stockholm: University of Uppsala.

Chapter 6

On interactivity
Consumers, citizens and culture

Andrew Barry

The relation between the contemporary science museum and its public is an interactive one. At the level of the institution, the museum is increasingly expected to respond to the public's demands rather than simply tell the public what it needs to know – the public needs to understand science but, before this is possible, the museum must first understand what the public wants. At the level of the gallery, museum staff aim to design exhibits which enable visitors to make choices and to experience a gallery 'in their own way' (Macdonald and Silverstone 1990: 184).[1] And at the level of the individual display, the museum seeks to develop and employ techniques which encourage greater dialogue with the visitor. As an influential Management Plan for London's Science Museum noted:

> Passive and poorly interpreted attractions will suffer at the expense of those that develop live demonstrations, provide participation, interactive displays, and give a quality of personal rather than institutional service to their visitors. Informality and friendliness will be valuable attractions.
>
> (Science Museum 1986)

In exploring the proliferation of forms and techniques of interactivity in the museum of science this chapter develops three themes. The first concerns the contemporary political resonances of interaction. There is no doubt, as Mark Poster notes, that the usage of the idea of interactivity can 'float and be applied in countless contexts having little to do with telecommunications' (Poster 1995: 33). Yet in the museum of science, interactivity can have a particular significance, drawing together concerns with, for example, both public 'participation', 'empowerment' and 'accountability' and with more specific questions and anxieties about the proper way to bridge the gulf between popular culture and the esoteric world of science and technology.

The contemporary concern with interactivity emerges at a moment when there is perceived to be a crisis in the relations between science and the public. The public are thought to be ambivalent about the authority of science and, at the same time, are said to be uninformed; a perception which ironically may serve, as Brian Wynne observes, to encourage even 'more public alienation, hence justifying and consolidating the neuroses' (Wynne 1992: 281; see also Wynne 1993). Some argue that interactive technologies can contribute to the solution of the problem of public misinformation by giving the public a practical and a creative understanding of what it is to be a scientist. Promoting a belief in the value of science to the wider social order depends, in this view, not just on the ritual public display of technological achievement, but on the development of the creative scientific abilities of the individual citizen.

The second theme of this chapter concerns the issue of interactivity as a theoretical concept. The idea of interactivity is one of a number of terms (including noise, feedback and network) which have acquired particular significance since the development of communications theory and cybernetics in the 1940s with the work of, amongst others, Norbert Wiener. In the cybernetic account there is no essential distinction between the capacities of the human and the non-human actor. Both the human and the machine act as sources and receivers of information thereby functioning as part of an interacting system. As Peter Galison reminds us, 'according to the cyberneticist, the world is nothing more than the internal relations of these incoming and outgoing messages' (Galison 1994: 255–6). Within the contemporary science museum, the technology of interactivity can be intended, if not necessarily to obliterate, at least to reconfigure the distinction between the human visitor and the non-human exhibit.

My final concern is with what we might call, following Foucault, the *political anatomy* of the museum visitor (Foucault 1979: 138; see also Schaffer 1992: 329). Although the interest in interactivity has to be seen in relation to the development of communications theory and technology, it can also be located in relation to a rather more longstanding concern with the body as source of experimental knowledge. Simon Schaffer notes that in the eighteenth and early nineteenth centuries the body of the natural philosopher, or of his audience, frequently functioned as an essential part of the experimental apparatus. The eighteenth-century Parisian lecturer Jean Antoine Nollet, for example, 'described "beatifying electricity", when sparks were drawn from victims' hair' (Schaffer 1992: 333). In 1800 the English chemist Humphry Davy reported on his experiments with the inhalation of gas. Davy 'lost all connection with external things . . . I existed in a world of newly connected and newly modified ideas. I theorised – I imagined that I made discoveries' (ibid.: 359).

Since the late nineteenth century, the significance of a scientist's body to experiment has changed. The body of the practising scientist has become disciplined, capable of performing meticulous practical tasks and making exact observations but no longer serving as an experimental instrument in itself. The process of science education is, at least in part, a matter of turning the untutored body of the student into that of a reliable technician. As John Law observes, the discipline of the scientist's body can play an important role in laboratory work (Law 1986: 21). Experimental events are no longer *experienced* by the scientist; they are *recorded* by the scientists' instruments (Barry 1995). By contrast, the relatively undisciplined body of the visitor has an increasingly important part to play both in the contemporary science museum and what is often called 'the science centre'.[2] Today, the visitor to the museum or the science centre is often encouraged to interact or to 'play' with an exhibit. In effect, the visitor is expected to make scientific principles visible to themselves through the use of touch, smell, hearing or the sense of physical effects on their own bodies (Durant 1992: 8). In a manner foreign to the practice of contemporary experimental science, the body is itself a source of knowledge (Gregory 1989: 4).

In exploring the significance and recent history of interactivity, this chapter focuses on two contemporary science museums or science centres; the Science Museum in London and the Cité des Sciences et de l'Industrie at La Villette in Paris.[3] In many ways these institutions are unique. In London, interactivity has developed in a museum which has evolved gradually over a long period of time and carries with it a complex historical legacy. This legacy consists not only of rich collection of material artefacts, but also a history of ways of displaying and visiting which goes back to the nineteenth century. In the first part of the chapter I focus on the key role that interactive devices are expected to play in breaking the museum away from what are regarded as some of the more problematic features of this past.

By contrast to the Science Museum, the Cité is a recent development, and the technology of interactivity is integral to the institution's conception and design. Whereas the Science Museum houses a vast collection of historical artefacts, the Cité displays little of the traditional curatorial interest in collection and the history of technology. In the second part of this chapter, I argue that interactive devices function in the Cité, not just as a presentational devices, but as a key element of the institution's vision of the technological present.

CONSUMERS AND CITIZENSHIP: THE SCIENCE MUSEUM AND THE EXPLORATORIUM

In Britain, the new emphasis on 'interactivity' can be understood, in part, in relation to broader changes in the public function of the museum. The modern science museum originally developed in the nineteenth century as a place where the successes of the imperial state could be displayed and where 'European productive prowess was typically explained as a justification for empire' (Bennett et al. 1993: 59).[4] But it was also intended to be a liberal space within which a bourgeois public would participate, and be seen to participate, in their own cultural and moral improvement. Thus, the population would be managed, as Tony Bennett argues, 'by providing it with the resources and contexts in which it might become self-educating and self-regulating' (Bennett 1995: 40). As an institution of government, the museum would act not so much through controlling and disciplining the public, but by enlisting its active support for liberal values and objectives.

Museums and expositions, in drawing on . . . techniques and rhetorics of
display and pedagogic relations . . . provided a context in which working and
middle-class publics could be brought together and the former – having been
tutored into forms of behaviour to suit them for the occasion – could be
exposed to the improving influence of the latter.

(ibid.: 86)

The complex of museums developed at South Kensington in the 1850s became
the paradigm of this liberal exhibitionary strategy (ibid.: 40).

In recent years, however, the liberal conception of culture as a means of
individual improvement has had to run alongside – if not compete with – neo-
liberal notions of culture as a consumer product (Silverstone 1992: 41). The
traditional museum has been accused of being too paternalist, too dominated by
the concerns of curators and the fetishism of the artefact, and too dependent
upon public subsidy.[5] What is said to be required is a new recognition of the
competitive character of the visitor business *in addition to* the older preoccupations with scholarship and public education. The museum is but a 'part of the
leisure and tourist industries' (Kirby 1988: 91).

For Neil Cossons, director of the London Science Museum in the late 1980s
and 1990s the new concern with the customer was a challenge that should
be welcomed, for, with the decline of state funding, 'spending power, and therefore choice, [would be put] into the hands of the people'. For the museums,
according to Cossons, the implications were clear: 'The battlefield will be the
marketplace and the casualties will be those museums that fail to adapt'
(Cossons 1987: 18). Seen in this context, 'interactivity' has a double function.
First, it is one of a range of technical methods – along with cost control, visitor
research, quality assurance, marketing and customer relations – which would
enable the museum to forge a more 'economic' relation both with its visitors,
and with private industry.[6] As one commentator has noted:

for interactive media the combination of: 1. multiplexing as a delivery mode;
2. interactivity as an intrinsically engaging form of media; 3. niche marketing
as an advertising strategy; 4. the affluent status of museum visitors as a
demographic group; 5. museums' status as pillars of respectability on
scientific, environmental and heritage issues . . . will greatly increase the
attractiveness of museums to sponsors.

(Nash 1992: 184)

Second, the technology of interactivity had a function in the context of broader
changes in political thinking on both the Left and the Right. Contemporary
political thinking is increasingly sceptical of the political and economic compe-
tence of the State and, in its stead, relies on the self-governing capacities of the
individual, the family, the enterprise or the community (Barry, Osborne and
Rose 1996). As Nikolas Rose observes, the subject of what he calls 'advanced'
liberal forms of government is given unprecedented responsibility for governing

his or her own affairs. For advanced liberalism, the task of the public authorities is not to direct or provide for the citizen but to establish the conditions within which the citizen could become an 'active agent in his or her own government' (Rose 1993: 296). Seen in this context, interactive devices have a function, for they may foster agency, experimentation and enterprise, thus enhancing the self-governing capacities of the citizen. Interactivity promises, in other words, to turn the museum visitor into a more active self (cf. Strathern 1992: 41–3, Macdonald 1993).

The association of the idea and techniques of interactivity with a broader conception of the public function of the science museum was not new. In 1969, the nuclear physicist Frank Oppenheimer, who had been blacklisted from practising as a scientist by the House Un-American Activities Committee, established the Exploratorium in San Francisco as an alternative to the traditional science museum. For Oppenheimer, existing museums in the United States often glorified the achievements of earlier scientists at the expense of enabling visitors to engage in a process of discovery themselves.[7] The radical message of the Exploratorium was one of *democratic empowerment* (cf. Cruikshank 1996). The public would be empowered through being able to *interact* with objects as an experimental scientist does in the natural world of the laboratory. According to Hilde Hein, 'interactive pedagogic technique contains a key to empowerment that could transform education on a broad scale and make an avenue of general self-determination' (Hein 1990: xvi). In short, visitors would be participants rather than mere observers. Increasingly concerned about the growing interest in mysticism, drugs and Eastern religions in the younger generation, Oppenheimer himself expressed the intellectual and political aspirations of the Exploratorium in these terms:

> The whole point of the Exploratorium is to make it possible for people to believe that they can understand the world around them. I think a lot of people have given up trying to comprehend things, and *when they give up with the physical world they give up with the social and political world as well.*
>
> (ibid.: xv, emphasis added)

If the idea of interaction was central to what the Exploratorium was trying to do, how was it possible to realize this in practice? What was an interactive technique and how could interactivity *empower*? In the early years, the Exploratorium's attempts to develop participatory and interactive exhibits were, no doubt, rudimentary. The Exploratorium staff had, themselves, to learn how to embody Oppenheimer's radical philosophy in a technical form. However, the centre was able draw on and translate other models of interactivity. One was a temporary exhibition of *Cybernetic Serendipity* which had originally been shown at the Institute of Contemporary Arts in London from August to October 1968 and which was designed to explore the relations between creativity and 'cybernetic' technologies such as computers, robots and mechanical feedback systems. For Oppenheimer and the Exploratorium the origins of the *Cybernetic*

Serendipity as an art exhibition accorded with the centre's modernist philosophy. First, neither Oppenheimer nor the exhibition organizers perceived a fundamental distinction between art and science. For Oppenheimer, science had an 'aesthetic dimension' and art and science were united in the 'human quest for understanding' (ibid.: xvi). According to the exhibition organizers, 'at no point was it clear to any of the visitors walking around the exhibition, which of the various drawings, objects and machines were made by artists and which made by engineers; or, whether the photographic blow-ups of texts mounted on the walls were the works of poets or scientists' (Reichardt 1971: 11). Blurring the boundaries of art and science was an important part of the Exploratorium's pedagogic strategy, for by doing so it was hoped that the centre's visitors might begin to understand that science was a *creative* activity.

In terms of the Exploratorium's philosophy, a second positive feature of the ICA exhibition was that it engaged with science at the level of material practice rather than merely at the level of metaphorical association. Visitors could have a practical as well as visual experience of technology. The instructions to one of the exhibits of *Cybernetic Serendipity*, for example, invited the museum visitor to interact with a machine by turning knobs that adjust the phase and frequency of two wave oscillations relative to one another in order to produce a variety of patterns (Hein 1990: 38). Thus, the relationship between scientific or mathematical truth and art would, through a process of interaction, be revealed to the uninitiated. This philosophy still persists. Addressing what he perceives to be the 'crisis in science education', the new director of the Exploratorium, Dr Goéry Delacôte has created a 'Centre for Public Exhibition' which 'provides informal science education through interactive exhibits which address and explore the relationship between science, art and human perception' (Délacôte 1992).

A further intellectual rationale for the idea of the interactive exhibit in the Exploratorium was found in the work of the psychologist Richard Gregory. In his Royal Institution Christmas lectures of 1967/8, Gregory had expounded a theory which held that visual perception entailed a complex integration of the perceivers' interpretive dispositions with external stimuli. According to Gregory,

> perception is not a matter of sensory information giving perception and guiding behaviour directly, but rather the perceptual system is a 'look up' system; in which sensory information is used to build gradually, and to select from, an internal repertoire of 'perceptual hypotheses'.
>
> (Gregory 1970: 174)

Translating this into practical terms, the Exploratorium 'let the visitor be the laboratory subjects of their own perceptual experiments' (Hein 1990: 72). The intended effect of this pedagogic strategy was not just to teach perceptual theory, but to encourage the visitor to experience the process of discovery and thus to become an experimenter.

The extraordinary enthusiasm for interactivity, which had been initiated by the Exploratorium in the late 1960s and subsequently spread across the United States, finally arrived in Europe in the mid-1980s with the opening of the Launch Pad gallery at the London Science Museum, the Cité des Sciences et de l'Industrie in Paris and Richard Gregory's own Exploratory in Bristol. By the early 1990s the growth of interactive science exhibits in Britain had been phenomenal (Stevenson 1994: 30). Indeed, a veritable interactives movement had emerged with the formation of associations such as the British Interactives Group (BIG) and the European Collaborative Science, Industry and Technology Exhibitors (ECSITE). Curators, educationalists and museum managers began to share their ideas about the function and design of interactives and encourage the use of interactives in exhibition spaces in which they had previously not been found, such as art galleries.

If the Exploratorium provided a model for the interactives movement in Britain it would be a mistake to imagine that the interactivity in Britain was simply a copy of the American original. As sociologists of technology have been at pains to argue, the process whereby a technology is 'transferred' from one place to another should be thought of as a form of translation or reinterpretation rather than merely a form of diffusion (Latour 1986). In the UK, the radical concerns of the American centre with the issue of empowerment were marginalized and, with exceptions, Oppenheimer's interests in the links between science and art were ignored. Instead, interactivity came to operate in relation to the failure of the traditional science museum to address a rather more mundane set of concerns with the public understanding of science and the attractiveness of the museum to visitors.

Criticism of the traditional science museum was most forcefully made by Richard Gregory, founder of the Bristol Exploratory and former adviser to the Exploratorium. For Gregory, 'looking at the traditional museums of science we find remarkably little science' (Gregory 1989: 7). Gregory saw the the essential feature of science as experimentation, so that in order to enable the public to get an 'intuitive feel for . . . the principles of science' hands-on interactive experiences were, he believed, critical. 'I suggest', wrote Gregory, 'that the major aim of interactive science centres, after stimulating interest and curiosity, should be setting up hand-waving explanations giving useful intuitive accounts' (ibid.: 5).

The new interactive science centres were certainly popular. 'Science centres attract visitors like magnets', noted the education officer at the Science Museum responsible for Launch Pad (Stevenson n.d.: 18). Interactive exhibits, whether located within science centres or in more traditional object-centred exhibitionary spaces were also consistently rated highly by the public according to visitor research. According to the Science Museum's own research Launch Pad receives 714 visitors per square metre of gallery space per year, while the entire museum receives only 44 visitors per square metre per year (Thomas n.d.: 3).[8] This popularity has proved both a benefit and problem for the development of interactive exhibitions. Certainly, the fact that interactives are popular is of considerable commercial and political significance in a period in which the museum or the science centre is increasingly understood as one part of a broader leisure industry and where the traditional curatorial concern with collection has been downplayed. Accusations that interactive science centres are merely expensive playgrounds that convey little of the tedious and difficult reality of science can be met with the response that this is what the public wants.[9] If interactive galleries enable the public to have fun and to enjoy some kind of experience of science then, in this view, that is sufficient justification for their development. In a period in which visitor numbers are taken to be one of the key performance indicators used in museums, then the case for increasing the space given to interactive exhibits within the museum can appear unanswerable (cf. Thomas n.d.).

However, the recognition that visitors came to interactive science centres and exhibitions to enjoy themselves created a problem for proponents of interactivity (Gregory 1989: 2). In the view of their designers, interactive exhibits were always expected to be as much instruments of informal education as a means of entertainment. The museum visitor was conceived of as an active learner, and not just as a consumer. Critics pointed to the lack of historical or industrial contextualization of many interactive exhibits and the frequent absence of any explanation of what scientific principles were supposed to be revealed through the process of interaction. Some exhibits, it was said, can be interpreted in ways which lead museum visitors to *false* conclusions.[10] Indeed, it is unclear whether any of the scientific principles that many interactives are meant to demonstrate would be grasped by any except those already possessing a good scientific education.[11] Moreover, some question whether many interactive devices are really interactive. Many so-called interactive touch-screen computers, for example, simply allow the visitor to select from a predetermined set of options. Far from providing the possibilities for experimentation, such interactive devices may merely serve to create the illusion of choice (Strathern 1992: 42).

There are, no doubt, many different interpretations and responses to this complex conjuncture. At the London Science Museum large numbers of human 'explainers' are employed to make sure that the interactive exhibits do the job they are intended to do. New galleries such as Health Matters and the temporary exhibition space, Science Box, incorporate increasingly sophisticated interactive exhibits as a matter of course.[12] There is now more emphasis on tailoring interactives to particular age-ranges so that it is possible to act on the specific technical competencies and interests of the young visitor. In these circumstances, gallery designers increasingly draw on the diverse insights of visitor research, ergonomics, sociology, developmental psychology and educational theory to ensure that the new interactive galleries prove to be educational as well as entertaining.[13] To an extent unparalleled in the past, the museum visitor has become the object of investigation. If interactive technologies are expected to enhance the agency of the visitor and to channel it in the most productive direction, then the specific dynamic of this agency must itself be known (cf.

Foucault 1979). The visitor, it seems, has been increasingly called on to interact with exhibits and respond to the growing number of explainers, actors and researchers who also inhabit the museum.

CYBORGS AND CULTURE: THE CITÉ

In what follows I want to look at a museum where 'interactivity' has a rather different set of resonances. At the Cité des Sciences et de l'Industrie at La Villette in Paris, 'interactivity' functions, I suggest, not just in relation to notions of the visitor as active consumer and learner, but in terms of a project which centres around a particular vision of the relation between humans and machines. Opened in 1986, La Villette was one of a number of other major construction projects – including the Bastille opera house and the Beaubourg – which dominated Parisian cultural policy in the 1970s and 1980s. Whereas, in the UK, the imperatives of cultural policy became increasingly understood in terms of notions of consumer demand and commercial viability, the ostensible objective of the developments in Paris was to broaden public participation in culture. As Nathalie Heinich has noted, one goal of the Beaubourg project was to 'democratise culture' and to somehow 'reconcile the imperatives of mass consumption with "higher" cultural production' (Heinich 1988: 199–200). Likewise, a key aim of the development of the site at La Villette was to enable a larger public to recognize the value and experience the excitement of science. Thus, the public would come to place as much value in science and technology as the French State itself.[14]

In practice, the techniques used at La Villette to encourage public interest in science obey no simple logic and are, no doubt, contradictory. On the one hand, the Cité tries to go to meet the wider public's taste not just through *vulgarisation*, but, by blurring the traditional boundaries between education and popular culture. Echoing the philosophy of many late nineteenth-century exhibitions, science is presented not just as knowledge but also as spectacle and entertainment:

> Above all the Cité des Sciences et de l'Industrie is a place to learn and a place to have fun.

> La Villette: a new way of seeing, listening, learning of amazement and emotion! A place for creativity and leisure, for discovery and play.
>
> (Cité: n.d.)

On the other hand, La Villette is not entirely without the conventional marks of cultural capital. In the park outside the Cité, there are a number of 'deconstructionist' architectural follies designed by Bernard Tschumi (Derrida 1986), an experimental postmodern garden, a research centre for the history of science and technology, as well the new national conservatory of music – 'a complex conceived as a stimulating environment and meeting place for the arts, sciences and music' (Cité n.d.).[15] Even in the Cité itself there is a multimedia library, an international conference centre and associated information services. In addition, mirroring the philosophy of the Exploratorium, is the 'Experimental gallery' which exhibits 'initiatives in art'.

> the Experimental gallery exhibits artwork closely related to the fields of science, technology and industry. Though these works are neither illustrative nor educational in nature, they do represent a certain poetry, myth, humour and even criticism. The artists do not share the same views on the world as do scientists but instead provide an answer to these views.
>
> (Cité 1988: 30)

At first sight, La Villette's gestures towards art and its flirtations with post-modernism appear to mirror the Beaubourg's enthusiasm for technology. Since its opening, for example, the Beaubourg has been associated with Pierre Boulez's Institut de Recherche et de Coordination Acoustique/Musique (IRCAM), a centre which carries out research in avant-garde computer music (Born 1995). And in 1984/5 the Beaubourg supported experiments in collective computer writing in an exhibit entitled *Les Immatériaux*, which provided a vehicle for the philosopher Jean-François Lyotard to speculate about the impossibility of consensus through communication (Poster 1990: 114).

Yet despite the apparent parallels between the cultural strategies of the two institutions their broader ideological resonances are quite different. In the case

Figure 6.1 La Médiatheque: Cité des Sciences et de l'Industrie (photograph by Jean-Yves Gregoire, courtesy of the Cité des Sciences et de l'Industrie)

of the Beaubourg, the centre's close relation to technology serves to legitimize its identity as an innovative cultural institution – reinforcing the image given to it by Richard Rogers' bold architectural design. By comparison, in the case of the Cité, 'art' will always remain at the margins of an establishment which is dominated by a vision of the information age, and which tries too hard to be futuristic. Ironically, it is the Cité which appears to be the more conventional of the two institutions: its high-tech structure immediately conjuring up not so much an image of innovation and creativity, but a history of so many earlier exhibitions and philosophies in which progress has been equated with technological change.

Although the Cité's relation to the future is only too familiar, its representation of technology is none the less distinctive. Whereas the museums of the nineteenth century articulated the evolutionary metaphors of biology and political economy, the Cité's taxonomies draw on the new ahistorical sciences of communications theory, cybernetics, psychology and ecology (cf. Jordanova 1989: 23). Exhibit areas are devoted to a whole series of topics concerned with the bodily and perceptual capacities of humans: sound, vision, light games, the representation of space, expression and behaviour. Moreover, although the Cité does possess the shiny rockets and cars to be found in all traditional science museums, its dominant images are those associated not so much with hardware, but with language, software and the metaphors of the 'information society'. This is a museum of information, networks, environment, multimedia, interfaces and participation (Cité 1995: 23).

In practice, these ideas are manifested in a number of different ways. At the most basic level, the Cité is full of 'interactive exhibits and audio-visual presentations', 'computer-based displays and games', 'participative, hands-on displays' and 'state-of-the-art museum technology'. Each of these devices has, no doubt, a specific didactic function and entertainment value. But collectively, the museum's interactive media also have a metonymic effect. As one curator put it to me, alluding to McLuhan, 'the medium *is* the message'. At La Villette, the future *is* interactive. Visitors to the museum purchase not a ticket but a machine readable smart card on which is written the demand 'Découvrez!'.

However, interactive technologies do not simply function as rhetorical tropes. They also serve to organize the internal space of the museum. As Roger Silverstone has argued, the visitor's experience of a museum may be understood as a narrative in space, the structure of which is governed, but not determined, by the spatial organization of the museum itself. This idea, derived from the work of Michel de Certeau, 'encourages us . . . to begin to analyze the rhetorical and narrative strategies which are present both in an exhibition's layout and in the routes which individuals construct through it' (Silverstone 1988: 235). In the case of the Cité, the internal space of the museum apparently takes a quite conventional form: the visitor is guided around a three-dimensional space divided into exhibitions, shops, galleries and cafés. However, the existence of 'interactive' devices and technologies creates discontinuities in this space,

Figure 6.2 Discover! Flight simulators in the Cité (photograph by Bernard Baudin, courtesy of the Cité des Sciences et de l'Industrie)

puncturing the visitor's route and establishing a further 'fourth' audio-visual dimension within which the visitor is encouraged to place him or herself, to participate and to interact. Thus, the visitor is not simply an observer of the museum's machines – he or she is positioned within them. In the 'Sound' exhibit area, for example, a computer game called a 'voice-actuated note-gobbler' serves to display the tone of a person's voice. The 'Light games' area includes a section devoted to the explanation of interference which brings together a number of 'hands-on' displays. In the 'Aeronautics' area some of the most popular exhibits are flight simulators. In the 'Environment' area computer based interactive multimedia allow the visitor to explore topics such as greenery, air and trees.

Just outside of the Cité, the position of the museum visitor in the museum's exhibitionary strategy is dramatically symbolized by a huge 3-D Omnimax cinema – La Géode – in which 'visual effects combine with sound effects to transport the spectators into the midst of the action surrounding them' (Cité 1988: 54). Reflecting on the significance of La Géode, Paul Virilio reminds us that 'the fusion/confusion of camera, projection system and auditorium in the Imax/omnimax process, is part of a long tradition of "mobile framing" in cinema, dating from the invention of the tracking shot in 1898' (Virilio 1990: 173). Placing the Omnimax in relation to the early history of cinema is certainly appropriate. Like the cinema of the 1890s and 1900s, contemporary IMAX/ Omnimax cinema is less concerned with narrative, than with exhibition, spectacle and affect (Elsaesser 1990). However, the economic conditions of IMAX and early cinema are quite different. Whereas small-scale production companies played an important role in the development of early cinema, the relative scarcity of IMAX/Omnimax auditoria and the expense of film production have meant that the development of IMAX/Omnimax depends on corporate sponsorship (Wollen 1993). In La Géode, one popular programme is a film of the Space Shuttle produced by NASA and the Lockheed Corporation. The Space Shuttle is a particularly appropriate subject at the Cité for its design is based on the view that it *matters* that research in space depends on the involvement of humans and does not rely solely on the operation of remote-controlled instruments. In the Shuttle, humans are 'explorers' pushing back the final frontier of space; they have the *Right Stuff*. However, equally significantly, the physical and perceptual capacities of their own bodies are the objects of the Shuttle scientists' experiments. Thus, at least some of the experiments performed in the Shuttle bear some comparison to those that might be found in the main body of the museum.

Figure 6.3 La Géode: futurism in the Cité (photograph by Arnaud Legrain, courtesy of the Cité des Sciences et de l'Industrie)

In the Cité the idea that science and technology reconfigure the boundaries between humans and non-humans is a pervasive one – represented not just in the ubiquity of 'interactive' techniques but in the vocabulary and taxonomy of the museum's exhibits. The Earth is understood as a 'machine' and as a 'space-ship'. Computers can 'talk'. 'Animal and vegetable kingdoms come to life in the form of automatons'. Robots and humans live in a 'cybernetic zoo'. And marriage is presented in terms of notions of 'trade' and 'system'.[16]

According to Donna Haraway, there is a tremendous political potential in the development of contemporary communication and bio-technologies. To be sure, she notes, such technologies have a crucial role in the conduct of modern states, multinational corporations, military power and labour-control systems (Haraway 1991: 165), but they also render obsolete the binary oppositions between organisms and machines, revealing that 'there is no fundamental, ontological separation in our formal knowledge of machine and organism, of technical and organic' (ibid.: 178). Thus, the idea of the cyborg provides the basis for challenging the essentialism of much contemporary political thought.

Perhaps. A visit to the Cité suggests, however, that rather less productive possibilities may often be associated with the fashionable figure of the cyborg. Instead of exploring the changing role of technologies in the constitution of the social and the individual, the Cité's exhibits freeze the relation in a series of disassociated and reified 'interactions'. Thus, in a double movement, science is popularized but, at the same time, mystified. Ironically too, although it has made huge investments in media and information technologies, the Cité often fails to make any reliable connections with debates about science in the world outside; and there is little sense of the agonistic relations which invariably mark scientific and technological change.[17] In brief, at La Villette, the interaction between humans and machines can all too easily become yet another object onto which celebratory high-tech fantasies can be projected.

CONCLUSION

There are two levels of criticism that can made of the development of inter-activity in the contemporary science museum. At one level, a series of questions have been asked about the use and effectiveness of interactives, not least by museum professionals and interactive designers themselves. As critics and researchers have pointed out, many interactives function as simple amusements or distractions and/or experimental games for the scientifically well-educated. However, the force of such criticisms has not been any decline in interest in interactives. On the contrary, criticism has provoked professionals to improve the design of interactive devices, tailoring their design more closely to the needs, capacities and behaviour of *real* museum visitors, and integrating them more carefully with the more traditional text- and object-based exhibits. In brief, the notion of interactivity has come to be the centre of a rapidly expanding cycle of intellectual, financial and technical investments in the public presentation of science and technology.

At another level, it is important to interrogate the forms of political reasoning which have justified this remarkable level of investment in interactivity. According to Michel Callon 'technical objects . . . more or less explicitly define and distribute roles to humans and non-humans' (Callon 1991: 137). Certainly, some of those associated with science museums and science centres have hoped that interactive devices could serve both to distribute roles to humans and to generate particular human capacities. Indeed, interactives have functioned as a kind of technical solution to the various problems that have emerged around the relations between science and the public. At the Exploratorium, for example, interactives were conceived of as ways of disseminating a sense of scientific experimentation to the wider public. In turn, the capacity to be an experimenter was taken to be equivalent to democratic empowerment. At La Villette, the idea and technology of interactivity connects together, in an ambitious project, the body of the individual visitor with a fantastic vision of a technological nation.

In contrast to France and the USA, British political and intellectual culture often appears be more ambivalent towards science and technology.[18] British critics have argued persuasively that museums should attempt to represent science and technology as complex political and cultural objects: as activities marked by contestation, uncertainty and undecidability. Indeed, far from emphasizing the importance of new forms of interactivity, such arguments point to the continuing centrality of *collections* to the public function of the contemporary museum of science.[19] According to Jim Bennett, although 'many of our former collection displays were uninspired, unimaginative and unchallenging . . . collections are the foundations of all great museums' and they should continue to have a central place in museum display (Bennett, Chapter 10). Although not entirely ignored, however, efforts to *rethink* the function of the museum collection have been secondary to a rather different set of concerns with questions of consumer choice and visitor behaviour. It has been the physical and perceptual capacities of the visitor, along with the development of new technologies of interactivity, which have come to be one of the dominant points of reference in contemporary debates about the design, function and future of the modern museum of science.

ACKNOWLEDGMENTS

Thanks to Sharon Macdonald and Roger Silverstone for their comments; to Stephen Johnston for his help and advice; and to all the staff at the Science Museum and La Villette who helped me with this research.

NOTES

1 According to one recent commentator: 'Museums are . . . inherently interactive multimedia. The visitor is in control of the paths along which they navigate through the artifacts, images, sounds and texts and they are under no obligation to follow the linear structure imposed by the curator' (Bearman 1993: 183).

2 Unlike the traditional science museum, the typical science centre does not house an historical collection but is likely to rely heavily on the use of interactive exhibits. For a discussion of the difference see Durant (1992).

3 Throughout this article I refer to the National Museum of Science and Industry (NMSI) as the Science Museum.

4 For a discussion of the history of the science museum in the eighteenth century see Hooper-Greenhill (1992). According to Schaffer the public presentation of science sometimes involved an extraordinary level of public debate: natural philosophers competed for patronage and audiences and 'critics sought to subvert the status of the lecturer's enterprise' (Schaffer 1993: 490).

5 See for example the article by the Science Museum director Dr Neil Cossons in the *Listener* (1987). According to one member of the museum staff at the time 'The inference in the article that the staff in the national museums are a load of dinosaurs with uncaring attitudes to the public was not well received' (letter to the author, 30 June 1987).

6 A combination of increasing attention to marketing and the development of a public controversy about imposing museum entry charges has given the Science Museum a higher public profile (cf. Cossons 1991: 185). However, its activities probably draw much less public comment than other museums of comparable size. As one museum curator noted: 'what is done by the National Gallery, the V&A, the Tate etc. is always subject to both media hype *and* informed comment, from layman and specialist alike. Alas the same cannot be said of the Science Museum' (letter to the author 18 June 1987; emphasis in original). The silence of the media and the public in relation to the politics of the Science Museum appears to be inversely related to the noise generated by visitors. According to one souvenir guide, '[The Science Museum] is somewhere where people feel free, and often excited; where they talk loudly (sometimes too loudly) and even laugh. It is different from most museums' (Riemsdijk 1980: 1).

7 According to Hein there were two important influences on Oppenheimer's thinking. One was the London Science Museum Children's Gallery (1936–94), which contained exhibits which could be operated by the child. The other was the Palais de la Découverte which, unlike traditional science museums, did not concern itself primarily with the preservation of artefacts. Created in 1937, the Palais described itself as 'a scientific cultural centre' in which a large number of scientific experiments were (and still are) demonstrated to visitors (Hudson 1987: 103). According to its founder, Jean Perrin, one of the objectives of the Palais was to realize the potential for scientific research which he hoped might be found in the population at large. For Perrin, those young people who had not been favoured by a good education, but who had a particular aptitude for research and who had enough enthusiasm and energy to make it their vocation, should be recognized and encouraged by the National Research Service (Maury 1994: 24).

8 For a overview of contemporary museum visitor studies see Bicknell and Farmelo (1993).

9 One widely cited example of such an accusation is Shortland (1987). One feature of this denigration of computer-based interactive museum exhibits is their association with interactive computer games. As Leslie Haddon observes 'moral panics about games, including fears of addiction, the "effects" of desensitisation and of escapism have spanned a range of political campaigns, media attention and academic, mainly psychological analysis' (Haddon 1993: 124).

10 One member of the Science Museum education staff remembered the example of an interactive where a light signal was interpreted by many visitors as the cause rather than the effect of the phenomenon that the interactive was meant to demonstrate.

Another suggested that many scientific principles which are supposed to be revealed by interactives would only be comprehensible by A-level students and above (interviews conducted at the Science Museum, London, June 1995).

11   As Sharon Macdonald suggests, the failure of interactives to communicate scientific principles may, in part, reflect the limitations of the museum as a medium: 'museums might not be particularly good . . . at getting across scientific facts and details, than furthering understanding through more general images and messages about the nature of science, its possibilities, its relevance *and* its limitations' (Macdonald 1992: 408; emphasis in original).

12   In the Science Museum there was considerable disagreement about whether this should be considered a problem or not. Proponents of interactivity noted that the Museum had a longstanding interest in interactivity from the opening of the Children's Gallery (1936) onwards. Many others thought that integration of interactives with historical objects could be a problem as it raises questions, for example, about how to define the boundaries between objects with which the public could and could not interact. More generally, the development of interactivity in the museum not only raised questions about the function of interactive devices but also about the function of traditional objects. On these points my thanks to Sharon Macdonald, Stephen Johnston and Gillian Thomas.

13   In Lash and Urry's (1994) terms the museum began to be engaged in a rather extensive process of reflexive modernization. In this process, the museum visitor was not necessarily conceptualized as an individual consumer. Many visitors came as part of family groups or in school parties and visitor research and exhibition design has to take this into account. In addition, the museum was aware that many of its adult visitors were male and middle class and, in this context, issues of class and gender have become a feature of exhibition design. A detailed examination of the ways in which different designs of interactive exhibits addressed specific kinds of museum visitor is beyond the scope of this chapter.

14   The post-war French State has, at least at the level of political rhetoric, tended to place great stress on the importance of science and technology for the modernization of France. By contrast, in the UK, interest in interactivity amongst scientists and museum staff developed at the height of what was perceived to be government hostility towards science in the mid-1980s.

15   The juxtaposition of scientific exhibitions and innovative architecture was not new in Paris (see Stamper 1989).

16   As Cornelius Castoriadis notes: 'Ordinary mortals are ensnared together with Nobel laureates in the coils of a new mythology ("machines which think", or "thought as a machine")' (Castoriadis 1984: 230).

17   Compare this with Bruno Latour's account of the need for democratic scientific institutions – a 'parliament of things' (Latour 1993: 142–5).

18   As David Edgerton observes, the situation in Britain is more complicated than this. In the twentieth century an important strand of political thinking in Britain has supported the development of advanced sciences and technologies – for military purposes (Edgerton 1991).

19   For accounts of the difficulties of representing controversy in science museums see Young and Levidow (1984), Macdonald and Silverstone (1992) and Ross (1995). One senior member of the staff of the Science Museum suggested to me that it was difficult for the Science Museum to respond to contemporary public controversies because of the high standards of professionalism (and hence time and expense) which were demanded of gallery designers. For a more general discussion of the importance of controversy to the public understanding of science see Wynne (1992, 1993). One of the successful recent attempts to incorporate recent approaches to the history and

sociology of science in museum design was undertaken at the Whipple Museum of the History of Science in Cambridge. (See Bennett *et al.* 1993 and J. Bennett Chapter 10).

REFERENCES

Barry, A. (1995) 'Reporting and visualising', in C. Jenks (ed.) *Visual Culture*, London: Routledge.

Barry, A., T. Osborne and N. Rose (eds) (1996) *Foucault and Political Reason: Liberalism, Neo-liberalism and Rationalities of Government*, London: UCL Press/ Chicago: Chicago University Press.

Bearman, D. (1993) 'Interactivity in American museums', *Museum Management and Curatorship*, 12, pp. 183–93.

Bennett, J., R. Brain, K. Bycroft, S. Schaffer, H. Sibum and R. Staley (1993) *Empires of Physics*, Cambridge: Whipple Museum of the History of Science.

Bennett, T. (1995) *The Birth of the Museum: History, Theory, Politics*, London: Routledge.

Bicknell, S. and G. Farmelo (eds) (1993) *Museum Visitor Studies in the 1990s*, London: Science Museum.

Born, G. (1995) *Rationalizing Culture. IRCAM, Boulez and the Institutionalization of the Musical Avant Garde*, Berkeley, CA: University of California Press.

Callon, M. (1991) 'Techno-economic networks and irreversibility', in J. Law (ed.) *A Sociology of Monsters: Essays on Power, Technology and Domination* (*Sociological Review Monograph*), pp. 132–61, London: Routledge.

Castoriadis C. (1984) *Crossroads in the Labyrinth*, Cambridge, MA: The MIT Press.

Cité des Sciences et de l'Industrie, direction de la Communication et du développement (1988) *Cité des Sciences et de l'Industrie*, Paris.

—— (n.d.) visitor information.

—— (1995) *Explora: Guide to the Permanent Exhibitions* (6th edition), Paris: Direction de la Communication et de la Promotion, la Villette.

Cossons, N. (1987) 'Adapt or die: dangers of a dinosaur mentality', *Listener* (16 April), pp. 18–20.

—— (1991) 'Scholarship or self-indulgence' *RSA Journal* (February) 139 (5415), pp. 184–91.

Cruikshank, B. (1996) 'Revolutions within: self-government and self-esteem', in A. Barry, T. Osborne and N. Rose (eds) *Foucault and Political Reason: Liberalism, Neo-liberalism and Rationalities of Government*, pp. 231–52, London: UCL Press/ Chicago: Chicago University Press.

Délacôte, G. (1992) http://www.exploratorium.edu/general/directors-vision.html.

Derrida, J. (1986) 'Point de folie – maintainant l'architecture', *AA Files*, 12, pp. 65–75.

Durant, J. (1992) 'Introduction', in J. Durant (ed.) *Museums and the Public Understanding of Science*, London: Science Museum.

Edgerton, D. (1991) 'Liberal militarism and the British state', *New Left Review*, 185, Jan–Feb.

Elsaesser, T. (ed.) (1990) *Early Cinema: Space, Frame, Narrative*, London: British Film Institute.

Foucault, M. (1979) *Discipline and Punish*, Harmondsworth: Penguin.

Galison, P. (1994) 'The ontology of the enemy: Norbert Wiener and the cybernetic vision', *Critical Inquiry*, 21 (Autumn), pp. 228–66.

Gregory, R. (1970) *The Intelligent Eye*, London: Weidenfeld & Nicholson.

—— (1989) 'Turning minds to science by hands-on exploration: the nature and potential of the hands-on medium', in Nuffield Interactive Science and Technology

Project *Sharing Science: Issues in the Development of Interactive Science and Technology Centres*, London: Nuffield Foundation/Committee on the Public Understanding of Science.

Haddon, L. (1993) 'Interactive games', in P. Hayward and T. Wollen (eds) *Future Visions: New Technologies of the Screen*, pp. 123–47, London: British Film Institute.

Haraway, D. (1991) *Simians, Cyborgs and Women: The Reinvention of Nature*, London: Free Association Books.

Hein, H. (1990) *The Exploratorium: The Museum as Laboratory*, Washington, DC: Smithsonian Institution Press.

Heinich, N. (1988) 'The Pompidou Centre and its public: the limits of a utopian site', in R. Lumley (ed.) *The Museum Time-machine: Putting Cultures on Display*, pp. 199–212, London: Routledge.

Hooper-Greenhill, E. (1992) *Museums and the Shaping of Knowledge*, London: Routledge.

Hudson, K. (1987) *Museums of Influence*, Cambridge: Cambridge University Press.

Jordanova, L. (1989) 'Objects of knowledge: an historical perspective on museums', in P. Vergo (ed.) *The New Museology*, London: Reaktion Books.

Kirby, S. (1988) 'Policy and politics: charges, sponsorship and bias', in R. Lumley (ed.) *The Museum Time Machine*, London: Routledge/Comedia.

Lash, S. and J. Urry (1994) *Economies of Signs and Space*, London: Sage.

Latour, B. (1986) 'The powers of association', in J. Law (ed.) *Power, Action and Belief*, London: Routledge.

—— (1993) *We Have Never Been Modern*, Hemel Hempstead: Harvester Wheatsheaf.

Law, J. (1986) 'On power and its tactics: a view from the sociology of science', *Sociological Review* 34 (1), pp. 1–35.

Levidow, L. and R. Young (1984) 'Exhibiting nuclear power: the Science Museum cover-up', *Radical Science*, 14, pp. 53–79.

Macdonald, S. (1992) 'Cultural imagining among museum visitors', *Museum Management and Curatorship*, 11, pp. 401–9.

—— (1993) 'Un nouveau "corps des visiteurs": musées et changements culturels', *Publics et Musées*, 3, pp. 13–27.

Macdonald, S. and R. Silverstone (1990) 'Rewriting the museums' fictions: taxonomies, stories and readers', *Cultural Studies*, 4 (2), pp. 176–91.

—— (1992) 'Science on display: the representation of scientific controversy in museum exhibitions', *Public Understanding of Science*, 1, pp. 69–87.

Maury, J-P. (1994) *Le Palais de la Découverte*, Paris: Gallimard.

Nash, C. (1992) 'Interactive media in museums: looking backwards, forwards and side-ways', *Museum Management and Curatorship*, 11, pp. 171–84.

Poster, M. (1990) *The Mode of Information: Poststructuralism and Social Context*, Cambridge: Polity.

—— (1995) *The Second Media Age*, Cambridge: Polity.

Reichardt, J. (ed.) (1971) *Cybernetics, Art and Ideas*, London: Studio Vista.

Riemsdijk, J. van (1980) *The Science Museum*, London: The Science Museum.

Rose, N. (1993) 'Government, authority and expertise in advanced liberalism', *Economy and Society*, 22 (3), 283–99.

—— (1996) 'Governing "advanced" liberal democracies', in A. Barry, T. Osborne and N. Rose (eds) *Foucault and Political Reason: Liberalism, Neo-liberalism and Rationalities of Government*, London: UCL Press/Chicago: Chicago University Press.

Ross, M. (1995) 'Museums and controversy: the case of passive smoking', *Science as Culture*, 5 (1), pp. 147–51.

Schaffer, S. (1992) 'Self evidence', *Critical Inquiry* 18, pp. 327–62.

—— (1993) 'The consuming flame: electrical showmen and Tory mystics in the world of goods', in J. Brewer and R. Porter (eds) *Consumption and the World of Goods*, London: Routledge.

Science Museum: the National Museum of Science and Industry (1986), 'Management Plan', London.

Shortland, M. (1987) 'No business like show business', *Nature*, 328, p. 213.

Silverstone, R. (1988) 'Museums and the media: a theoretical and methodological exploration', *The International Journal of Museum Management and Curatorship*, 7, pp. 231–41.

—— (1992) 'The medium is the museum: on objects and logics in times and spaces', in J. Durant (ed.) *Museums and the Public Understanding of Science*, London: Science Museum.

Stamper, J.W. (1989) 'The galerie of machines of the 1889 Paris World's Fair', *Technology and Culture*, 30 (2), pp. 330–53.

Stevenson, J. (n.d.) 'The philosophy behind launch pad', Science Museum, *Journal of Education and Museums*, 8, pp. 10–18.

—— (1994) 'Getting to Grips', *Museums Journal*, May, pp. 30–2.

Strathern, M. (1992) *Reproducing the Future: Anthropology, Kinship and the New Reproductive Technologies*, Manchester: Manchester University Press.

Thomas, G. (n.d.) 'The National Museum of Science and Industry: facing the future', mimeo.

Virilio, P. (1990) 'Cataract surgery: cinema in the year 2000', in A. Kuhn (ed.) *Alien Zone: Cultural Theory and Contemporary Science Fiction Cinema*, London: Verso.

Wollen, T. (1993) 'The bigger the better: from cinemascope to IMAX', in P. Hayward and T. Wollen (eds) *Future Visions: New Technologies of the Screen*, pp. 10–30, London: British Film Institute.

Wynne, B. (1992) 'Misunderstood misunderstandings: social identities and the public uptake of science', *Public Understanding of Science*, 1, pp. 281–304.

—— (1993) 'Public uptake of science: a case for institutional reflexivity', *Public Understanding of Science*, 2, pp. 321–37.

Chapter 7

Supermarket science?

Consumers and 'the public understanding of science'

Sharon Macdonald

In Britain during the 1980s the metaphor of the museum as a kind of shop seemed to catch the imagination of many of those involved in trying to find a place for the museum in an apparently increasingly hostile environment. In 1985, Sir Roy Strong, then director of the Victoria and Albert Museum, famously said that the V&A could be the Laura Ashley of the 1990s. For Sir Roy, this seems to have been a statement of democratizing intent, albeit a rather conservative one; something missed by the museum's marketing manager who later 'corrected' Sir Roy's ambition to the V&A being the 'Harrods' of the museum world (Hewison 1991). While analogies between museums and shops were not without precedent,[1] Sir Roy's characterization seemed to be part of a broader movement in which the metaphor of the shop was expressive, and increasingly constitutive, of an attempt in museums (particularly national museums) to reformulate their relationship with 'the public' and with the State. In a climate of dwindling state support and the introduction of admission charges at many nationals, museums began to a new extent to regard exhibitions as products to be marketed and visitors as 'customers' with the discretion to spend as they chose. In defining their future directions, museums came to foreground the question of what the public would 'buy'; and talk was increasingly of 'packaging' exhibitions as 'products' or 'brands', of identifying 'unique selling points', and of the importance of 'corporate image' and 'market niche'. As part of this redefinition, many museums employed marketing staff and carried out market and visitor research for the first time or on a new scale; they adopted corporate logos and images; they mounted unprecedentedly large advertising campaigns; they tried to make their exhibitions and facilities more 'user-friendly'; they expanded their shops and restaurants; they set up trading companies and mail-order catalogues; and they redeployed, restructured, retrained and sometimes lost staff.

In this chapter I explore some of the politics and implications of this way of conceptualizing museums. How does it influence the content of exhibitions? In particular, how does it affect representations of science and technology? And is the casting of visitors as 'customers' and the emphasis on 'consumer choice' democratizing and enabling for the public?

Figure 7.1 Heritage shopping: 1920s Sainsbury's in *Food for Thought: The Sainsbury Gallery*, Science Museum, London (photograph by Sharon Macdonald)

My focus in the chapter is an exhibition which opened in the Science Museum, London (part of the National Museum of Science and Industry) in 1989. This exhibition, *Food for Thought: The Sainsbury Gallery*, is an especially apt example in which to explore such questions for, not only was it created within a new attempt by the Science Museum to market itself and employ consumerist ideas, it also dealt in part with the subject of shopping, and had as its main sponsor a trust linked to the supermarket chain Sainsbury's. I spent just over a year before the opening of this exhibition carrying out ethnographic research with the exhibition staff charged with creating it. My account draws on my participant observation fieldwork, interviews conducted with museum personnel, documentary sources (such as files concerning the exhibition and press reviews), and interview research with visitors to the exhibition subsequent to its opening.[2] My aim here is to examine some of the very detailed ways in which the shopping metaphor could reach into the presentation and content of an exhibition; to explore some of its consequences, which were often un-anticipated by the exhibition's creators; and to discuss its politics, which were, I argue, ambivalent.

LOCATION

Food for Thought was the first exhibition begun and completed after the Science Museum's Corporate Plan of 1987. The first such plan after the appointment of a new director, Dr Neil Cossons, the plan made the museum's 'mission statement' 'the public understanding of science'. The Corporate Plan also instigated extensive managerial restructuring in the Science Museum and new arrangements for the creation of exhibitions (see pp.122–6). These developments were all acknowledged as being intended to give 'the public' a new priority in the museum's conduct. As such, they were part of the more widespread movement in museums to be more 'user-friendly' – or in the words of the title of the press release in which Sir Roy made his infamous Laura Ashley comments – more 'consumer-oriented' (Strong 1985). Moreover, *Food for Thought* was the first major exhibition to be opened in the Science Museum after the introduction of admission charges. As such, it was intended as an exhibition which would be seen as sufficiently appealing to the public to entice them to pay for what formerly had been free, and which was, perhaps, something of a flagship for future directions of Science Museum exhibitions.

At the time of its opening, *Food for Thought* was the most expensive exhibition the museum had ever mounted. It cost £1.2 million (excluding staff costs), the majority of which came from food industry sponsors. The Sainsbury Family Charitable Trust provided £750,000, and Tate and Lyle, British Sugar, the Meat and Livestock Commission, the National Dairy Council, Mars and *Good Housekeeping* all contributed smaller, though substantial, sums. Opened in October 1989 as part of both the British Year of Food and Farming and Museums Year, it was a 'permanent' exhibition, intended to be in place for at least 10 years. It covers 810 square metres, contains 160 panels of text and images and numerous three-dimensional exhibits, including many state-of-the-art multimedia and interactive technologies.

Food for Thought was carried out under new managerial arrangements. Instead of being organized from a curatorial, collections-based department, as had been the case with most exhibitions previously, it was managed within a new 'division' of 'Public Services'. As its name implies, 'Public Services' was concerned primarily with the public (rather than with the museum's collections of artefacts, which were the remit of a new, slimmed-down 'Collections Management Division'). As one curator, disgruntled with the new arrangements put it, now exhibitions were to be organized under the same 'line-manager' responsible for organizing 'cleaning the toilets' rather than those responsible for scholarship. Although the six women who constituted 'the exhibition team' were experienced curators, for the duration of their secondment to 'Public Services' to work on the exhibition their job title was 'interpreter' (a relatively new term in museums at that time): their task was not primarily 'caring' (curating) for museum objects but providing attractive displays for the public. Moreover, their curatorial expertise was not for the most part considered particularly important in selecting them to work on the exhibition. What seemed to be the most important qualification for the task was their personal commitment to creating an exhibition for lay people (Macdonald 1996) and, to this end, expert knowledge tended often to be regarded not merely as irrelevant but as a potential inhibition to communicating with the public. As one of the interpreters explained: 'I think it actually *helps* to be starting from scratch because then you're more in touch with what, well, what an ordinary person might know – what they're thinking – rather than just knowing everything already.'

As well as 'the Team', who wrote the script of the exhibition and were primarily responsible for deciding upon its content and endeavouring to make sure that everything got done that was supposed to get done, numerous other people were also involved. These included a specialist museum design company, staff of which worked closely with the Team, as well as various technicians within the museum and outside it: educationalists, interactives experts, nutritionists and other food advisers, food companies, consumer organizations, the sponsors, the Team's managers, picture researchers, photographers, joiners, builders, shop-fitters, companies specializing in stuffed animals and replica foods, companies specializing in period dress, companies specializing in food aromas, and others. Clearly, there was much more going on – and many more human and non-human actors jostling in on the action – than my brief account here can convey. These, together with such other vital factors as time, space and money, all played a part in shaping the finished exhibition, leading it in directions not always anticipated by those who were officially charged with constructing the exhibition's 'messages', as the ideas which visitors were intended to acquire were referred to.

The Team members were all strongly committed to creating an exhibition which would be directed at lay people rather than specialists. The 'public understanding of science' approach provided them with an opportunity to create what they regarded as a new democratic type of exhibition in the Science Museum – an exhibition which would not 'preach from on high', as one Team member put it. For the most part, Team members described themselves as essentially lay people, sometimes emphasizing, for example, how they had 'accidentally' ended up working in the Science Museum and how they were really not especially interested in science. They expressed their 'non-expert' status in terms of both their gender (detailed interest in science and technology being sometimes talked of as 'boys' stuff') and their relatively low status in the museum hierarchy; and regarded the exhibition as, in part, an opportunity to create an exhibition on behalf of some of those (including themselves) marginalized by previous museum representational strategies. In expressing the way in which their exhibition would differ from those that had gone before, they sometimes talked of the 'sexism' of museum displays and institutional culture; and of the ways in which staff (generally men) who claimed to be 'experts' had tended, especially before the 'new regime', to get promoted ahead of them and to have been given 'the jammy jobs', of which exhibition-making was one. Many of the exhibitions produced earlier were, they said, 'boring'; they were 'basically a Ph.D. thesis pasted onto panels' or 'intended for the other two people in the universe who are interested in the topic'. Their exhibition was to be different. It was to be 'accessible' and 'fun'. Although the Science Museum had a long history of interactive educational technologies in the Children's Galleries (opened in the 1920s) and the area known as Launch Pad (opened in 1986; see also Barry Chapter 6), *Food for Thought* was seen as being innovative in mixing interactive exhibits with displays of artefacts, audio-visual technologies and reconstructed scenes, all connected by the theme of food. Interactive technologies would not, therefore, be contained within a discrete bounded area but would be integrated into a mixed-media gallery.

There was a strong sense of flouting established museum conventions among the Team during the planning of the exhibition. They enjoyed the consternation that rumours about the exhibition caused in the Science Museum and they themselves hinted – misleadingly – that it would feature a giant tea-cup dangling over the museum's central atrium, and – not misleadingly – a McDonald's and an outsized pot of chocolate mousse. To some extent, the depiction by the Team of *Food for Thought* as very different from previous exhibitions was overstated, and indeed from my experience of other exhibition teams this kind of contrast seems rather typical during exhibition-making. Exhibition-making is, after all, regarded as a particularly creative aspect of museum work, and creativity in much of Western culture is generally thought of in terms of difference, distinctiveness and individuality. Nevertheless, the emphasis put upon 'fun', 'entertainment' and 'accessibility', and upon the visitors or 'consumers' was carried to an extent which was unusual in the Science Museum at that time and which entailed a conceptualization of the museum, and the exhibition itself, as shop-like, which was distinctive from most earlier exhibitions.

So how did the Team try to create a democratizing, consumer-friendly exhibition? What kinds of shopping metaphors did this entail? And how did that same exhibition also come to be read – as it has by various reviewers, commentators and visitors – as containing a rather less-than-democratic politics of enterprise culture and individualistic consumerism?

EXHIBITIONARY STRATEGIES

Familiarity and fun

The Team's decision to foreground consumption – shopping and eating – was part of a technique intended to present people first with familiar, everyday experiences so that science and technology would be made familiar rather than esoteric. Foodstuffs that it was thought likely that lay people would eat – selections confirmed through a small visitor survey – were chosen to exemplify different production processes: baked beans to illustrate canning, fish-fingers and frozen peas to illustrate freezing, and so forth. The incorporation of a high proportion of interactive exhibits was envisaged as helping break down barriers between the museum/science and the public through encouraging the active participation of visitors. More generally, the inclusion of popular culture – for example, McDonald's and a juke-box – and exhibits more readily associated with a fun-fair than a national museum – such as the giant chocolate mousse and distorting mirrors – were seen as likely to be attractive to visitors and a challenge to the fusty authoritative image of museums.

Interactives and popular cultural exhibits were also frequently talked about by the Team as being 'fun'. This exhibition was not only to be about learning but also about entertainment and pleasure. There was during the making of the exhibition an attempt to include and retain exhibits which were thought to excite feelings of wonder and surprise, and which were judged beautiful. Exhibits such as a sculpture made of sugar, a picture of a woman made of fish, and a Greek vase, as well as the chocolate mousse, found their way into the exhibition principally on the basis of such judgments. Interactives too, whilst often justified in terms of learning, were also talked of in terms of 'play'; and the Team themselves admitted that some of these – such as a proposed exhibit in which the visitor would be buffeted by cold air like a pea being frozen – had much more 'entertainment value' than 'learning content'. What was involved here, I suggest, was a conflation of pleasure and democracy – a conflation that Jody Berland has identified in other contemporary cultural technologies (Berland 1992: 47).

The idea of 'choice' was also implicated here. The use of 'pick-and-mix' strategies, such as 'multi-level' text, a range of media involving different senses and skills, and a layout with no fixed direction or predetermined route, were planned in order to involve the visitor in making choices. Visitors were to be invited to 'shop around' in the exhibition, to make their own selections, to 'decide for themselves' what they wanted, metaphorically, to 'take home'.

Many of these strategies can be seen, and were seen by the Team, as analogous with shopping. More specifically, and appropriately given the case at hand, they employ supermarket strategies. In particular, there is an emphasis on consumers making their own selections amongst a range of attractively presented and easily reached goods. The exhibition avoids having a single 'storyline' which visitors must follow in order, but has instead themed areas, rather as supermarkets have shelves and counters devoted to particular products. Originally, most of these areas in *Food for Thought* were to be organized around particular foods: thus it would have been possible to go to, say, 'Bread' or 'Meat and Fish'. In the finished exhibition the close link with particular foodstuffs has been severed to some extent, but the organization of the exhibition into themed areas remains. Early ideas for the exhibition also included the possibility of visitors taking a shopping trolley around with them (something restricted in the finished exhibition to the use of shopping baskets to fill for passing food products over a supermarket checkout; and the static display of filled trolleys); and of the exhibition containing numerous market-style counters (as has been adopted by some contemporary supermarkets in order to look more homely).

An active and differentiated public

The kind of visitor envisaged here is rather different from that of traditional glass case and diorama display techniques. Where these allowed visitors, rather as in the early department stores, to gaze reverentially and deferentially at sanctified objects, *Food for Thought* invites visitors to get close to the objects, to handle – and even to smell – at least some of the goods, to enjoy themselves, to make a noise, to have fun, and – an adjective frequently used by the exhibition-makers – to be 'busy'. The customers in *Food for Thought*, just as the customers in Sainsburys, are assumed to be active and discriminating purchasers, who will take their business elsewhere if there is insufficient choice. And just as supermarkets in the post-Fordist, consumerist era must think of their customers not as a homogeneous market but as varied and 'segmented', so too does *Food for Thought*. Through different levels of text visitors are segmented by age and literacy; through the different media they are segmented by sensory and participative preference; through the layout they are segmented by their choice of subject-matter. Moreover, even though there is a focus on Britain within the exhibition (something deemed appropriate for a national museum), it nevertheless strives to represent 'the British public' as diverse. To this end, it contains various images of women and people of Asian and Afro-Caribbean background, and shows the foodstuffs of a number of ethnic and religious groups. While this may seem a fairly token inclusion of 'difference', it was accorded considerable importance by the Team, who saw themselves as disrupting Science Museum conventions in this regard too. Moreover, ethnic diversity is also made part of one of the exhibition's main organizing themes: that of the expansion of food choice in Britain over the past 100 years. Immigration, the exhibition is meant to imply, has been an important factor in bringing new foods to, and thus expanding food choices in, Britain today. Difference and choice are, then, conceptually intermeshed in the exhibitionary narrative.

Diet and choice

The themes of activity, choice and the heterogeneity of the public are also extended to some aspects of science, particularly the controversial subjects of nutrition and diet. Here, the Team's aim was not to prescribe what should and should not be eaten; rather, the exhibition states: 'Diet is as individual as a person's clothes – what suits one person does not necessarily suit another.' Diet is presented as a matter of personal image and lifestyle; and these in turn are understood as essentially matters of individual choice.

The idea that members of the public should choose for themselves is also given some emphasis, though made problematic, by the exhibition's depiction of some scientific claims as variable and unstable. If science cannot be relied on to give reliable and unequivocal answers, consumers must 'decide for themselves', as the Team stressed. One panel states: 'Not all scientists agree about a "healthy diet". Information and ideas about which foods you should eat have changed over the years and are still changing.' Two markedly different sets of calorific intake guidelines (UK and US) are presented to highlight the divergence of views. A panel headed 'Controversy or consensus?', also intended to highlight different nutritional ideas, shows mug-shots of nutritionists together with sample statements of their views. However – in an unexpected intervention from the world of science – the expert statements are neither controversial nor contradictory. In the knowledge that their views were to be on public display for the next 10 years or more, the professors (who also acted as advisers to the exhibition) selected rather bland assertions of their positions.

Democratizing strategies?

The original intention of this representation to redistribute some of the authority to determine a proper diet from nutritionists to the lay public could be regarded as empowering of lay people – and this is how the Team saw it. Their exhibition would help to show that science and technology were part of the world which lay people also inhabited and in which they might already have expertise. It would show that some aspects of science were subject to change and different opinions. It would, literally as well as figuratively, attempt to remove some of the barriers usually employed to keep visitors at a distance from the 'learning displayed' The hands-on interactive exhibits, and the lack of, or minimal, barriers around many of the other objects on display, were just some of the means by which this idea was materialized in the exhibition. Visitors were to be turned from passive spectators into active participants; they were to experience as few boundaries as possible between themselves and science; they were to 'have fun'. As such, the exhibitionary strategies used by the Team could be conceived of as part of a democratizing of both science and the Science Museum. Their populist intentions coincided with the Science Museum's corporate strategy; and although they did not agree wholly with that strategy (for example, they all disagreed with the introduction of admission charges), they grasped it as a useful opportunity to create the kind of exhibition which they had long wanted to create.

In many respects *Food for Thought* can be regarded as democratizing in the ways the Team intended. The exhibition has proved popular, with large numbers of visitors attending and many saying that they like its hands-on accessibility (Macdonald 1993a). Like the Team, these visitors often contrast *Food for Thought* favourably with more specialist-orientated Science Museum exhibitions. Moreover, the very fact of finding this exhibition in the Science Museum does seem to make some visitors reappraise their vision of science as necessarily distant and difficult (ibid.).

Yet the democratizing potential of *Food for Thought* can also be argued to be limited or even contradicted by other dimensions of what one reviewer referred to as the exhibition's 'supermarket logic' (Cooper 1989). Its predominant motif of consumer choice is also very much part of the broader commercial or enterprise culture in which the exhibition was created (see Keat and Abercrombie 1991; Heelas and Morris 1992a; Abercrombie *et al.* 1994). And although consumerism can be seen as democratizing – as being a means through which 'the people' express themselves and, perhaps, challenge elitism – it can also entail shifting responsibility onto the individual consumer while masking malpractices of production. This is very much part of the supermarket logic. As David Harvey writes: 'We cannot tell from contemplation of any object in the supermarket what conditions lay behind its production',

> The conditions of labour and life, the sense of joy, anger, or the frustration that lie behind the production of commodities, the states of mind of the producers, are all hidden to us as we exchange one object (money) for another (the commodity). We can take our daily breakfast without a thought for the myriad people who engaged in its production. All traces of exploitation are obliterated in the object (there are no finger marks of exploitation in the daily bread).
>
> (Harvey 1989: 101)

The supermarket logic of *Food for Thought*, and more generally of the 1980s' shopping model of the museum role, may also entail a similar effacement of production. As we shall see, this means that despite the appearance of a great wealth of choice, there may be a restriction on what we are told – for example about conditions of production – which means that we are not in fact able to make fully informed choices. Moreover, there are questions to be asked too about the democratizing potential of the emphasis on entertainment and on choice.

OBJECT FETISHISM AND SANITIZING PRODUCTION

In *Food for Thought* there is some attention paid to food production. However, this is not made nearly as prominent as food consumption because of the exhibitionary philosophy of emphasizing practices, in this case eating and shopping, which were judged likely to be familiar to visitors. The approach of beginning with the familiar was thought likely to be attractive to visitors as well as helping them to feel less alienated from science. This meant, however, that the amount of space and detail which it was possible to devote to production was restricted; and as constraints during exhibition-making become more pressing, it was the sections dealing with production that were particularly squeezed. Moreover, a decision not to deal with primary production was made because of proposals underway for a new national museum of farming, and because it was argued that a gallery in the middle of London was not a good place in which to deal with these matters. Although these were clearly reasonable arguments, this led to a severing of the connection between food consumption and the primary production of food; and this in turn meant that some of the issues which are of the greatest cause for concern among consumers (e.g. diseases such salmonella in eggs and BSE in cattle) could not be tackled except in terms of rules for individual hygiene and cursory notes on possible causes (see Macdonald and Silverstone 1992).

Secondary production – factory processing of food – does feature in the exhibition. It is presented in sections each dealing with particular processes in relation to a food typically produced by the method – freezing (peas), canning (baked beans), jam-making, juice extraction, tea and coffee production, margarine-making, pasteurization and bottling (milk), sausage-making, sugar production and baking (bread). These occupy a central area of the exhibition, one juxtaposed with 'Food in the Home', where some similar processes are illustrated on a domestic scale.

Originally, these 'production' sections were not intended as such. The Team had planned to organize the exhibition around different foodstuffs, each of which would be used to illustrate a whole range of things, from particular nutritional ideas (e.g. carbohydrates in the bread section, vitamins in the juice section) to historical, sociological and folk life themes (e.g. the revolting original recipes for margarine, local customs about throwing salt). However, the nutritional advisers regarded the idea of particular foods as exemplary of certain nutritional principles to be old-fashioned and misleading, preferring to emphasize the combination and range of nutrients in particular foods. Thus nutrition – or 'Food and the Body' as it came to be called – became a separate section in

Figure 7.2 Sanitized technology: sausage machine in *Food for Thought* (photograph by Sharon Macdonald)

the finished exhibition. This effectively presented nutrition as a matter primarily to do with 'the body' – with individual eating habits; and disconnected it from the potentially more political matters of socio-historical changes in eating patterns, global trade networks, and food production, which are dealt with elsewhere in the exhibition

Later, the sheer amount of varied detail in these middle food-based sections of the exhibition was criticized by the Science Museum Director. The Team decided that they must 'rethink' the exhibition and edit these sections severely. In the pressure of doing so, and having already acquired a number of processing machines and organized the design of interactives to illustrate processes, these sections became 'Food in the Factory', with a stated aim to 'show the variety of preparation and preservation techniques which lend themselves to industrial production'. Some of the earlier details remain, but the rethinking procedure, which followed a strict managerial logic to create 'single unambiguous messages' for each section, largely cleared the sections of their social and historical dimensions. As such, they become rather sanitized representations of factory production – monumentalized machines largely removed from their workers or their hazards. For the Team at the time, these decisions seemed to be made purely within the practical and logical constraints of space, the objects they had committed themselves to, the exhibition philosophy of messages and – increasingly invoked as the going got tough – the fact that 'we are the Science Museum, after all'. In what was an extremely fraught and hectic period of exhibition-making and in the face of competing exhibits for a finite space, those which continued a Science Museum tradition of showing 'how things work', and which could more readily be thought to be somehow 'value-free' and technological, usurped other contenders. Perhaps because the reasons for the decisions seemed primarily pragmatic rather than ideological, the Team did not particularly pursue at the time the consequences that the changes would have in terms of the implicit messages in the finished exhibition.

However, the consequence of the changes was that factory production is uncritically represented. This is something which some visitors comment upon. For example, comments included: 'Why doesn't it mention meat-stripping?'; 'I don't think they were addressed enough, though – like the mass-production aspect'. Most visitors, however, seem to be lulled into a rather non-interrogative frame of mind by the exhibition – something which some attributed to the exhibition's style: 'It doesn't go into that great depth. You sort of think, "Oh well, that's that"'; 'you have to make a selection. And in the end you just zonk out, you have too much. And so you look for some trivial thing that catches the eye'; 'it was something that kept you moving'. Like a trip to the supermarket, the consumer in *Food for Thought* seems so caught up with making choices and participating that there is little opportunity to ponder the politics of what is on offer (Macdonald 1995). This is also emphasized by the pervasive commodity fetishism of the supermarket-like exhibition. Objects on display are not for the most part presented as 'objects of men's hands' but 'appear as independent beings endowed with life' (Marx 1974: 77; Jordanova 1989: 38). Their value – and their interest to the visitor – is mainly defined in the exhibition not in relation to where they have come from but in relation to their place in the revered experience of consumption.

More specifically, the exhibition itself makes no hints that we should have any concern over production processes. Linked with the section on 'Food in the Home', factory production is familiarized and domesticated and, as such, depicted as wholly benign. The production sections are also curiously disconnected from consumption in the exhibition, in particular from issues of the nutritional or gastronomic qualities of factory-produced foods. This is mirrored in the layout, 'Food in the Factory' being separated from sections such as additives, food poisoning and nutrition. And although the factory section is physically central in the exhibition, it is easily by-passed, as it was by half of the visitors observed in our survey. Moreover, it is relatively lacking in the popular culture, dummies and fun interactives of much of the rest of the exhibition; and this too serves to make it seem separate from the subjects that are dealt with elsewhere: eating, nutrition and shopping. Food and eating are predominantly portrayed as fun, they are about individuality, variety and lifestyle, rather than the relatively boring and lifeless matters of production.

CHOICE, CONSUMERS AND KNOWLEDGE

To be an active consumer is only possible, of course, in a world in which there are products which can be chosen between. Although the exhibition was given the stated aim 'To help people understand the impact of science and technology on our food', during the rethink, the Team also employed a theme of changes in Britain over the past hundred years which 'have brought us more choice in our food'. This infuses many of the sections of the exhibition. Thus, 'Trading Food', while containing a small section on famine, highlights the way that global transport systems bring us an expanding variety of foods from around the world. The representation of different ethnic groups in Britain becomes subsumed to a story of how immigration has brought us a greater range of goods in our shops. And the supermarket at one entrance to the exhibition, where the visitor is invited to put foods in a basket and run them over a checkout, can easily be seen (by contrast with the decrepit street-seller a little further along) as a glorious culmination of this upward trend of variety-bringing improvement.

Not only, however, is this exhibition *about* consumption and choice: visitors themselves are cast as choice-making consumers. This is both in relation to food – putting their own selections of goods in the shopping basket, being told that diet is a matter of their own selections – and in relation to the exhibition itself. Visitors are invited to select their own routes through the exhibition, the levels of information that they get out of it (both through the multi-level text and a computer terminal available for additional information), and the kinds of media they prefer. If the visitor of the traditional exhibition was supposed to be orderly and silent, like the ordered displays and hallowed galleries (Bennett 1995: ch. 2), the visitor in *Food for Thought* is supposed to take part, to be flexible enough to cope with the multimedia and to use all of his or her senses. What is more, many of the interactives go beyond pushing buttons and involve the visitor either in tests of sensory acuity (as in guessing foods or spices from their smells or sounds) or performance (as in exercise bikes which show the number of calories expended). If the visitor in the traditional gallery was being enlisted through the displays as an orderly citizen, the visitor in *Food for Thought*, it might well be argued, is being enlisted as an enterprising consumer and enterprising worker – relentlessly active and energetic, capable of making swift decisions, flexible enough to cope with the multiple demands of change and innovation, and willing to have their skills tested and their performance monitored (cf. Martin 1994; Macdonald 1993b). Again, modern supermarket shopping, which has sought to transform itself from a matter of housewifely drudgery to an opportunity to perform, to demonstrate skills of discernment, bargain-spotting and personality, is an apt analogy for the visitor practice which exhibitions such as *Food for Thought* attempt to promote.

Knowledge is also reconfigured in the supermarket model. Rather than being a body of accumulated truths, it becomes a matter of *information* (cf. Lyotard 1984) from which consumers select that which best suits their purposes. Like consumers themselves, it is segmented and localized. This can be seen, for example, in the treatment of diet described above, and also in the general

Figure 7.3 Hands on: visitors check out in the Sainsbury Gallery
(photograph by Sharon Macdonald)

'pick-and-mix' strategies of the exhibition. And in a move which takes knowledge yet further into the non-transferable realms of the individual, it becomes fetishized into *experience*. This is evident in many of the exhibits in *Food for Thought* in which the kind of 'information' that is provided is not only difficult to generalize, it is also difficult to convey in words. For example, an exercise bike exhibit provides the rider with a sense of the amount of effort required to use up one calorie of energy; a set of slightly distorting mirrors offer the individual viewer the opportunity to confront his or her self-perceptions; a 'smellerama' and spice cabinet entice the visitor into a game of sensory recognition. These exhibits are not providing visitors with a set of facts or principles which they can take away and apply elsewhere (as was the case for the interactive exhibits of older educational galleries) – instead, they provide a sense of the sensory self, an individualized experience.

THE SHOPPERS

Visitors to *Food for Thought* were among the first visitors to the Science Museum who had effectively already acted as the kind of discerning consumers that the museum wished to encourage by choosing to pay the newly introduced admission fee. The majority were, from their own accounts, not looking for specific information but were, rather, on days out, hoping to add an educational dimension to what was primarily a leisure activity.[3] A few had specifically intended to visit *Food for Thought*, but most had happened upon it as part of a more general visit to the Science Museum. This leisure framework is important, for, as I have argued elsewhere, the configuration of visitors as seekers of leisure, entertainment and experience – a configuration which is increasingly emphasized by exhibition-makers, as in the case of *Food for Thought*, and which seemed largely to accord with the self-definition of these visitors[4] – has consequences for the kinds of questions visitors ask and, in effect, for the politics of public understanding of science (Macdonald 1995). As I have noted, while some visitors did ask questions about what they perceived as silences in the exhibition, the majority did not; and many seemed readily to produce the kind of 'busy' account of various activities that could be seen as an 'experience-near' (cf. Geertz 1983: 57–8) exhibitionary encounter. Yet to imply that visitors fully fitted the enterprise model of performing, experience-focused choice-makers not only ignores those who did ask questions or were reluctant to get their hands on, it also overlooks several other common patterns among many of the visitors who in some ways appeared to be enterprising consumers.

Many of the visitors to *Food for Thought*, in contrast to the expectation that they would feel enabled by being presented with choices, seemed unsettled by the offer to select their own routes. They often complained of the lack of clear direction in the exhibition, and sometimes assumed that they had somehow 'got it wrong'. For example:

I found it quite confusing – perhaps because we came in at the output end of it. There's no clear direction indicating which end you should approach the gallery . . . That's a bit confusing.

I had difficulty following a theme through it. So it wasn't – there didn't appear to be a predetermined way of walking through it. And I might have preferred that – they were taking me through a sort of ordered thing. Maybe they were and I just didn't pick it up that easily.

You feel a slight bewilderment, a bit like a rat in a maze, not quite knowing which way to go.

Such visitors clearly did not feel empowered by the choice built into the exhibition layout. What they seemed to seek was a clear 'story'; and indeed, many of them reconstructed the exhibition into the story that they supposed was guiding the layout of the exhibition.

Among these stories, one of the most prevalent in the interviews is of particular interest in relation to the exhibition's attempts to present diet as a matter of lifestyle choice. For many visitors, what they perceived the exhibition as doing was telling them about 'good foods and bad foods' (phrases which resonated through many interviews) – and this despite the fact that one panel explicitly stated 'Most scientists agree that no one food in isolation is "good" or "bad"'; that is, these visitors perceived the exhibition to be prescribing and promoting a particular kind of diet:

Telling you more about food than just eating it. It tells you more about it. What's good for you and what's bad for you, ain't it?

I suppose it's trying to promote healthy eating.

Showing you what's right to eat and what's not right to eat.

Likewise with science, few visitors related the message of disagreement among scientists over food in relation to the exhibition, though some talked of the variability of nutritional advice more generally. Partly at stake here perhaps was an assumption that the Science Museum would surely be providing a scientifically reliable presentation of 'the facts'. Certainly, there was much in the exhibition that was presented in such terms, and visitors did refer to nuggets of information that they had gleaned. The point, however, is that visitors did not embrace the invitation to 'choose for themselves' as readily as the exhibition-makers might have anticipated.

However, while visitors were not so willing to position themselves as choice-makers in relation to the routes and nutritional messages of the exhibition, they did seem to welcome the familiarization and the fun dimension of science. In doing so, many made a contrast, akin to that made by the Team themselves, with some other Science Museum exhibitions:

A lot of this museum is very sciency and if you're not particularly interested in that then it's hard to relate to. I thought this was more sort of open to everybody, not just people who are interested in science.

It didn't strike me as being too scientific, or off-puttingly so. It was just sort of fun sort of thing.

For some, this worked just as the Team had hoped, conveying a message, as one visitor put it, 'that there's quite a lot of technical issues at stake in food. But it's done in a way that's easy'. Yet while many said that they enjoyed the exhibition and the fact that it was not 'off-puttingly' scientific, this seemed for a considerable number of visitors to imply that this exhibition was not to do with 'real science' at all. *Food for Thought*, many visitors told us, was not 'deeply scientific' or 'purely scientific'; it was instead, more a matter of 'common sense'. Nevertheless, even if *Food for Thought* dealt with common-sense and everyday matters that many visitors had not regarded as science, they found themselves grappling with the fact that as an exhibition in the Science Museum it surely must be 'scientific'. As one said: 'I just didn't think that food was science, but now I know.'

For visitors, then, the exhibition did have the potential to disrupt expectations to some extent, though what is perhaps more notable is the way in which many visitors read the exhibition through a lens of expecting, and even perhaps desiring, prescription and authoritativeness from the Science Museum. They did so, however, while simultaneously accepting at least some of the invitation to play and perform, within the exhibitionary space. Some did, perhaps, go away with a sense that they knew more science than they had previously realized, though for many 'real science' remained in those 'difficult' exhibitions elsewhere. And while some visitors did ask political questions about food, they did so only against the grain of the exhibition,[5] by interrogating its own representations rather than through the choices offered by the exhibition itself.

Although most visitors seemed to have expectations and perceptions of the Science Museum as authoritative and politically disinterested, they held these views while simultaneously regarding the museum as part of the marketplace. This arose especially in connection to questions of sponsorship. Here, virtually all visitors recognized that Sainsbury's had provided financial support and many even assumed that Sainsbury's was responsible for the content of the exhibition (an idea supported by the presence of Sainsbury's goods and the reproduction of a Sainsbury's store). Yet, although this was perceived by a minority as a source of 'bias' in the exhibition, the majority talked of it only in terms of the financial advantages for the museum. Moreover, few seemed to think that sponsorship might affect the exhibition in anything other than superficial ways. Sponsorship was seen as offering a company 'advertising', but this was not in itself regarded as detrimental to what was on display. Advertising, according to the comments of these visitors, was perceived as a readily identifiable and transparent matter which consumers could take or leave as they chose: 'I don't think people are necessarily going to rush out and buy all the Sainsbury's things because they've seen it.' Here, then, the model of the exhibition as shop was very pertinent: visitors perceived themselves as being presented with 'products' which they could choose whether to 'buy' or not. What this mode of perceiving and appropriating the exhibition did not do, however, was to lead them to ask questions about the production of the exhibition or the politics of what was, and was not, on display.

POLITICS OF THE SUPERMARKET

The supermarket model that *Food for Thought* exemplifies so well can, then, be argued to have rather different possible political potentials. It might be seen, as the Team hoped, as a welcome democratizing of museums, a break-down of the idea of the canon, a recognition of the value of local and lay knowledges and an acceptance of the popular and of pleasure. Yet, as this analysis suggests, the 'shift of authority from producer to consumer' (Abercrombie 1991: 172) can also mean laying responsibility for social and individual ills at the door of the individual while ignoring the part that producers and the State may play.[6] There are other problems, too, inherent in the supermarket model, and more widely in uncritical celebration of consumerism as democratizing. This is not to deny that consumerism *can* have democratizing effects; the argument is that if it is to do so, then there are more questions that need to be addressed.

Partly as a consequence of playing down production, the rhetoric of consumer choice skates over questions of the determination of the 'choices' on offer. Clearly, these have been determined by producers, even if they have taken the believed preferences of consumers into account. Moreover, the post-Fordist legitimization of available choices in terms of being 'what people want' conflates desire and democracy in such a way as to 'deproblematize' democracy, and deny connections between pleasure and power: 'fun is fun, and has nothing to do with power' (Berland 1992: 47). As such, 'the popular' and the choices on offer are positioned beyond critique.

There are, nevertheless, questions to be asked about which consumers are being authorized to make choices and have pleasure. Sir Roy Strong, in looking for a shop as analogue for the future V&A, selected one which caters for a rather specific population segment: the fairly well-off, respectable and traditionally inclined – preferred V&A visitors no doubt (Hewison 1991: 162–3). The cosmopolitan, enterprising shopper at Sainsbury's might well be argued to be analogous to the visitor defined by *Food for Thought*. This rhetoric of consumer choice, however, evades awkward questions of differences – of income, of education, of mobility – which may affect the capacity of individuals to make choices – to be consumers. Instead, it projects the message that 'choice is . . . the only source of difference' (Strathern 1992: 37) – we are all equal but for the different choices that we have made. And, consequently, we are all responsible for our fates. What is more, as Marilyn Strathern points out, we are given no choice *not* to choose: consumerism is prescriptive (ibid.: 38), it is how personhood is being defined in enterprise culture.

Although consumerism may have broadened the range of consumer interests provided for, these are undoubtedly still limited; and alongside a trend towards differentiation there seems simultaneously to be a homogenization of many products and a routinization of production which makes catering for the specific demands *more* rather than less difficult. This routinization is referred to by George Ritzer as 'McDonaldization', a term he coins by reference to the fast-food chain McDonalds which epitomizes such processes (Ritzer 1996). One consequence of McDonaldization is that if your needs or desires are perceived as so singular that they do not constitute a 'market segment' – if, as in an example given by Leigh Star, you are allergic to onions, say – then your choices will not be catered for (Star 1991). This 'constituency problem', as it is sometimes called, can also be seen as a version of the so-called 'philistine critique' or 'lowest common denominator effect' of enterprise culture (Heelas and Morris 1992b: 14). Knowledge, in such a framework, will not only tend to be commodified into 'useful information', but minority interests and cultural pursuits which entail more than a swift passing enthusiasm will find it increasingly hard to get backing in a competitive market (ibid.). And, as the intervention of the State recedes in enterprise culture, there is more reliance upon the benevolence of those who do well within it (ibid.: 11). Sponsorship – so vital now for museums, as in *Food for Thought* – is one symptom of this. It comes with another set of constraints upon what is on offer, however, for some interests and subjects are considerably less attractive than others, and sponsorship may come with strings attached (Levidow and Young 1984; Kirby 1988; Davies 1989). An exhibition on the malpractices of factory production would be unlikely to find industrial backing. In effect, this may extend the power of successful producers as they look for projects to boost their corporate image in post-Fordism's increasingly subtle battles for popular taste and prestige (Harvey 1989: 160).

The Team primarily responsible for making *Food for Thought* embraced the supermarket model for its democratizing potential. So how did it come to have another potential too? Although I have described some of the ways in which forces beyond the Team intervened in the development of the exhibition, its shaping was not openly contested. The Team was not forced to go in directions with which they fundamentally disagreed. Rather, different political inflections never really emerged. The enterprise connotations of the exhibition presented themselves during exhibition-making not overtly but in the managerial procedures of rethinking the exhibition, in the scientists' reluctance to become dated, in the resort to Science Museum authoritativeness, in images of technologies as value-free, and in decisions over such matters as the exhibition layout and display media.

The alternative political potentials were also masked by the fact that the different 'strands' of consumerism have a good deal in common; in particular a shared common rhetorical vocabulary, incorporating phrases and terms such as 'public understanding of science', 'widening access', 'public accountability', 'visitor participation' and 'choice'. They can also both inhabit the same physical exhibits – such is the possible multiple semantics of the material. Moreover, the alternative politico-semiotics of the exhibition were also already written into many of the cultural notions that the Team themselves embraced. They were there already in assumptions about consumption as a key means of expressing individuality, activity as choice, objects as commodities, fun as democratizing and museums as part of the marketplace. Many of these assumptions are also shared by visitors.

Of course, it might be argued that the 'exhibition-as-supermarket' model is no less democratizing than the more prevalent earlier models of museums as temples, schools, penitentiaries or glossy department stores.[7] This may be so, though, as Tony Bennett argues (Chapter 2), the authoritative, educational model *was* seen by those involved as part of a liberal democratic production of citizenship. My view, however, and this is an argument which might equally apply to other exhibitionary models, is that an exhibition can contain alternative – though not necessarily contested – political motivations and potentials; and that the visions of some (such as the exhibition-makers) can, through subtle processes, be given a rather different political inflection. We have in recent years heard much about exhibitions as 'contested' (Lavine and Karp 1991: 1), and about the politics of such contests; there is, however, also political potential, alternative and effect in that which has not been subject to disagreement. It is to further understanding of some of the processes and cultural assumptions involved in this, that this chapter is intended as a contribution.

NOTES

1 See Chantal Georgal (1994) for an interesting discussion of analogies and relationships between museums and shops (particularly department stores) in nineteenth-century France.

2 The research was funded by the Economic and Social Research Council under its 'Public Understanding of Science' programme (award no. Y418254003). It was directed by Roger Silverstone and most of the visitor study was carried out by Gilly Heron. Gratitude to Roger and Gilly, and only limited responsibility, are intended by my use of 'our research'. I would also like to thank the Science Museum – especially the *Food for Thought* team – for so generously and bravely agreeing to be subjects of the research.

3 Comments and quotations are derived from the visitor study carried out on *Food for Thought*. This entailed conducting interviews (in a semi-structured format) with groups of visitors (42 groups in all) after they left the exhibition. Because the aim of the analysis was more to identify prevalent patterns in visitors' appropriation of the exhibition ('cultural projects'), the issue of precise numbers or proportions of visitors is not relevant and hence I use general terms such as 'the majority' or 'many'. For a much more extensive analysis of the data see Macdonald (1993a).

4 It might be argued that visitors interviewed in this study were more likely to describe themselves in such terms as they were interviewed just after leaving *Food for Thought*. I think this is too deterministic a suggestion, however, and note that the way in which visitors expressed their intentions were usually through touristic discourses such as 'doing London', rather than in terms offered by the exhibition.

5 For a discussion of 'reading against the grain', a concept derived from feminist theorizing, see Porter (1996).
6 More generally, this can be argued to be an ambivalent political potential of postmodernism (see for example Bauman 1992; Lash and Urry 1994: 113).
7 For a discussion of the museum as temple, see for example Duncan (1995); as school, Hooper-Greenhill (1994); and as department store, Georgel (1994). The model of the museum as penitentiary has been discussed by Tony Bennett, especially in his contribution ('The Museum as Penitentiary') at a conference on 'Museums as Contested Zones' in Milton Keynes, November 1996. See also Bennett (1995, ch. 2).

REFERENCES

Abercrombie, N. (1991) 'The privilege of the producer', in R. Keat, N. Abercrombie and N. Whitely *Enterprise Culture*, pp. 171–85, London: Routledge.
Abercrombie, N. *et al.* (eds) (1994) *The Authority of the Consumer*, London: Routledge.
Bauman, Z. (1992) *Intimations of Postmodernity*, London: Routledge.
Bennett, T. (1995) *The Birth of the Museum*, London: Routledge.
Berland, J. (1992) 'Angels dancing: cultural technologies and the production of space', in L. Grossberg, C. Nelson and P. Treichler (eds) *Cultural Studies*, pp. 38–55, London: Routledge.
Cooper, D. (1989) *The Food Programme*, Radio 4 BBC broadcast, 9 October.
Davies, M. (1989) 'Sponsorship threatens museum role', *Museums Journal* (December), pp. 13–14.
Duncan, C. (1995) *Civilizing Rituals: Inside Public Art Museums*, London: Routledge.
Featherstone, M. (1991) *Consumer Culture and Postmodernism*, London: Sage.
Geertz, C. (1983) *Local Knowledge*, New York: Basic Books.
Georgel, C. (1994) 'The museum as metaphor in nineteenth century France', in D. Sherman and I. Rogoff (eds) *Museum Culture: Histories, Discourses, Spectacles*, pp. 113–22, London: Routledge.
Harvey, D. (1989) *The Condition of Postmodernity*, Oxford: Blackwell.
Heelas, P. and P. Morris (eds) (1992a) *The Values of the Enterprise Culture: The Moral Debate*, London: Routledge.
—— (1992b) 'Enterprise culture: its values and value', in P. Heelas and P. Morris (eds), *The Values of Enterprise Culture: The Moral Debate*, pp. 1–25, London: Routledge.
Hewison, R. (1991) 'Commerce and culture', in J. Corner and S. Harvey (eds) *Enterprise and Heritage: Crosscurrents of National Culture*, pp. 162–77, London: Routledge.
Hooper-Greenhill, E. (ed.) (1994) *The Educational Role of the Museum*, London: Routledge.
Jordanova, L. (1989) 'Objects of knowledge: a historical perspective on museums', in P. Vergo (ed.) *The New Museology*, pp. 22–40, London: Reaktion Books.
Keat, R., N. Abercrombie and N. Whitely (eds) (1991) *Enterprise Culture*, London: Routledge.
Kirby, S. (1988) 'Policy and politics: charges, sponsorship and bias', in R. Lumley (ed.) *The Museum Time-machine*, pp. 89–101, London: Routledge/Comedia.
Lash, S. and J. Urry (1994) *Economies of Signs and Space*, London: Sage.
Lavine, S. and I. Karp (1991) 'Introduction: museums and multiculturalism', in I. Karp and S. Lavine (eds) *Exhibiting Cultures: The Poetics and Politics of Museum Display*, pp. 1–9, Washington, DC: Smithsonian Institution.
Levidow, L. and R. Young (1984) 'Exhibiting nuclear power: the Science Museum cover-up', *Radical Science Journal*, 25 (1), pp. 53–79.
Lyotard, J-F. (1984) *The Postmodern Condition: A Report on Knowledge* (trans. G. Bennington and B. Massumi), Minneapolis, MN: University of Minneapolis Press.

Macdonald, S. (1993a) 'Museum visiting: a science exhibition case study', Keele University, Department of Sociology and Social Anthropology Working Papers.

—— (1993b) 'Un nouveau "corps des visiteurs"?: Musées et changements culturels', *Publics et Musées*, 3, pp. 13–27.

—— (1995) 'Consuming science: public knowledge and the dispersed politics of reception among museum visitors', *Media, Culture and Society*, 17 (1), pp. 13–29.

—— (1996) 'Authorizing science: museums and the public understanding of science', in A. Irwin and B. Wynne (eds) *Misunderstanding Science? The Public Reconstruction of Science and Technology*, pp. 152–171, Cambridge: Cambridge University Press.

Macdonald, S. and R. Silverstone (1992) 'Science on display: the representation of scientific controversy in museum exhibitions', *Public Understanding of Science*, 1 (1), pp. 69–87.

Martin, E. (1994) 'The end of the body?', *American Ethnologist*, 19 (1), pp. 121–40.

Marx, K. (1974) *Capital: A Critical Analysis of Capitalist Production*, Vol.1, London: Lawrence & Wishart.

Porter, G. (1996) 'Seeing through solidity: a feminist perspective on museums', in S. Macdonald and G. Fyfe (eds) *Theorizing Museums* (*Sociological Review* monograph), pp. 105–26, Oxford: Blackwell.

Ritzer, G. (1996) *The McDonaldization of Society* (2nd edition), Thousand Oaks, CA: Pine Forge Press.

Star, S. L. (1991) 'Power, technologies and the phenomenology of conventions: on being allergic to onions', in J. Law (ed.) *A Sociology of Monsters* (*Sociological Review* monograph 38), pp. 26–56, London: Routledge.

Strathern, M. (1992) *Reproducing the Future*, Manchester: Manchester University Press.

Strong, R. (1985) 'Towards a more consumer-oriented V&A', Press release, V&A.

Nations on display
Technology and culture in Expo '92

Penelope Harvey

THE FRENCH PAVILION

The entrance to the French pavilion was on the top floor. The room was lined with cabinets filled with examples of French cultural production, evidence of France's high culture, particularly all that is associated with literature, opera, history and scientific discoveries from ancient geometry to holograms. The floor of this room was glass. The drop, which was visible, was broken by a model of eighteenth-century Paris. Visitors stood on the glass floor and looked down through 200 years of French history. As they walked, they walked over a model of the city, in fact over layers of cities from different periods. Many people, including myself, were rather nervous about walking on the floor. The drop induced vertigo. At the far end of the room there were TVs, holograms and computers with more information available from the video-disks on the Paris exhibition of 1900.

Down on the second floor the model of the French city appeared at shoulder height. As we walked backwards in time through the exhibit, it was clear that the model was in fact hanging upside down and reflected in a mirror. What had been seen from above, and what could still be seen by looking to the side and down was the mirror image. This was the pavilion of mirror technology. The ground floor was dominated by a mirrored film pit. The films advertised French companies, and the research they had sponsored as their contribution to 'our world of the future'. I watched a film about space that depicted the world as watched by a satellite, setting off from Spain looking over America. Communications technology united the globe. As the film played, as well as watching it from around the sides, people floated over the pit on a moving walkway. Some walked backwards to prolong the experience, or came in from the wrong end to walk through slowly, against the force of the walkway. I began to feel that the vertigo I had felt on stepping onto the glass floor at the top of the pavilion was a planned pre-figuration of the vertigo yet to be experienced as a result of the intellectual free-fall which would take place in the consumption of this hyper-reflexive exhibit.

WORLD'S FAIRS AND INTERNATIONAL EXHIBITIONS

The technological innovations of the twentieth century have had dramatic effects on the political and cultural relationships that sustain and constitute the nation-state and its modernist institutions of cultural display, the museum and national exhibition. The most flamboyant of these, the World's Fair, provides a particularly vivid image of the changes and continuities in representations of world, nation and citizenship over the past century. As temporary yet monumental exhibits, these fairs are extremely flexible institutions of display. Unlike museums, they can operate as sites of innovation, and provide opportunities for the demonstration of new technologies and their effects.[1] Change and progress, however, are only visible in a context which also marks continuities and traditions. Thus, although the idioms of power in Expo '92 were quite openly directed towards a corporate model of the nation-state, to the global competition for markets and control of the most advanced information technologies, the values of culture, tradition and identity were also central to national exhibits. Nation-states were produced as cultural entities in Expo '92 through an interplay between innovation and tradition. Technology played a crucial role in this process and influenced the terms on which participants competed in this theatre of global display.

Expo '92, granted 'Universal' status by the Bureau of International Expositions in Paris, is the most recent of a series of events which started with the Great International Exhibition held in London in 1851 at the Crystal Palace. In this first 'global' exhibit, mass production was on show in the very fabric of the event. Itself the product of machine technology, the first Great Exhibition celebrated high capital and empire. By the late nineteenth century these exhibitions had reached their apogee. The idea of totalizing paradigms, and the full and 'physical realisation of previous knowledge' in the exhibits was established as the ideal form (Greenhalgh 1989: 89). Culture and technology were the objects of display, economic and political power the motivations for the very costly sponsorship of participation. Up until the First World War, such exhibitions were defined not only by their scope but also by their optimism, their extravagance and their spirit of international competition (Benedict 1983; Greenhalgh 1989).

It was technological developments themselves which changed the nature of the International Exhibition in subsequent decades, reducing their importance in the public eye and altering their internal appearance. The wonder of seeing things for the first time was diminished by the spread of communications technologies which gave immediate mass access to innovation via other channels such as newspapers, radios and, more recently, television. The economic benefits for exhibitors also had increasingly to be measured against the advantages of more widespread and effective advertising media and the more specialized trade fairs. Finally, and perhaps increasingly since the 1950s, World's Fairs seemed to have lost that central element of international competition and had become simply business fairs and amusement parks (Benedict 1983: 59).

However, despite declining visibility in the crowded contemporary field of promotional activity, the Universal Exhibition continues. National pavilions remain the focus of these World's Fairs, with nations investing millions in order to participate. And while multinationals underwrite much of this national activity, they do not erase the presence of the nation-state. Fujitsu, Siemens and Rank Xerox, the largest multinational corporations to participate in Expo '92, were sited alongside and in a complementary relationship to their nations of origin. Thus, the Fujitsu high-tech spherical cinema stood opposite Japan's wooden pavilion. Siemens was located next to Germany, Rank Xerox opposite the United States of America. There are strong continuities from previous eras and modernist values are still very much on show. Expo '92 was optimistic, extravagant and outward-looking; its general thematic focus was 'The Age of Discoveries' and participants were encouraged to reflect on human history and human futures in grandiose terms. What has changed is the public understanding of the nation-state itself and its place in the wider global context. If the imperial exhibitions were about realist representational practices[2] and 'the celebration of high capital, as enhanced by machine technology' (Greenhalgh 1989: 94), then the post imperial exhibition, while still celebrating capital, is now enhanced through electronic communications technology and an excess of imagery which affords little or no promise of access to the real. The nation-state is in many ways redundant to this exercise, yet it remains as the central pivot of the exhibition, the enduring legitimization of what was a crucial statement of identity for one nation – Spain – while simultaneously constituting a rather less focused marketing identity for the particular business interests of other participants.[3]

The process through which Spain secured the exhibition and produced Expo '92 was a long one. King Juan Carlos made a speech in Santo Domingo in 1976, shortly after his reinstatement and before the death of Franco, expressing his wish that a Universal Exhibition be celebrated in Spain on the occasion of the fifth centenary of the discovery of America. Amid speculation that Spain had paid the crucial membership fees for the Latin American nations, securing their voting rights and their votes, the International Bureau decided in 1983 that the 1992 World's Fair should be held jointly by Seville and Chicago. But with the successful Olympic bid and the increasing focus on Spain, Chicago decided against the investment. In 1987 the Spanish Government set up three state corporations, Expo '92, the V Centenary Commission and the Olympics Commission. Spain was set to reproduce the Great Exhibitions of Paris (1900), St. Louis (1904) and London (1908), the three previous World's Fairs to be held in conjunction with the Olympic games. State invitations were issued and the terms of participation negotiated.

The instigation of this process was reminiscent of the Ibero-American Exhibition held in Seville in 1929 and Barcelona's International Exhibition of 1888: outward-looking politics on the back of internal disorder, an attempt to assert an effective world presence, to claim a position of parity among the nations of the European Community. As the press dossier states:

> The Universal Exposition means for our country the opportunity to appear before the international community as a modern, efficient country, capable of organizing a project of the size of the Exposition. A country with competitive businesses and a highly-qualified labour force, capable of involving all economic sectors and public administrations in a common project.

More pragmatic perhaps than the Eiffel Tower or the Statue of Liberty, the architectural monuments of Expo '92 are the bridges, the elegant and daringly conceived connections between the old quarter of the city of Seville and the exhibition site, the Island of Cartuja. The bridges were a literal connection and a powerful symbol. In the run-up to the Expo, the island was converted from a parched area of Andalusian countryside into the latest image of the 'idealised consumer city' (Benedict 1983: 5). The construction project involved 650,000 square metres of buildings, 500,000 square metres of parks and gardens, mile upon mile of networked cabling and a completely new infrastructure of transport links. The small island was now connected to global networks, both electronically and by road, rail and air, an image of the ways in which Spain sought to link itself to its European neighbours and the more distant sources of international capital. These centres were the future; Latin America the past.

WORLD'S FAIRS/EXPOSITIONS AS TECHNOLOGIES OF NATIONHOOD

As Haraway argued so forcefully with reference to New York's Natural History Museum (Haraway 1989), celebratory public exhibits do more than simply represent life, they recreate their object of attention in a perfect and desirable form. The Expo was produced through processes of standardization and integration which rendered the world not only accessible but also recognizable. As a technology of contemporary nationhood, Expo enabled the simultaneous appearance of cultural tradition and innovation, cultural unity and difference, stereotypes and challenges to the preconceived. Expo also enabled the sensation of movement in time and space, and the sensation of an accessible global culture through the spectacularization of our relationships with the world to which it refers.

The 112 participating nations displayed culture, but culture in a particular commodified form which was, within certain standard variations, quite uniform. Expo '92 was unlikely to produce culture-shock in any visitor even mildly conversant with leisure industries and heritage culture. The exhibitors offered mild sensation, through the film technologies, simulation techniques and accessible knowledge, made attractive by interactive displays, variety of media and clarity of explanation.

One of the standard fantasies in which visitors were obliged to participate was the redrawn map of the world. Spain dominated this new ideal world with its commanding focal site at the head of the Avenue of Europe on the edge of the

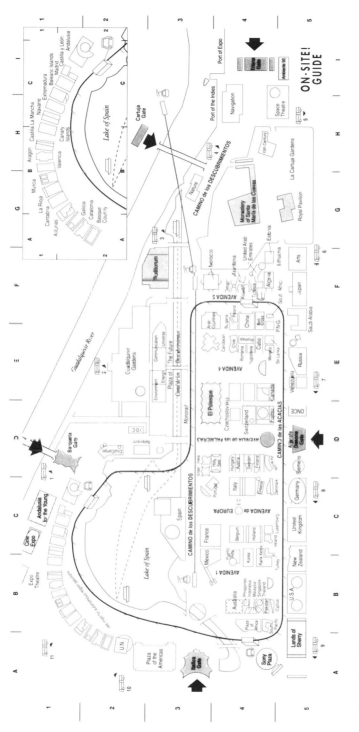

Figure 8.1 Map of Expo '92

newly constructed Lake of Spain. The space it occupied was doubled by the display of its disaggregated component parts, the 17 autonomous regions, ranged around the far shores of the lake. The pavilion of the European Community occupied a position in the centre of the European Avenue. The exhibition space was underground, not visible from the outside. What could be seen was the multicoloured tower designed to display simultaneously the flags of all the Community members in the order of their affiliation. The 12 nations of the Community were also literally attached to the tower by cloth awnings which spanned the walkway. Arab nations, included for the first time at a World's Fair, were grouped at the eastern end of the precinct, including in their midst the most expensive pavilion of the Expo, the hand-crafted ($35 million) Moroccan palace.

The western end of the site was dominated by a large office-style building, the Plaza of America, the subject of intense pre-Expo negotiations which well illustrate the politics involved in drawing up the final world map. The Expo organizers were concerned that Latin American nations should have a high profile. It was for this reason that they built this multiplex pavilion, not simply to house all those Latin American nations that wished to participate but also to secure for them a dominant position equalled only by that of Spain itself. There were, however, unfortunate implications in this design. In the first place, the pavilion did appear to be integrated into the Spanish section of the site. Furthermore, even if it were argued that the positioning could indicate an equivalence of status between the Americas and Spain, the effect was to reduce a whole continent to a single locale. Not all the Latin American nations were prepared to accept this arrangement. It was argued that they would appear as the poor relations which would give a negative image of the economies which they had come to Spain to promote. Mexico, Chile, Venezuela and Cuba opted to build pavilions at their own expense on separate sites outside the Americas building. Things were beginning to look bad for the Expo management. The building was already constructed and it seemed possible that they might not be able to fill it. Expo subsidized participation in this building. For many of the nations it was not just the venue they provided but the transport and insurance of the exhibits, and the travel and accommodation of personnel. Further temptations of privileged business agreements for the shops and restaurants which some of the nations wished to set up secured the crucial presence of Colombia, Argentina and Brazil, three nations which might have been able to finance a separate participation. It is noteworthy that throughout these negotiations the economies of Mexico and Venezuela were respected in their own right, but there were fierce struggles with Cuba, which wished to remain independent despite the cost. For Cuba, the fact of independent survival was one of the primary messages which they wished to convey. Chile was openly elitist, their Commissioner declaring in public that Chile did not wish to be associated with the Blacks and Indians inside the Plaza.

The concern of the Latin Americans about their portrayal as the poor of the Expo, was echoed in the concerns of the African nations. There were those who argued it was worse for the Latin Americans because they could be seen to be poor, while the Africans with their north-facing position, looking away from the main site onto the newly built motorway, could not even be seen and therefore had less to worry about in terms of negative effect! The African nations were also housed in an Expo building, another permanent structure built with future purposes in mind – hence, its somewhat alternative orientation. Unlike the Latin American states, not all African states were represented, a sample was enough to provide the world context in which to set Spain and Europe. The Expo management defended themselves from criticism with the argument that Africa was a lesser priority than South America, or alternatively that they had spent more on the participation of Third World countries than any previous Expo.

Quite apart from the physical siting of the pavilions, the exhibits themselves demonstrated that the uniformity of a particular commodified global culture prevails despite the process of individuation which it entails. This theme of unity and diversity was the principle vehicle for the expression of national histories, national integration with wider polities and the multiculturalism contained within national boundaries.[4] Spain provided the most visible example with the independent participation of its 17 Spanish autonomous communities. As might be expected, the theme was also part of the rhetoric of the EC pavilion. This exhibit dealt specifically with the tension between a European history of civilization and the simultaneous disruptive nationalism, the local competition that had led to the two World Wars. Through this image of conflict the EC produced itself as the way forward for a future harmonious, peaceful and productive Europe. In similar vein, many nations chose to stress the links that they had with other nations as individual entities acting in a wider social universe. Portugal, for example, displayed maps which showed the diverse European cities in which their most famous scholars had studied and which also depicted the trade routes through which they had for the past 500 years interacted with the rest of the world. Israel stressed that not only was Jerusalem a sacred centre for Jews, Christians and Muslims but that the five million Jews in Israel had come from 40 separate nation-states.

A further way in which the boundaries between nations were blurred by the exhibits was in the explicit challenge that was made to the differentiating stereotypes that distinguish one nation from another in popular imagination. Japan rejected its association with technology and produced its tradition, a wooden pavilion, traditional arts, paper models instead of electronics. Britain, on the other hand, worked explicitly against an image of the isolationist tradition-bound nation of Beefeaters, Welsh ladies, Scottish kilts and Morris dancers. Late-twentieth century Britain is the nation constructing the Channel Tunnel, linked to continental Europe with the latest communications technologies, a vibrant economic force in the contemporary world.

Other challenges to the stereotype were more radical and worked against the concept of the nation altogether. Switzerland, for example, greeted pavilion visitors with a Ben Vautier artwork from 1935 consisting of the message:

'Switzerland does not exist'. The accompanying explanation pointed out that there was no common culture or language in Switzerland. The threat to national identity posed by the lack of a common linguistic and cultural denominator was explicitly addressed in the exhibit and the solution found in communicative multiplicity, summed up in the slogan 'Je pense donc je suisse'.

The Czechs also made a radical statement about the relationship between a nation and its history. The pavilion housed a glass sculpture which was exhibited through a show of light and sound. The Communist government had been over-thrown during the planning stages of the Expo and the new organizers had held a competition for the design of the interior of the pavilion. The judges had liked this abstract modern sculpture because they believed it would produce a memorable experience for those who came to look at it. They thought that the experience of engaging with the exhibit, of using it to explore one's own fantasies and associations, was a more creative way of engaging with the idea of nationality than the alternative accumulation of cultures and histories. Most importantly, they wanted to find a way to leave the culture and history of their recent past behind them. The commissioner with whom I spoke, who had been on the selection panel, had himself favoured an even more radical exhibit which would have consisted of a patch of grass, a flagpole and the Czech flag - no pavilion, no structure, a Czech identity with no content, no past, just a new future.

This exhibit also served as a reminder that the harmonious world of the Expo was in contact with the world of contemporary politics, where the structures of the nation-state are constantly under challenge and review. Expo personnel had to work hard on occasions to maintain the image of global collaboration. A ban on South Africa was lifted at the last minute to enable their participation, and an attempt to exclude Yugoslavia, represented in the end by the Serbs, was side-stepped by the Expo management. The Russians and subsequently all the Eastern European participants had to redesign their pavilions at very short notice. The British government seemed oblivious to the Department of Trade and Industry's attempts to claim unwavering support and commitment to Europe as they withdrew from the Exchange Rate Mechanism and began to distance themselves from the Maastricht agreement. And, as always with Expo, there was someone explicitly including such critiques in their exhibits. In this case it was the Dutch, who had mounted a dramatic exhibition of photo-journalism in what might be described as a display of famous and memorable images of world horror. This exhibit had no national orientation; it was a statement about global connections.

TECHNOLOGY AND CULTURE

Throughout the history of World's Fairs the political and economic motivations and agendas have been underplayed in the displays of technology, art and science which are produced as the universal goals and values of human endeavour. In this sense, the World's Fairs have a deep and intrinsic commitment to the values of modernism. However, technological developments have produced a situation in which these values are easily undermined, particularly in the possibilities they afford for certain kinds of postmodernist expression, such as that characterized by Featherstone as 'the celebration of the depthlessness of culture, the decline of the originality/genius of the artistic producer and the assumption that art can only be repetition' (Featherstone 1991: 8). My interest here is to look at how contrasting relationships between technology and culture create these contrary effects.

Invisible techniques of assistance for the expression of cultural forms

The most conservative manifestation of this relationship is the display of 'high culture', valuable original pieces, in high-tech exhibition spaces. The technologies behind the display of high culture are invisible techniques of assistance designed to enable the fullest expression of the beauty of the cultural form. The Expo site contained several exhibits which brought culture and technology together in this way: the pavilion of the fifteenth century, the 'Treasures of Spain', (within the Spanish pavilion), and the art collection at the Holy See, the Vatican pavilion. Authentic indigenous art was most prominently represented by the 'Gold Exhibition' in the American Plaza and the 'Treasures of Nigeria' in the African Plaza.

The pavilion of 'Art and Culture around 1492' contained an exquisite display of late-fifteenth-century pieces. The gallery space was itself an art object, the restored fifteenth-century Carthusian monastery where Columbus is known to have stayed, and where his remains were once held. This building is described as the 'nerve centre' of the Universal Exposition, the 'symbolic focal point', which served as a tangible, concrete historical presence in an event which was otherwise comprised of only semi-permanent structures most of which would be dismantled. History in this exhibit was presented through a display of original forms in contrast to the use elsewhere of models and mirrors, and a pervasive state-of-the-art technology such as high-resolution TV, Imax and spherical projection, holograms and virtual reality. The technology is, of course, there in the 1492 exhibit, in the control of light, heat and humidity, in the restoration of the building and in the transport and surveillance of the objects; however, it was the art objects, not the technology, which visitors were invited to wonder at. In this conservative model technology is used to reveal latent truth or beauty but is not in any way modifying the intrinsic cultural form.

Innovations and improving cultural life

An alternative relationship between technology and culture is that of liberal rationalist thought which posits culture as a way of life and technology as innovation and improvement. In this model there is a causal and developmental relationship between technology and culture. Several pavilions explored this relationship.

The Italians, for example, had mounted an exhibit on perspective which discussed and illustrated the new theories and laws of vision which altered notions of reality in the fifteenth century. They then suggested that that sense of reality was itself challenged by contemporary technology. In what appeared to be a booth to listen to the high-quality sound of an operatic performance which you could also watch on screen, visitors unknowingly allowed themselves to be filmed and the image of them as viewers was played back on banked TV screens just out of their sight. It was not clear who was watching and who was being watched, nor indeed what exactly anyone was looking at. Following the exhibit on perspective, the visitor entered a display which discussed the relationship between communication technologies, memory and culture. Devices such as the eye glass and the pendulum were presented as objects designed to thwart space and time. Paper was shown to have acted as the main support for human memory and culture until the recent move into the electronic age, where hypertexts hold millions of pieces of information in computerized systems. The message was that technologies designed for medical and military purposes affect the generation of cultural knowledges more widely.

The Siemens exhibit was even more explicit about this connection between communications technology and contemporary cultural practices. Siemens, one of the high-profile corporate participants, was the supplier of the communications system to the Expo site and had also led the German–Spanish consortium responsible for the electrical engineering and the installation of telecommunications equipment for the high-speed rail link from Madrid to Seville.

The Siemens exhibit was focused on company history, on corporate culture, 'the evolution of technology at Siemens from the pioneering days to modern innovations'. This was a company with a tradition of innovation and their multi-media exhibit was a survey of the history of electrical engineering, electronics and microelectronics as they have affected the world of work. The tradition which the exhibit evoked was one of innovation. Evolutionary change was presented as progress, rather than adaptation, a natural process of development through which the quality of life is enhanced. A history is presented in which transformations in communications technologies developed until isolated systems reached their limits. Then came the most recent transformation, the evolution of networks and the merging of systems. The message of this exhibit was that if we use our technical resources properly, a Utopian future lies within our reach. We cannot predict the future, they mused, but we can invent it.

The other distinctive message that the Siemens pavilion stressed was the need to recognize and reinforce the symbiosis of man, nature and technology. The greater the connection the less environmental damage or waste of energy. In fact, their film stated quite explicitly that the human race will destroy itself if it does not learn to act in the terms of integrated systems. Technical progress was explicitly rendered analogous to biological process as the theme of 'Evolutionary networks, technology and biology in parallel' was expounded. This message was picked up in the ecological responsibility embraced by the company, their involvement in searches for alternative sources of energy and their commitment to use the potential of technological evolution in the service of mankind. Their call was for holistic thinking to avoid the conflicts that have arisen between man, nature and technology in the past. Siemens, they boasted, is the company which has made it possible to do away with monotonous and arduous work, enhancing the flexibility and efficiency of the productive process. They are involved in developing networked transport systems and modern electro-medical technologies.

The general themes of the Siemens exhibit were echoed in that of Rank Xerox. The role of the individual, their human values and their functioning within their social, cultural and economic context is a vital one in creating a better future for coming generations. Communication is a key factor in all this. And what is the essential tool for storing and transmitting knowledge, experience, even the ephemeral qualities of poetry? Unquestionably, the written word, the document.

Rank Xerox, the official supplier of the office computer systems to the Expo presented a multimedia rendition of the history of documentation. Again, the process was evolutionary, this time the visitor watched a video of the evolution of the written word that pointed towards the possibility of a fantastic future. They had a copy of the message which was launched by satellite into space in the hope that an extraterrestrial might one day find it, interpret it and visit Earth.

In these examples it is clear that there is an integral relationship between technology and culture. Human history is the history of technological development. Neither Rank Xerox nor Siemens made reference to the nation-state in their historical approach to the development of technological systems. These systems developed as if in isolation from their specific economic and political environments, just as the specificity of the emergence of particular nation-states was not referred to in the national exhibits. Without a specific social context through which to evaluate the social effects of such progress, the technology is presented as a neutral agent in the pursuit of improved lifestyles for the human race in general.

All the multinational exhibits stressed the ways in which the technologies they were responsible for producing and which they were promoting at the Expo were technologies which operated for the benefit of humanity generally, for the global community in which the deterritorialized multinationals operate. The attitude of the Fujitsu personnel was particularly strong in this regard. Despite my insistence, the personnel officer denied the importance of the special relationship between Japan and Fujitsu. They were not serving the partial interests of particular constituencies, nor were they engaged in the nightmares of modernist technological development, developments in which technology stood in opposition to art, replacing and working against human and spiritual values. The presentation of technology at World's Fairs was ever thus, as Rydell has noted:

The century-of-progress fairs represented a powerful defense of corporate capitalism as a modernizing agency that would lead America out of the depression towards a bountiful future . . . Fundamental to this effort was an assault on remaining vestiges of values that were associated with what some historians have called a 'culture of production'. To hasten the dissolution of this older emphasis on restraint and inhibition, already under siege by world's fairs at the beginning of the century and by the steady barrage of advertising that saturated the country during the 1920s, world's fair builders injected their fantasies of progress with equally heavy doses of technological utopianism and erotic stimulation. In pavilions like 'Decocracity' and 'Futurama' at the New York World's Fair, technology appeared as a democratizing force that would simultaneously require a cadre of experts to assure the rational operation of intersecting social, economic and political forces.

(Rydell 1993: 117)

The idea of technology as a modernizing and democratizing force was, as you might now expect, contested in other Expo exhibits, although there was no direct challenge to the transnational companies' presentation of themselves not merely as good global citizens but as guardians of life itself. The Dutch pavilion had mounted an exhibition of press photographs of world atrocities, the outcomes of certain uses of military technologies, particularly in Europe and in the Gulf War. Needless to say, the causes of war and the interests of the arms manufacturers were again not alluded to. But technological innovation was not presented as necessarily progressive or liberating. The display at the pavilion of the environment presented the problems that human activity has created in the environment, again using compelling and innovative film technology, which presumably diverted attention from what these technologies presented.

Just as concepts of tradition and innovation are equally constitutive of the modern nation-state, so too the conservative and liberal models of the relationship between technology and culture can coexist without contradiction. Technological innovation is a precondition for the preservation of antiquity, the distinction between the ancient and the modern itself a hallmark of modernity. Progressive technologies enable history to be held stable, to be preserved as a point of origin from which to measure progress and change. The innovative and the traditional necessarily coexist, each requiring the other for its own visibility.

Technology as cultural artefact

There was, however, a third way in which the relationship between technology and culture appeared at the Expo. In this guise, technology existed as cultural artefact in its own right. Here, technology is culture, not assisting or causing but substituting, referring only back to itself. One of the Russian exhibits combines these last two possibilities and enables their comparison.

The Novosibirsk Medical Research Centre presented 'HELIOS', a prognosis expert system in which man discovers outer space in himself through the new cosmogony. The computer's helio-geophysical data-bank, with an input of 60–70 years of data, allowed you to reconstruct real outer-space events at any time of your embryo development (for those currently aged between 15 and 65). This information enabled you to forecast the level of your biorhythms which are dependent on these concrete helio-geophysical factors. Was this an instance of knowledge and progress or an ironic collapse of science and fantasy?

There were many more examples. The Canadians showed a video montage, a blatant spoof on national promotional films. 'The taxpayer of Canada presents . . . another government movie', ran the opening credit. National symbols were ridiculed, the obligatory Mounty was a cardboard figure that collapsed on screen. References to Canadian life were made in a style of deliberately whimsical modernity. A woman cycled through a remote rural landscape making calls on her cell phone. The modern igloo was equipped with remote control TV, microwave and telephone, and the owner sat in the middle of the living-room floor, fishing through the ice. The spoof was on the way that nations tried to promote an image of themselves at Expo, and could even be seen as a take-off of the dramatic Imax movie which followed in the central venue of the pavilion. Visitors were thus warned in advance that the images were simply artificial constructs.

By far the most spectacular exhibits at the Expo were those which offered sensation or experience with little or no specific cultural referent. People queued all day to watch the film in the Spanish pavilion where the seats moved to convey the sensations of movement associated with the images on the screen. The images were in the genre of the travel film, a variety of landscapes that could involve the visitor in hang-gliding, ski ing, kayaking and horse-riding. But the landscapes of Spain were not particular to Spain and were hard to distinguish from those of Australia, Venezuela and Canada, who also offered the big-screen experience. Finally, there was the dramatic Fujitsu production, 'Echoes of the Sun', packed with technology that you could not see, yet here, unlike the *Art and Culture* exhibit, it was the technology that people queued to experience. And it was the proximity of experience, not the distance offered by representation, that drew people to these displays.

Fujitsu

Discover the art in technology. And the technology in life . . . Fujitsu welcomes you to a world where the only frontiers are in your mind, and where art, technology and life become one.

(Official Guide: 240)

Fujitsu, the world's second-largest manufacturer of information processing systems, generates telecommunications and microelectronics devices throughout the world. Their territory is global, their corporate population quantifiable: 145,000 employees world-wide, installing and manufacturing their systems in over 100 countries.

Working with the theme of art in technology, Fujitsu stunned Expo visitors with the computer-generated graphics of the process of photosynthesis and glycolysis, the basis of all life on Earth. The show, entitled 'Echoes of the Sun' was the world's first IMAX SOLIDO TM, full-colour, 3-D, wrap-around motion picture, and it set out to show how the possibilities for human motion lie in sunlight. Visitors were immersed in images projected in three dimensions on a giant wrap-around screen. They watched the 30-minute film wearing what were referred to as 'futuristic 3-D glasses'. The central figures of the film were three puppets, a chameleon, a caterpillar and a ladybug, living in a vineyard. Grapes dangled apparently within the reach of the viewer. As the story of how plants convert sunlight into energy progressed, viewers felt forced to duck to avoid the molecules which hurtled towards them from the screen. Visitors screamed as the chameleon's tongue shot out towards each one of them as they watched.

Throughout, the emphasis was on the possibilities that Fujitsu technology affords for making things visible. Thus, while the film renders visible a process not visible to the naked eye, so, they warn you, the film 'Echoes of the Sun' is packed with technology that you cannot see. The guidebook to the pavilion in turn reveals this information. It contains explanations of how the images on the screen were produced. We see photographs of the puppeteers as well as details of how computers generate graphics. The complexity of the processes involved are stressed. These images are not photographs. We are in the presence of a technology that is not simply reproducing originals but generating idealized and imaginary forms, concrete versions of scientific abstractions which nevertheless can simulate the movements and the relationships of the original forms. The guide book also explains how the 3-D glasses work, the effects of the wrap-around screen, even how a raccoon was rehearsed to walk over and eat a grape for one of the film sequences.

There were thus three relationships between technology and culture on show at the Expo '92: (i) invisible techniques of assistance for the fullest expression of the beauty of authentic form; (ii) techniques of innovation and improvement for culture as a way of life; (iii) technology as cultural artefact, providing sensational evidence of its own enterprise. These in turn entailed two basic representational paradigms. On the one hand, there are technologies to represent the world and, on the other, technologies of simulation provoking a reflexive awareness of artificiality and simulacra. The first of these conceives of technology as enabler, and is the concept that lies behind the notion of the Expo as a technology of nationhood. Technology enables a perspective that can produce wholeness from fragmentation. Expo enables the appearance of the world as whole, through the revelation of the fragments that are cut from it and the apparent celebration of their differences. As Strathern has noted:

> The realization that wholeness is rhetoric itself is relentlessly exemplified in collage, or collections that do not collect but display the intractability of the disparate elements. Yet such techniques of showing that things do not add up

paradoxically often include not less cutting but more – a kind of hypercutting of perceived events, moments, impressions. And if elements are presented as so many cut-outs, they are inevitably presented as parts coming from other whole cloths, larger pieces, somewhere.

(Strathern 1991: 110)

However, this is not the end of the story, because Expo is not simply a technology for producing wholeness through the emergence of apparently incommensurable fragments. It is also about spectacle, a process that does not produce its object by a cut from a ground that still remains as founding referent, but rather a process through which ground is in fact erased and all we are left with is culture, culture as the ubiquitous effect of social processes whose particular conditions of emergence are no longer visible.

The technique is quite familiar in contemporary art, and is one which centres on the use of copies and discernible artifice to challenge essential identities and reveal constructs: Cindy Sherman's photographic series of self-portraits, for example, in which she dresses up in the guise of already-known feminine stereotypes

Her self is understood as contingent upon the possibilities provided by the culture in which Sherman participates, not by some inner impulse. As such, her photographs reverse the terms of art and autobiography. They use art not to reveal the artist's self, but to show the self as an imaginary construct. There is no real Cindy Sherman in these photographs; there are only the guises she assumes.

(Crimp 1980: 179)

Much of Expo's most spectacular technology of display works in this way: the laser show over the Lake of Spain in which computer-generated figures dance flamenco on the water; the Fujitsu 3-D cinemascope where the objects depicted hang before your eyes and where images move past you as you watch; the ubiquitous holograms – all are examples of these ethereal absent presences. The use of these technologies no longer aim to represent the world as we know it to be. Instead, they celebrate the possibility of producing a simulated world, a world of images more real than the real, a fascination with the hyperreal, pretensions to realities that were never there in the first place, or at least not in such perfect form, concrete manifestations of abstract possibilities.

It will be noted in this regard that representational technologies are those which provide context to render culture visible, while simulation technologies do not require context, they simply produce effect and in so doing they erase the social conditions of their production. Technology, for Fujitsu, is art; technologies generate beauty, they bring people together, enable communication, produce the essence of life itself as outcome not origin.

As Haraway has pointed out, 'micro-electronics is the technical basis of simulacra' (Haraway 1991: 165). There are technologies that take us into a world which Expo does not need to spell out, it simply exists through them. Haraway alludes to the pervasiveness of such effects:

> Communications technologies depend on electronics. Modern states, multi-national corporations, military power, welfare state apparatuses, satellite systems, political processes, fabrication of our imaginations, labour-control systems, medical constructions of our bodies, commercial pornography, the international division of labour, and religious evangelism depend intimately upon electronics.
>
> (ibid.)

Unlike the displays of technology in the nineteenth- and early twentieth-century exhibitions, these contemporary technologies are not the focus of the displays. Thus, it is neither product nor process but the effects of simulation which people wonder at and seek out.

Through these technological displays the spectacle of contemporary exhibitions are of a different kind than in previous decades. The display of the exotic produced a sense of self in the viewer through an exaggeration of difference achieved through decontextualization and lack of information. The exotic has been replaced by the proximity of simulated experience. World's Fairs used to display the exotic alongside the technological to convince people of the necessity of imperial economies for the general progress of mankind (Rydell 1984). Technological possibilities were associated with national potentials and agendas, themselves objectified in the racial hierarchies on display. Today's technologies generate effects apparently without regard for cultural or racial difference. Thus, while spectacle always provoked emotion and allowed the viewer to experience vicariously without responsibility or involvement, the spectacle of Expo '92 suggests a new chapter in the narrative which tells of human liberation through technology (see Lyotard 1984). But the myth of equal access hides or displaces the ways in which all have equal access to what are, for some, only images – a range of choices or options which themselves reinscribe hierarchies of value and reproduce the differences of class and race. For not all can produce image to the same effect; parody is not available to all participants; not all are able to convincingly conflate image with life itself.

THE INFORMATICS OF DOMINATION

This use of simulation technology within Expo revealed its own rather sinister politics. As Haraway has written:

> we are living through a movement from an organic, industrial society to a polymorphous, information system – from all work to all play, a deadly game.
>
> (Haraway 1991: 161).

It was apparent in Expo that not all nations were playing the same game, not everyone had moved from identities to networks, and it was the less powerful nations who were still playing within the earlier frame of reference. In Haraway's analysis, representation, bourgeois realism, and White capitalist patriarchy are contrasted with simulation, postmodernist science fiction and the informatics of domination (ibid.: 161–72). The latter phrase refers to the restructuring effects of technological innovations on social relations: labour relations, gender relations, representational practices. These may reproduce existing social relations, but in so doing they also change both their value and their visibility. Computerized technologies make information a political quality (Lyotard 1984), and it is the political effects to which I now turn.

The difference between the exhibits of the African Plaza and the high-tech displays of Spain and Fujitsu could be seen as the difference between representation and simulation, between shops and spectacle, material goods and ephemeral images. There was no hyperreality in the African Plaza, the representational techniques were stunningly literal. Many national pavilions operated basically as souvenir stalls. Within the African Plaza the objects on sale were barely distinguishable from one nation to the next, wooden animals and printed cloth being the most common. Expo organizers had had to put considerable pressure on the Nigerian government to get them to bring their exhibit from the Lagos museum, and this 'high culture' was not displayed in Nigeria's allocated national space, but apart as a separate concern. Nigeria's pavilion was also dedicated to selling local crafts and to low-tech displays of development projects. Many of the African nations had wanted to show themselves to the world by bringing fresh samples of their produce. Senegal had wanted to display fresh fish, many other countries had wanted to bring peanuts, palm oil, corn. In their place, they tended to display packaged products, soap powder, beer. There were very few videos and those there were appeared on single TV monitors rather than the banked monitors that converted the single image into spectacle in other venues. Displays of modernization projects were done through photographs, designers' plans, maps.

The African organizers were quite explicit about their motives for being at Expo and in their explanations they revealed an understanding that separated culture from business, 'Expo is not only about culture', they claimed. As far as the more powerful participants were concerned, this was, of course, an inappropriate assessment. Expo was exclusively about culture, but culture as commodity which the technologies of simulation could now generate and market without concern for relationships of production and reproduction.

Thus, despite the fact that Europe was so clearly presented as occupying a space at the centre of the world, we are not dealing with a simple metropole/colony opposition as was the case with the earlier World's Fairs. In these events the relationships of colonial production were central to the exhibits, and not only in terms of the international division of labour underlying industrial capitalism. The colony also provided the metropole with exotic peoples and goods which once displayed constituted the spectacle through which the metropole could witness its own control, and marvel at the 'Other'. In Expo '92 the metropole produced intrinsic spectacle, in many cases from within its own former colonies as, for example, in the cases of Venezuela or Mexico, which could now be assimilated as simply further perspectives, more difference.

Within this scenario, images of technological progress were used by participants to make connections between the particular and the universal. In this Expo '92 continued the tradition of previous World's Fairs. But technological innovation has had effects and in terms of World's Fairs the difference it has made is linked to the ability of electronic technology to render social relations invisible. Technology as a link to the universal has always been treated as culturally neutral, as 'culture without culture' (Haraway 1996). Haraway's concept of the informatics of domination draws our attention to the power relations that operate through these apparently culture-free zones and reminds us of the political effects of the division of labour in which some emerge as technologically (not culturally) more advanced than others. This technoculture denies culture and concerns itself instead with ownership. It is through the ownership of knowledge that categories of cultural distinction are created in the otherwise bland environment of Expo's homogenized cultural forms. There are thus strong resonances here with the ways in which branding operates as a way of securing market visibility through the ownership of essence. Thus, while universal exhibitions are concerned to display the overwhelming reality of technology itself, the human narratives to which these technologies are harnessed have changed. We no longer find, therefore, an unambiguous commitment to the relationship between technological development and human liberation, let alone the prospective unity of all knowledges which, according to Lyotard (1984) characterize modernist narratives on technology. The (postmodern) technical and commercial aims of optimal performance are more visible.

The mechanical age of reproduction produced objects, and display was about their control. In this sense, the World's Fairs operated much like museums, displaying 'the peculiar preoccupation of modern Western societies with mastering "objects of knowledge", and then publicly commemorating the victory by putting them on show' (Jordanova 1989: 40). As Rydell (1984) has argued, World's Fairs were about the dissemination of ideas which had direct bearing on the status of the nation-state. Scientific paradigms, the emphasis on classification, evolution and racial and cultural hierarchies, were produced for popular consumption in the categorization and display of people and objects. The new communications technologies produce sensations. The emphasis is no longer exclusively on categorization as the concern is no longer to display people and objects. In this paradigm, the nation is superseded and exists only as a presence made visible through the workings of invisible networks of power, like a hologram or laser image. These two possibilities for conceptualizing the nation coexist at the Expo.

Global culture in the Universal Exposition of 1992 did not look the same as it did in the Great Exhibition of 1851, despite the fact that many other aspects of these institutions of display have remained very stable. Culture is now not simply something to acquire but also something to experience, something to consume on the spot. It is no longer displays of goods that produce visible hierarchies of value.

The ironic commentaries on the Fairs themselves, which always existed, but which were previously a critical reaction to the Fairs, articulated from the outside, are now integrated as further perspectives. Audiences are encouraged to interpret and make national cultures for themselves, and new technologies thus appear to encourage greater participation and reflexivity. Yet those same technologies also produce new techniques of exclusion and control.

World's Fairs have always been about consumption and about commodification. I have suggested that there has been a move away from the commodification of goods to the commodification of nations and the concept of culture itself. Thus, ironically, while in the representational model technology makes culture more visible, as it enables more relationships and more history, more technology also produces less culture in the simulation model where diversity works against choice and individuation.

ACKNOWLEDGMENTS

This chapter is based on research funded by the British Academy and carried out in Seville in 1992 with Laura Rival. The full account of this research can be found in Harvey 1996. Much of this chapter is reproduced in chapter 4 of that work.

NOTES

1 See Macdonald and Silverstone (1992) for a discussion of the problems museums face in renewing information.
2 For a parallel argument concerning museums see Donna Haraway (1990) and Ludmilla Jordanova (1989).
3 See Michael Ames (1992) on the relationship between Expo '86 and the Canadian State.
4 See Maryon McDonald (1996) for a recent discussion of this theme in relation to EU rhetoric.

REFERENCES

Ames, M. (1992) *Cannibal Tours and Glass Boxes: The Anthropology of Museums*, Vancouver: University of British Columbia Press.
Benedict, B. (1983) 'The anthropology of world's fairs', in B. Benedict (ed.) *The Anthropology of World's Fairs: San Francisco's Panama Pacific International Exposition of 1915*, London: Scolar Press.
Crimp, D. (1980) 'The photographic activity of postmodernism', reprinted in T. Docherty (ed.) (1993) *Postmodernism: A Reader* pp. 172–9, London: Harvester Wheatsheaf.
Featherstone, M. (1991) *Consumer Culture and Postmodernism*, London: Sage.
Greenhalgh, P. (1989) 'Education, entertainment and politics: lessons from the great

international exhibitions', in P. Vergo (ed.) *The New Museology*, London: Reaktion Books.

Haraway, D. (1989) *Primate Visions: Gender, Race, and Nature in the World of Modern Science*, London: Routledge.

—— (1991) *Simians, Cyborgs and Women: The Reinvention of Nature*, London: Free Association Books.

—— (1996) *Modest_Witness@Second_Millennium.FemaleMan©_Meets_OncoMouse™: Feminism and Technoscience*, New York: Routledge.

Harvey, P. (1996) *Hybrids of Modernity: Anthropology, the Nation State and the Universal Exhibition*, London: Routledge.

Jordanova, L. (1989) 'Objects of knowledge: a historical perspective on museums', in P. Vergo (ed.) *The New Museology*, London: Reaktion Books.

Lyotard, J-F. (1984) *The Postmodern Condition: A Report on Knowledge* (trans. G. Bennington and B. Massumi), Manchester: Manchester University Press, reprinted in P. Brooker (ed.) *Modernism/Postmodernism* pp. 139–50, London: Longman.

McDonald, M. (1996) '"Unity in diversity": some tensions in the construction of Europe', *Social Anthropology*, 4 (1), pp. 47–60.

Macdonald, S. and R. Silverstone (1992) 'Science on display: the representation of scientific controversy in museum exhibitions', *Public Understanding of Science*, 1, pp. 68–87.

Rydell, R. (1984) *All the World's a Fair: Visions of Empire at American International Expositions, 1876–1916*, Chicago: University of Chicago Press.

—— (1993) *World of Fairs: the Century-of-Progress Expositions*, Chicago: University of Chicago Press.

Strathern, M. (1991) *Partial Connections*, Lanham, MD: Rowman & Littlefield.

—— (1992) *Reproducing the Future: Essays on Anthropology, Kinship and the New Reproductive Technologies*, London: Routledge.

Chapter 9

Strangers in paradise
An encounter with fossil man at the Dutch Museum of Natural History

Mary Bouquet

ANCESTRAL KEEPERS

Under what circumstances could an exhibition be construed as an affront to the scientist whose work it was supposed to honour? This chapter will discuss the *Pithecanthropus* centennial exhibition, to commemorate Eugène Dubois' discovery of the first fossil 'missing link' between apes and men, a century ago.

The guardians of human origins, in so far as these are embodied in fossils, are predominantly male: two exceptions, Maeve Leakey and Marie-Antoinette de Lumley, custodians through marriage to Richard Leakey and Henri de Lumley, respectively, are exceptions which prove the rule. *Pithecanthropus erectus*, discovered by the Dutchman Eugène Dubois a century ago on Java, and now classified as the type specimen of *Homo erectus*, is a case in point. Dubois' collection was transported to Holland in the late 1890s, where it has already passed through the hands of three generations of curators at the Dutch National Museum of Natural History. The collection comprises some 12,000 Pleistocene faunal fossils, including the skull-cap, molar and thigh-bone of *Pithecanthropus erectus*. Only specialists are usually granted access to the collection, which obviously adds extra piquancy to any public display of the fossils.

The year 1993 was the centenary of Dubois' identification of his fossils as *Pithecanthropus erectus*, the upright-walking ape-man, rather than *Anthropopithecus erectus* (the upright-walking man-ape), as he had at first surmised. Dubois' originality lay in searching for concrete proof of the 'missing link' between ape and man, heralded in evolutionary theory by Darwin, Huxley and Haeckel (Theunissen 1989). Dubois' removal of the fossils from the Dutch East Indies was almost a matter of course 100 years ago. It would not happen today.

Celebrating the centennial in Leiden in 1993 was an opportunity, a challenge and an embarrassment. Embarrassing in so far as the fossil is clearly out of context in the Netherlands in 1993; a challenge precisely because of this. How would the organizers legitimize this ancestral presence – especially at a time of deteriorating relations between Indonesia and the Netherlands? It became an opportunity for many different people to display their ingenuity – not least the conceptualizer (myself) and the designer of the exhibition – both women

– in worlds (palaeoanthropology and the museum) under the almost exclusive guardianship of men. We were understandably excited, as a British social anthropologist and a French interior architect, about getting our hands on *Homo erectus* in Holland. How, you may ask, did the ancestral keepers ever allow events to come to such a pass? Some institutional background is required.

The Dutch National Museum of Natural History is developing a new site to house both collections and permanent exhibitions due to open to the public in 1997. There has been a change of policy over the last few years, comparable to that which has taken place in many science museums, away from being a purely scientific institution towards developing a 'clear orientation towards the public' (Van der Weiden 1993). There has been a shift in the balance of power between the scientific staff and those responsible for making exhibitions and organizing educational activities. The New Presentations Department (Afdeling Nieuwe Presentaties), comprising a biologist, a botanist, two geologists and a social anthropologist, is responsible for conceptualizing the future permanent exhibitions. The scientific staff are supposed to provide supportive rather than directive (as in the past) advice.

The proposal for a centennial exhibition to commemorate Dubois' find presented the Museum of Natural History with something of a dilemma. The proposal came from a specially constituted *Pithecanthropus* Centennial Foundation, comprising representatives of the Dutch Royal Academy of Sciences, Leiden University and the Dutch Geological Service. The exhibition was to be part of the centennial celebrations, dominated by a scientific congress on the theme of 'Human Evolution in its Ecological Context', to be held in Leiden in June 1993. Dubois was to be rehabilitated as an ecologist *avant la lettre*, with the *Pithecanthropus* fossils as a kind of talisman: either human beings adopt a more responsible attitude towards their environment or the course of human evolution will be arrested (see Leakey and Slikkerveer 1993). The chief sponsor was Mobil Oil who, as their invitation to the reception and private view of the exhibition held on 28 June 1993 put it, have been 'discovering fossil fuels for over 100 years'.

The Museum of Natural History's initial response was tepid. The New Presentations Department had its hands full with work on the permanent exhibition for 1997. Investment in a temporary exhibition of this kind would only distract from the major project in hand. The alternative, allowing 'the scientists' to dictate the form the exhibition would take, was clearly contrary to the long-term objective of reformulating working relations among curators, *commissaires d'expositions* and designers. The only suggestions for an exhibition to have emerged by late 1991 appealed neither to the Presentations Department nor to the newly appointed director of the museum. These proposals came from 'scientists' and lacked all the ingredients for the kinds of exhibition the museum now wished to make. Yet there were obvious advantages for both the new director and the museum to fall in with the plan for a major exhibition in 1993. It could be used to publicize the new permanent exhibitions of 1997, especially if it were as successful as the dinosaur exhibit held in 1990.

It was at this juncture that I was invited to draw up a preliminary proposal for an exhibition (November 1991). My experience of exhibition-making to date was documenting (with a view to exhibition) a small collection of Melanesian artefacts, originating from the former German colony of Kaiser Wilhelmsland and dating from the late nineteenth/early twentieth centuries, for the Museu de Etnologia in Lisbon, Portugal (Bouquet and Freitas Branco 1988). My proposal was vetted by the Museum and the *Pithecanthropus* Centennial Foundation. Whilst the latter supported the outline, the former divided into several factions, a minority in favour, others lukewarm and a strong contingent against. I was taken on by the Museum of Natural History and assigned a temporary base in the Presentations Department, on the understanding that I would accept the advice of the Centennial Commission and would work in consultation with members of the scientific staff (the curator of the Dubois Collection, and the curator of Mammals) as well as my exhibition-making colleagues. I was to begin working with an as yet unidentified designer as soon as possible – that is, as soon as the concept permitted. It was to be a delicate balancing act.

Although based in the New Presentations Department, I had to spend quite a lot of time at the Dépendance where the Dubois Collection is housed, about half a kilometre from the main museum buildings. Here the curator allowed me to see the *Pithecanthropus* fossils and the rest of the Dubois Collection, and directed me towards other material and literature that I required to prepare the exhibition script. I periodically faced the (all-male) Centennial Committee with my exhibition storyline (14 February 1992), proposal for an exhibition (15 April) and later, with the exhibition designer Isabelle Galy, with the sketch design for the exhibition (5 October 1992). It was rather like delivering a series of seminar papers, with the crucial difference that the outcome of the debate would determine the shape of a future display.

I was compensated for my minority status by being allowed to discourse, both verbally and in the various documents I had to produce, in English. I have commented elsewhere on the hegemony of the English language in academic anthropology (Bouquet 1991a), and in Dutch anthropology in particular (Bouquet 1991b). There were none the less complex skirmishes over the meanings to be put on the 'high ground of public display' (Macdonald and Silverstone 1990: 77) right up until November 1992, when the exhibition ought long to have moved into the production phase.[2]

But what was the problem with the conceptualization of *Pithecanthropus erectus* that was gradually taking shape on paper?

ANCESTRAL CONCEPTIONS

My perception was that *Pithecanthropus erectus* had undergone the same kind of sea changes as the Melanesian artefacts and therefore entailed some of the same museological problems for exhibiting 100 years on. The Melanesian artefacts became Sleeping Beauties of sorts in an ethnological museum in Portugal (Bouquet and Freitas Branco 1988: 21). The fossilized skull-cap, thigh-bone and molar of *Pithecanthropus erectus* have also endured 100 years of solitude amidst a paradise of once-living animals, preserved in various shapes and forms at the Dutch National Museum of Natural History.

Developing the *Pithecanthropus* centennial exhibition at the Dutch National Museum of Natural History was something like being a stranger in paradise. I became fascinated by the imprint of the surrounding culture on a setting dedicated to the monumental preservation of nature (cf. Haraway 1989). Why should a human fossil that is classified as a type specimen of a now extinct human species (*Homo erectus*) be kept in a natural history museum rather than (say) an ethnographic museum – where the spectacular Sepik and Asmat ancestral skulls are housed? Why should a fragment of human anatomy in this form belong to nature? This perception was encouraged by Gould's remark that,

> organisms have, through their evolution, an irreducible and inalienable status in and for themselves. But we can only speak of them in terms of their meaning for us; culture and mind permeate our world of discourse . . . Why not admit that we cannot see natural objects except in our terms, and struggle instead to make the union instructive?
>
> (Purcell and Gould 1986: 13)

Rosamond Purcell's photography of the N.N.M. historical ape and monkey collection in storage (Purcell and Gould 1986), as well as elements of the Dubois Collection (Purcell and Gould 1992) dwells upon these added layers. The importance of photographic imagery in training us to see was as fundamental in conceptualizing *Pithecanthropus* in Het Pesthuis as, in a different way, it was for the exhibition of Melanesian artefacts (cf. Bouquet 1992). Purcell comments on natural history photography:

> We have rendered (animals) as gods, as totems, as auguries. We have devised peculiar rites for these creatures in natural history museums – inscriptions in ink on bone, chemical baths to render them translucent, systematic placement on shelves, often in the dark, often in shrouds of dust or moth crystals. I think of these treatments as forms of burial, but I think of the animals as expressing, in various ways, life after death.
>
> (Purcell and Gould 1986: 116)

The museological problem as I saw it was to show up the layers of meaning added to the *Pithecanthropus* fossils, much as Gould describes Purcell's photography as doing (ibid.: 13). I found a parallel with Vogel's approach to Mijikenda memorial posts in the Art/artefact exhibition at the Center for African Art in New York 1988, which considered the contexts in which Westerners have seen African art (Vogel 1991: 195–201). The challenge of the *Pithecanthropus* centennial exhibition was, to my mind, to consider some of the *many* contexts and forms in which Westerners have viewed the ape–man (ape-man) relationship. The emphasis lay on the plurality and diversity of environments and ecologies that would encompass their culturally constructed dimensions.

Hence, one might look at images of apes, men and the ape-man in late-twentieth century popular culture – in films, cartoons, and toys – that coexist alongside scientific findings as conveyed through similar media. Or at the idea of the ape-man as the missing link between a common ancestor of apes and men in the writings of nascent evolutionary theorists. *Pithecanthropus erectus*, the fossil, was seen by Eugène Dubois as *the* concrete evidence of man's common ancestry with the apes. The ape connection has been shifted even further back in time over the century that has elapsed since Dubois, with the Australopithecines now viewed as the earliest transitional form. The ape-man also figures in phylogenies, genealogies of man extended back through geological time. Sculptures of ape-man record changing visions of prehistoric man's appearance over a century. Finally, there is the cultural mirror that historical taxidermic preparations of monkeys and apes holds up for the viewer.

I could thus conceive of at least seven different settings through which one might track the ape–man relationship in various forms. These seven elements were staged through the seventeenth-century square Pesthuis building, with its eight divisions, as a kind of narrative. This storyline comprised a series of environments, some artificial, some natural and some internal to the museum itself. Different visions and versions of the ape man and the ape–man relationship were presented in each.

The first room, The Movies, showed film and cartoon images of the ape-man, apes and men, that are part of the artificial environment at the end of the twentieth century. Scientific and popular conceptions of ape and man relations were jumbled together to pose the question why, given the growth in knowledge of human origins since Dubois' discovery a century ago, do characters like King Kong and Tarzan remain so popular?

The second room, The Library, introduced Dubois through a reconstruction of his library. Ten different strands of nineteenth-century thought on man's place in nature materialize along the outer walls beneath portraits of the respective writers. There was, at the beginning of the nineteenth century, no fossil man, according to Cuvier. Dubois' originality lay in searching for concrete fossil evidence to prove evolutionary theory as developed by (Lamarck), Darwin, Wallace and Haeckel, and supported by Huxley and Vogt during the nineteenth century. Skeletons, embryos, microcephales and birds of paradise were among the objects used to evoke approaches from the selected thinkers.[3]

The Fossil Collection, the third room, presented a selection of the Dubois Collection, that is not usually open to the public. The *pièce de résistance*, *Pithecanthropus erectus*, stood in a bomb- and bullet-proofed vitrine at the far end of a room lined with relics of extinct elephants, deer, cows, pigs, tortoises and tigers. Thus, there was a first fossil man in 1893. Apart from the display of

III. The Fossil Collection

The story of Dubois' journey to the East Indies and his discovery of the fossil 'ape-man', is told at each end of a room filled with fossils of prehistoric animals from Sumatra and Java, and dominated by *Pithecanthropus erectus*, discovered in 1890 - 1892.

IV. The Island and the World

The discovery of *Pithecanthropus erectus* heralded a century of spectacular human fossil finds throughout the world. Mankind is now thought to have evolved 2-3 million years ago in Africa, migrating to populate diverse environments throughout the world (including Java, then connected to mainland S.E. Asia) about 1 million years ago.

V. The Forest

The tree diagrams showing the course of evolutionary history employ a familiar western European cultural form, the genealogy, itself related to the religious Tree of Jesse. Scientific depiction of evolution is embedded in a specific cultural view of ancestry.

VI. The Art Gallery

A century of artistic reconstructions illustrates that the changing face of prehistoric man is conditioned by socio-cultural factors that filter scientific ideas about the past.

VII. The Depot

A 19th century museum collection of apes and monkeys illustrates that the reconstruction of once-living animals for scientific purposes is also conditioned by the wider culture in which it is situated.

II. The Library

The reconstruction of Eugene Dubois' library evokes various currents of 19th century thought on man's place in nature. The Library introduces Dubois' decision to go in search of fossil evidence for the missing link between apes and man.

I. The Movies

Introducing the exhibition are fragments of films, cartoons and toys all of which illustrate the ape-man relationship. The appropriation of evolutionary theory by popular culture draws attention to the cultural context of western science.

NATIONAAL
NATUURHISTORISCH
MUSEUM

PITHECANTHROPUS **APE - MAN MAN - APE** IN HET PESTHUIS

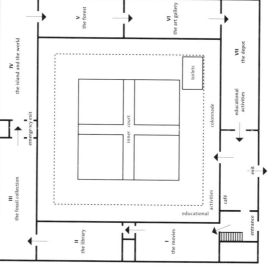

Figure 9.1 Plan of Man–Ape, Ape-Man exhibition (courtesy of the Nationaal Natuurhistorisch Museum, Leiden, The Netherlands)

fossils, there was also information on Dubois' initial work on Sumatra as well as on his return to the Netherlands. Portraits of the three curators of the collection were also on view.

The fourth room, The Island and the World, dealt (on the island) with the question of how *Homo erectus* managed to reach Java one million years ago, when sea-levels fell as a result of the ice ages permitting an influx of fauna – including mankind – from South East Asia. After a century of palaeoanthropological finds (the world) *Pithecanthropus erectus* is reconceptualized as the type specimen of *Homo erectus*, while the ape connection (the Australopithecines) has been pushed back in time to around three million years.[4] There are, in the late twentieth century, many fossil men. These were portrayed as a line of *National Geographic* men running from the left (out of prehistory) towards the right (*Homo sapiens*), into the next room. This line of running men, showing the various anatomical stages through which mankind is deemed to have passed on the basis of the fossil finds to date, is conventionally represented as a phylogeny, and some recent examples were shown (together with some historical ones) in the following room.

The fifth room, The Forest, took up the question posed at the beginning of the exhibition about the relationship between science and popular culture. It began with phylogenies, the diagrammatic story of human evolution that can be taken in at a glance. The tree form of the phylogeny is borrowed from the historical genealogy, projected into geological time. Phylogenies (such as Haeckel's oak) and genealogies (such as the Schaap family oak) are both akin to the Christian depictions of Christ's earthly ancestry (again sometimes an oak, but this time referring to Biblical chronology), known as the Tree of Jesse (see Bouquet 1995). The scientific representation of human ancestry borrows a culturally specific genealogical model that is by no means universal. This was a first illustration of science borrowing a representational form from the wider culture (and its art forms) in which it is embedded.

The Art Gallery, the sixth room, displayed a dozen visions and versions of prehistoric man's appearance, aestheticized in such a way as to disrupt any natural association between fossil and reconstruction. Dubois' own reconstruction of *Pithecanthropus erectus*, made for the 1900 Paris World Exhibition, was surrounded by (amongst others) a Belgian *Javamens* dating from the First World War, a Hungarian *Pithecanthropus* made at the time of the Second World War, a Mexican illustration for the cover of a children's series (1959) purporting to show Dubois' reconstruction but actually presenting a Neanderthal! The aim of the reconstructions was to educate the general public about scientific discoveries of prehistoric man. Yet the aggregate vision is far from consistent. Mascré's *Javamens* is hairier than either Dubois' *Pithecanthropus* or the 1980s' reconstruction of *Homo erectus* from Museon in The Hague. The Mexican view of Dubois' reconstruction also illustrates how images could be transformed in the course of their travels around the world. The collaboration between artist and scientist implied just that: fitting scientific information into artistic genres.

The Depot, the final room of the exhibition, inverted the aestheticism of the Art Gallery, giving instead a glimpse behind the scenes of the historical (late-eighteenth and nineteenth-century) monkey and ape collection in storage. The aim here was to show the imprint of images received from the natural history texts of the late eighteenth and early nineteenth centuries upon the taxidermist's work of mounting collected specimens – again for the instruction of the public. The striking anthropomorphism of many of these artefacts reiterates the infiltration of wider cultural ideas in daily practices taking place at the very heart of a scientific institution in the nineteenth century.

The idea was that the visiting public, *Homo sapiens*, was also the main subject of the exhibition moving through the seven environments. This subjectivity was underlined in the last section where, as the visitor walked along a reconstructed gallery of mounted prosimians, monkeys and apes dating from the nineteenth century, he caught sight of his own reflection in the mirrors running parallel to the display.

The artefactual character of *Pithecanthropus* was underscored by the changes of form and fields of meaning that precede and succeed the date of the fossil's appropriation (see, for example, Bouquet and Freitas Branco 1988; Bouquet 1992; Thomas 1991). Its history as a museum object was no longer relegated to background status, but rather construed as part of the object itself. Seen in this way, the fossil belongs to a class of widely different objects, generated at different historical moments: cartoons, films, books, skeletons, embryos, microcephales, fossils and casts of other *Homos*, genealogies, reconstructions. *Pithecanthropus erectus* was originally appropriated from Java and brought back to the Netherlands because of a specific set of European ideas about man's place in nature, and the nature of man. The exhibition tried to make *this* specificity visible through the various kinds of context created.

BONES OF CONTENTION

Transposing this notion of artefact onto a human fossil in the Dutch National Museum of Natural History was an absorbing, although by no means a pacific, operation. The poetic interpretation of the term environment caused an equal commotion among those with a vested interest in retrieving Dubois as a prophet of the ecology movement (see Bouquet 1993b). These may have been logical steps for a cultural anthropologist and a designer to make. They were much less straightforward for palaeoanthropologists and geologists. The respective notions of object and context could not have been more discordant. Geology provides the 'natural' context for interpreting palaeoanthropological finds; the de-naturalized contexts proposed for the fossil in this exhibition could all too easily be interpreted (as one American palaeoanthropologist put it) as 'an insult to Dubois'.

In what did the insult consist? Mainly, perhaps, in the insistence on contextualizing science itself, in this case exemplified in Dubois' find that is often (certainly in the Netherlands) paraded as the inception of the science of palaeoanthropology. Instead of telling a classic tale of progress (from Cuvier's assertion at the beginning of the nineteenth century that there is no fossil man, through Dubois' discovery of *the* fossil ape-man, to the multiple human fossils of the late twentieth century) and leaving it at that, all kinds of diluting mixtures were introduced. There is room to do no more than indicate how science, art and culture had permeable boundaries in The Movies, The Forest, The Art Gallery and The Depot. Worse still, these contexts surrounded the tale of Dubois and his find, and the tale of *its* place in the story of palaeoanthropology. The composition was contrapuntal and upset any hope of presenting a unidirectional story of progress. It gave a new and unintended twist to the notion of human evolution in its ecological context.

The expression of so much (male) concern over the centennial exhibition of what is now classified as the type specimen of the species *Homo erectus* is, of course, in itself fascinating. Yet I cannot claim to have been a dispassionate observer of all that took place. I had a stake in making my own predilections materialize. The cultural environment(s) that the audience had to traverse before reaching the promised land of coffee and apple tart,[5] placed them centre-stage at a piece of theatre where they had expected to be spectators. The closing sentence of the exhibition catalogue is quite explicit about this: 'The visitor to *Man ape Ape man* is an intrinsic part of this exhibition as of no other' (Bouquet 1993a: 87).

One of the criticisms of the exhibition concept was that it was 'too intellectual': nobody (aunts, uncles, fathers, and young nephews were constantly invoked as witless members of the Dutch general public) would understand it.[6] My basic assumption was (and remains) that visitors are capable of understanding at *various* levels (i.e., a heterogeneous public) and that instant gratification is not necessarily a sound pedagogical principle. Exhibitions should make people *think*, not simply spoon-feed them information. In place of the Sainsbury consumer model, with the visitor loading a trolley (cf. Macdonald, Chapter 7), one might (for example) try to explain how Dubois reached his decision to search for the missing link by staging a kind of conversation among different nineteenth-century thinkers in a reconstruction of his library. Why should the (Dutch) man in the street be unable to grasp the different strands of nineteenth-century thinking on man's place in nature if these were attractively and clearly presented? Why should a museum simply reproduce what is seen as 'information' (here, a popular version of the theory of evolution) in familiar terms? One of the challenges for those with access to elite culture (or specialist knowledge) is surely to identify points of articulation with popular cultural forms with which everybody is familiar, and to use it to pedagogical purpose.

A bilingual guide to the exhibition (catalogue is not part of current vocabulary in this kind of museum), where the concept could be pinned down by anyone (Dutch or English speaking) interested or unable to fathom what it was all about, was a second string to this argument. This kind of detachable document can be taken away and read *after* the actual visit to the exhibition. Time spent in visiting an exhibition could be measured according to how long or often the visitor thought about what they had seen after leaving rather than simply the length of time they had been 'busy' in the exhibition. We are, after all, dealing with *Homo sapiens*, and making the audience reflect on what they have seen is a *leerzaam* (educative) exercise, especially if the experience of walking through the exhibit (the design) had been enjoyable (*leuk* and *boiend*). There was little room for special effects (like the climate room proposed by the geologists, where the audience would experience the warming and cooling temperatures by blowing hot and cold air into the room) and the kinds of interactive devices that clog many exhibitions. This assumes that the experience of an exhibition is not necessarily reducible to what visitors can get their hands on. This was the idea behind calling the guide a souvenir.

My reply to the charge of insulting Dubois was that the composition of the exhibition placed Dubois, his originality, his finds and his position in the history of palaeoanthropology at the centre of the exhibition (Rooms II, III and IV). The surrounding rooms framed the centre-piece to its greater exaltation. Despite its much-lamented lack of museum facilities, the astonishing beauty and aptness of the seventeenth-century Pesthuis building was a source of inspiration for both the concept and the design of the exhibition, and, of course, its scale was fitting for an occasion like the centennial.

The designer, Isabelle Galy, made sketches on the basis of my concept during September and October 1992. It was by no means an easy exercise, but it was certainly a most instructive dialogue. The designer's ideas about space, atmosphere and the kinds of objects required rendered the concept at once more elaborate and more concrete. The formality of The Library with its portraits and strictly symmetrical arrangement of Dubois' books and his desk at the centre, is one of the best examples of the designer's hand. I then reformulated the text that accompanied the sketch design on the basis of those sketches and notes. The Library, for example, translates the newly discovered perception of geological time that opened up in the nineteenth century into space: the dimensions of Room II contrast sharply with the claustrophobic corridor preceding it, where we referred to the Biblical chronology of 5000 years since the creation by juxtaposing the Bible and Darwin's *On the Origin of Species*.

A Dutch (male) manager was appointed in August 1992 – to keep the *meiden* (*lit.* girls) in hand, as it was put. This meant establishing and securing deadlines; and drawing up a budget, which enabled the marshalling of resources and personnel to proceed.

Once the concept design had been approved (end of October 1992), there followed something resembling the scramble for Africa: the designers needed specific information now (measurements and descriptions of objects) as well as the exhibition texts. The experience of moving from concept to object was a traumatic one for me. My role changed abruptly from composer to provider of highly specific information about objects. This, in turn, required knowledge and decision-making abilities that I often did not have. Objects are, furthermore, always mediated by persons, and some of the objects I required were guarded by people who were reluctant (because of the shape the exhibition was taking on) to give access. At this point the exhibition entered its social phase: the language of teams and groups, routine meetings and briefs, forced the unwilling to comply by transforming an idea that had been all too closely associated with one or two persons into a collective enterprise.

The physical construction of the exhibition began in December 1992/January 1993, while the pursuit of objects and the writing of exhibition texts and the catalogue texts proceeded apace. The exhibition that was unveiled on 15 May met with mixed reactions. Interestingly enough, the Dutch press focused almost exclusively on the three rooms concerned with the growth of knowledge as visible in the Dubois story. This emphasis underlined the sanctity that the story of human evolution has acquired in the late twentieth century, pruning off the problematic frames we had put around it. This reaction reflects specific expectations about science museums among Dutch ('science') journalists, especially the handful that cover topics related to human evolution. How far those responsible for public relations within the museum, who avoided mentioning conceptual factors and design, let alone innovation, dwelling instead on *Homo erectus* as a scientific discovery, succeeded in casting the die is a question worthy of attention. The visitors' book, on the other hand, attests to much more varied public reception, including appreciation for the design. International interest in the exhibition in English also seemed much more prepared to take on board the other accents present in the exhibition (see for example Franklin 1993).

The deconstruction of the exhibition began, appropriately enough, on All Souls' and All Saints' Days (1 and 2 November 1993), with *Pithecanthropus erectus* returned to its seclusion, along with many of the other items on display. The Pesthuis was emptied. What remains of this event? Such immortality as the exhibition can hope to achieve will crystallize in the photographic images and texts that serve as souvenirs – reminders – in the long unfinished generation of ideas about ape, man and ape-man.

POST MORTEM

The anxieties of the ancestral keepers over the exhibition concept and design were gradually transformed as increasing numbers of people became involved in its making. What had been construed initially as an 'insult' in terms of concept, later became a matter of 'injury' when the director declined to list (on the board at the end of the exhibition, and in the catalogue) every individual within the Museum of Natural History who had worked on the project, preferring instead a global acknowledgment. I hope that I will be forgiven for drawing a metaphorical parallel between conceptualizing this human ancestor for exhibition and biological conception. The seed of an idea, invisible at the outset, gradually acquired shape and form within the confines of the space available. The birth, like the revelation of a child, was a surprise – shortcomings are always painful for the mother in particular. The social existence, coming of age, autumnal decline and eventual demise of the exhibition left behind them feelings not unlike those aroused by a living being. Yet this socially constructed entity engendered equally intense emotions in those who saw it as fundamentally 'about' the three fossilized relics of *Homo erectus* and the sacred story of human evolution. In claiming paternity for that part of the exhibition which dealt with this aspect of human evolution, one can understand how seriously guardianship of human origins in the shape of fossils is taken by those unable to conceive of ancestry in any other way.

ACKNOWLEDGMENTS

I would like to express my gratitude to the philosopher and anthropologist Raymond Corbey, and to the historian of science (and Dubois' biographer) Bert Theunissen, for their encouragement and for generously providing expertise from their respective fields.

NOTES

1 The paper I presented at the E.A.S.A. Conference in Prague in 1992 ('Natural History and Cultural Stories: Exhibiting *Pithecanthropus erectus* in 1993') focused on the centrality of texts in the initial phase of exhibition development. Reactions to this piece, based on the practical experience of the first six months at the museum, were (to me) surprisingly critical, apparently discerning 'the sort of "fashionable" items we now find in every deconstructionist piece' (Jean-Claude Galey in letter to the author).

2 'Minority status' refers here to (relative) age and sex. The complexity was heightened by my being an academically well-qualified woman in Holland which had, until quite recently (at the end of the 1980s), the second-lowest rate of married women on the labour market after Spain. My linguistic advantage was compensated by (to me surprising) attention to personal details. I recall being quizzed by the Centennial Committee Secretary about my husband's *achternaam* (surname) and the reasons why I use my own. Male employees would scarcely be questioned as to why they chose to use *their* own surnames!

3 Thus, for example, Huxley's frontispiece from *Man's Place in Nature* materialized as the skeletons of a man, a chimpanzee, a gorilla, an orang-utan and a gibbon, illustrating the argument based on comparative anatomical evidence of man's similarity to the great apes.

4 The Australopithecine (Southern Ape) discoveries in Afar, Laetoli and southern Africa are dated around 3 million years old. *Pithecanthropus erectus* is dated at around a million years by some (De Vos and Sondaar), and between a half and three-quarters of a million years by others (Day).

5 I refer to three things here. First, the importance of consumption (eating and drinking) as part of a museum visit, referred to by Macdonald and Silverstone (1990) as the 'Ace Caff' syndrome. The restaurant facilities available during the *Pithecanthropus* exhibition were scarcely of that order, but the symbolic attached to the consumption of coffee – especially in a Dutch context – is unaffected. Second, there is an echo of

an advertisement placed by an insurance company during the winter of 1992/3: it showed a purplish depiction of a steaming cup of coffee accompanied by the text: '*Is er koffee na de dood?*' (*lit*. 'Is there coffee after death?'). This refers to the practice of offering coffee to those who have attended a funeral.

6 I became adept, in time, at conjuring up my own 3-year-old son as a potential visitor to the exhibition. Although this strategy proved useful in dampening the idiom of kinship, I gained something of a reputation for being a severe and heartless mother! I felt like one of Schama's travellers to the Republic, 'surprised and disconcerted by the softness with which children were treated' (Schama 1987: 485), only in the style of the late twentieth century!

REFERENCES

Bouquet, M. (1991a) 'On two-way translation', *Man*, 26 (1) pp. 162–3.
—— (1991b) 'Anthropology at home', (review of J. Boissevain and J. Verrips (eds) *Dutch Dilemmas: Anthropologists look at the Netherlands*, Assen: Van Gorcum), *Amsterdamse Sociologisch Tijdshrift*, 17 (4), pp. 144–51.
—— (1992) 'The photographic "blind spot" between words and things', *Critique of Anthropology*, 12 (2), pp. 193–207.
—— (1993a) *Man-ape Ape-man*: Pithecanthropus *in Het Pesthuis, Leiden*, Leiden: Nationaal Natuurhistorisch Museum (exhibition catalogue).
—— (1993b) 'Exhibiting *Homo erectus* in 1993', in R. Corbey and B. Theunnissen (eds) *Man, Ape, Apeman: Changing Views since 1600, Proceedings of the* Pithecanthropus *Centennial Congress* (Session F), Leiden: Leiden University Press.
—— (1995) 'Exhibiting knowledge: the trees of Dubois, Haeckel, Jesse and Rivers at the *Pithecanthropus* Centennial exhibition', in M. Strathern (ed.) *Shifting Contexts: Transformations in Anthropological Knowledge*, pp. 31–55, London: Routledge.
Bouquet, M. and J. Freitas Branco (1988) *Melanesian Artefacts, Postmodernist Reflections/ Artefactos melanésianos, Reflexões pós-modernistas*, Lisbon: I.I.C.T./Museu de Etnologia (exhibition catalogue).
Corbey, R. and B. Theunissen (eds) (1993) *Man, Ape, Apeman: Changing Views since 1600, Proceedings of the* Pithecanthropus *Centennial Congress* (Session F), Leiden: Leiden University Press.
Franklin, S. (1993) 'Imaging and imagining the missing link', *The Times Higher Education Supplement* (26 June) p. 19.
Haraway, D. (1989) 'Teddy bear patriarchy: taxidermy in the Garden of Eden', in D. Haraway *Primate Visions. Gender, Race and Nature in the World of Modern Science*, pp. 26–58, New York and London: Routledge, Chapman & Hall.
Karp, I. and S. D. Lavine (eds) (1991) *Exhibiting Cultures: The Poetics and Politics of Museum Display*, Washington, DC and London: Smithsonian Institution Press.
Leakey, R. E. and L. J. Slikkerveer (1993) *Man-ape Ape-man: The Quest for Human's Place in Nature and Dubois' 'Missing Link'*, Leiden: The Netherlands Foundation for Kenya Wildlife Service.
Macdonald, S. and R. Silverstone (1990) 'Rewriting the museums' fictions: taxonomies, stories and readers', *Cultural Studies*, 4 (2), pp. 176–91.
Purcell, R. W. and S. J. Gould (1986) *Illuminations: A Bestiary*, New York: W. W. Norton & Co.
—— (1992) *Finders Keepers: Eight Collectors*, New York: W. W. Norton & Co.
Schama, S. (1987) *The Embarrassment of Riches: An Interpretation of Dutch Culture in the Golden Age*, London: Fontana.
Theunnissen, B. (1989) *Eugène Dubois and the Ape-man from Java: The History of the First 'Missing Link' and its Discoverer*, Dordrecht: Kluwer Academic Publishers.

(First published as *Eugène Dubois en de Aapmens van Java*, by Rodopi, Amsterdam 1985).

Thomas, N. (1991) *Entangled Objects: Exchange, Material Culture and Colonialism in the Pacific*, Cambridge, MA: Harvard University Press.

Van der Weiden, W. G. (1993) 'The identity of the National Museum of Natural History: past and future', paper presented at the symposium, 'The Identity of Natural History Museums', 1 April 1993 (De Nederlandse Museum Vereniging: Sectie Natuurhistorische Musea).

Vogel, S. (1991) 'Always true to the object, in our fashion', in I. Karp and S. D. Lavine (eds) *Exhibiting Cultures: The Poetics and Politics of Museum Display*, pp. 191–204, Washington, DC and London: Smithsonian Institution Press.

Chapter 10

Can science museums take history seriously?

Jim Bennett

Never before has the history of science had such opportunities and confronted such challenges in the world of museums. On the one hand, recent trends in science history offer new involvement for museum collections and their interpreters. On the other, fashions in the public presentation of science seem to deny historical sensibilities by seeking to isolate transcendent principles from the contingencies of their creation, use and development. Just when historians of science are moving towards material culture, influential lobbies in science museology are retreating from it.

Where science historians formerly sought to trace histories of ideas and to fashion communities of interest on mutualities of theory, they now embrace a much broader scientific culture. Education, popularization, instrument development and manufacture, laboratory training, and professional and industrial practice are a few elements in this larger view of science where museums can contribute. Museum collections are an important resource for the historians' programme, since only a tiny proportion of the instruments they contain were ever research tools: the great majority were made for education, training, entertainment, professional practice, and so on. Indeed, it may have been their very comprehensiveness that formerly marginalized collections in the academic discipline of the history of science; in the former historiography the crux of a theory might be conveyed in part by the instrument used in a critical discovery, but it is less clear where the many cloned instruments might stand in a discipline most truly exemplified by disembodied ideas and their inferential formalism.

The attitudes of historians have changed profoundly and museum practice will have to change to make use of the opportunity for collections to count in the history of science. We need to find ways of representing the generation and use of instruments, whether the work they performed was in the laboratory, the factory, the classroom or the gentleman's library. Work here comes in many forms – making the results of experiments, making trained practitioners, making entertainment for customers, making status for a patron or making authority for a professional such as a surveyor or a physician. These are only a few examples, but to approach the new challenge our displays will have to aim at being – so far as it is possible – both inclusive and contextualized.

Recent developments in collections management and display have not always been helpful. As the goal broadens to no less than a presentation of science in history and society, the trend to reduce the number of instruments on display will have to be reversed. Design imperatives have enforced a norm of fewer and fewer instruments in showcases and less and less supporting material. Minimalist presentations, for all their value in focusing attention on the qualities of particular objects, will not help us to show science as a pervasive and multifaceted influence in the formation of modern culture and so will eventually undermine the purpose and mission of the museum. Worse still is the trend actually to remove collections from galleries and replace them with designed environments themed for representations of contemporary science. Many of our former collection displays were uninspired, unimaginative and unchallenging, but collections are the foundations of all the great museums, and to forget our responsibility to mediate them to our public is to fail. Displayed storage is a welcome and positive idea, but as an addition to the techniques of object management, not as a substitute for exhibition.

So we must have more objects on display and more information available to make sense of them. We must also be creative in the stories we tell about them. Linear accounts of conceptual development are the most straightforward for the museum staff to devise and probably for the visitor to read, but only because they are consistent with ingrained assumptions about development and progress. They have their place, since they are appropriate to a good many topics in science history, but we should be prepared to develop other models, other dynamics to inform our displays. Two recent exhibitions in the Whipple Museum of the History of Science in Cambridge have addressed these issues by experimenting with the use of the exhibition as a medium.[1]

EMPIRES OF PHYSICS

All science historical exhibitions must try to contextualize, to say that science was formed in history with all the contingencies that this simple but apparently disturbing truth implies. Do our public see this message in our exhibitions? Probably not. We all know that visitors reach for the safe resource of the quaintness, the naivety, even the stupidity displayed in the past – it is something other, and thankfully not a part of what science has become. Even though science has indeed evolved from this primitive state, it has become something different, of which its former condition is no part – the model for its development is not so much developmental growth as the emergence of a perfect butterfly from an unpromising chrysalis. So the historian is thwarted and science remains ahistorical: such ideas and practices were all very well then, but we know better now.

We tried to approach the problem of contextualizing science in a different way, which made it less easy for the thoughtful and sensitive visitor to avoid. We made use of the topography of the Whipple Museum to present two views of the same subject and displayed late-nineteenth century physics simultaneously in two galleries. The galleries occupy the same floor area, one directly above the other, and are linked by staircases at either end. Our special exhibition thus came in two instalments – the first, on the lower floor, with the sub-title 'The Laboratory', the second 'The Exhibition'. Downstairs, then, was the private world of the experimental physicist, upstairs the public space of the many science displays of the time, often linked to international exhibitions. Downstairs we evoked the Cavendish Laboratory and the Cambridge Scientific Instrument Company in the late nineteenth century; upstairs was derived from the generality of exhibitions, but with some particular reference to the Electrical Exhibition in Paris in 1881. Downstairs demonstrated that a great deal of training of operators and refining of delicate instruments and arcane techniques has to take place to create a successful laboratory science; upstairs all this work and difficulty had been lost in a presentation that was direct, engaging and untroubled.

The visitor was not meant to feel completely comfortable in the 'The Laboratory'. He or she had trespassed into a private world, which was not designed to entertain or to assist the outsider. Thus, the environment was not particularly helpful. There were no labels as such, though we contrived to leave around such clues as instrument catalogues, laboratory instruction manuals, and shelf labels for insuring that apparatus was correctly replaced after use. Rather, the serious visitor used a guide, like a tourist in a foreign country. Giant photographs successfully evoked the laboratory and workshop ambience. Some cases were lined with wood, like cupboard interiors, to hold all manner of instruments and apparatus – contrary to current designer dogma, these cases were as crowded as possible. Experiments from the teaching laboratory were set up ready for use with manuscript instruction books, and schedules were posted allocating pairs of students to individual experiments. Everything was done to create a sense of suspended activity, and to suggest an unstable compromise between the ordered regime of education and the unpredictability of experiment. It was just this instability that so worried some college tutors in Cambridge, who saw students of experimental physics engaged in a dubiously insecure and contingent regime, instead of challenging themselves with the intellectual and moral certainties of classics and mathematics.

Another area in 'The Laboratory' dealt with the research project that was central to the work of the Cavendish in this period, namely, the production of a standard of resistance. It was here that the title of the special exhibition, *Empires of Physics*, began to take meaning. In the lower gallery it was a metaphor for the kind of influence that the creators of such standards sought to exert, from the imperial centre of the laboratory workshop through the burgeoning electrical networks of communication and power. This project, centring on delicate electrical measurement and the development of the instruments and apparatus to carry results and techniques into the world outside the laboratory, linked directly with the work of a manufactory – the Cambridge Scientific Instrument Company – displayed nearby.

Visitors emerged from the dim and disorientating 'Laboratory' into the well-lit 'Exhibition' upstairs with some relief. Here they could be much more at ease – this really was an exhibition, and here they knew how they were expected to behave. The display reinforced this difference. Colour was eschewed downstairs, embraced upstairs. Black curtains characterized the 'Laboratory', rich red the 'Exhibition'. There were roughly made, bare, pine display stands downstairs, finished, painted stands upstairs, and so on. Three stars of exhibition technology – the telephone, the telegraph and the phonograph – were presented upstairs, each in an engaging way with a working exhibit for the visitors to try. The telephone display, for example, recreated the live relays of opera performances that so astonished visitors to the Paris Electrical Exhibition in 1881.

We showed also that the exhibitions were competitions, with medals awarded as prizes, and we highlighted the rivalry between Great Britain and Germany. Here, then, the imperial theme took on a more overtly political significance, but one that mirrored the struggle over standards already encountered downstairs. National displays from Germany and Britain dealt mainly with electrical and optical instruments. Other echoes from downstairs were noted as the Cavendish was seen to buy sets of German thermometers through the Special Loan Collection Exhibition in London in 1876, and the Cambridge Scientific Instrument Company to display its wares and win a medal in Paris in 1900. Throughout we tried to remind visitors that this apparently very different world, where all the training and work were lost to view, in fact depended on the world of the lower floor.

As visitors then returned downstairs, as they had to do to leave the museum, they saw the 'Laboratory' world in a different perspective. Moving between the two presentations of the same subject – presentations derived from the period – their view was to some degree contextualized. They had, we hoped, been seduced by the exhibition, and so might engage more thoughtfully with what it obscured. At this point, if they were going round in one of our organized workshops, visitors were invited to attempt a replicated experiment of the period. We decided that providing an opportunity for laboratory experience was important in an exhibition which argued that the work of making physics is part of what physics becomes, and cannot be hidden without an enormous loss of context. The experiments on offer were measuring Joule's mechanical equivalent of heat or measuring an unknown resistance by a Wheatstone bridge. Both used carefully replicated apparatus. It may sound as though the Whipple had joined the 'interactive' vogue, and in terms of encouraging active visitor involvement this was so, but our expectations were very different. Far from making experiments untroubled and fun, we relished the enormous difficulties both we and our visitors experienced in getting anything like the 'expected' results, for it sensitized all of us to a more realistic appreciation of both 'The Laboratory' and 'The Exhibition'.

It is true that visitors required guidance from demonstrators, but the experimental adventure was as open-ended as possible. We allowed visitors to come to a realization of the unwritten practical and tacit skill that must be integrated into the total virtuosity of the experimenter. This in itself gave them some sense of the assumptions unspoken in the world above. Visitors who raised questions and difficulties about the integrity of the experiments clearly expected, from their laboratory training at school or elsewhere, a resolution of the problems from the demonstrator. Instead, their difficulties were taken seriously, implications for the integrity of the experimental result were discussed and the questioners, in turn, were invited to consider the consequences. We were applying disciplinary techniques of the humanities to a practical study of experimental science – a risky strategy and one to which our visitors were unaccustomed. In offering a different channel of appreciation of science past, we were able to show that tacit skill comes to be taken for granted and that other kinds of negotiation must be undertaken, beyond appealing to the transparency of an empirical result, to secure something so complex as the mechanical equivalent of heat.

In using the topography of our exhibition galleries to present the message of *Empires of Physics*, we sought to promote the special potential of the medium of the exhibition; too often the model of the book is unthinkingly transferred to the gallery. The dynamic of the exhibition was thus not progressive or chronological. The visitors moved freely between the private and public worlds, examining afresh their relationships and their constructed distinctions. The showcases were filled with instruments – not there only to represent a result, an insight or a discovery, but to evoke a broader scientific culture as it appeared in the laboratory and the exhibition.

Empires of Physics was a challenge to the slight resources of the Whipple Museum; it was also a challenge to our public. We tried to make it accessible in a variety of ways. The 'guide' deliberately did not follow the usual conventions of an exhibition catalogue – it was more a combined tourist guide and a workbook or resource book. The style was that of a French *cahier*, to indicate that even the visitor had to do some work at this exhibition. There were public lectures, the first a re-enactment of a lecture on the subject of the telephone given by Maxwell in Cambridge in 1878. There were workshops for student and school parties and for any visitors who signed up; these included sessions with the experiments. There was, finally, a lecture course for our own students in the Department of History and Philosophy of Science.

Our initiative provoked critical attention as well as interest and discussion from fellow museum professionals and historians of science. Certainly, the exhibition served to raise the Whipple Museum's profile as an institution of commentary and criticism in an increasingly unchallenging science museum environment. Our visitors, however, it must be admitted, often did not get the rather subtle point at the centre of the whole project. But we did discover that if someone spent a few minutes outlining the structure and the significance of the two levels before they entered the special exhibition, they responded very positively, saw what we were trying to do and felt obliged by that simple human contact to give the idea a chance. This was one reason for our increasing such contact in the second exhibition.

THE NEW AGE

The second of our pair of exhibitions, *1900: The New Age*, also experimented with presenting different views of a subject in two galleries. Here, visitors were taken back to 1900 and upstairs were presented, as observers, with a technological programme for the twentieth century; downstairs, in a reversal of roles, they were then the objects of observation in a complementary human programme.

1900: The New Age showed how the twentieth century was anticipated at its very beginning – a natural source of curiosity in our own *fin de siècle*. To present the prospect of the twentieth century in 1900, we chose one of the most spectacular and ambitious of the extraordinary series of Universal Exhibitions which followed from the Great Exhibition in London in 1851. This was the enormous Exposition Universelle in Paris, one of the largest and most extravagant the world has seen.

Visitors were transported to Paris in 1900 in the Whipple Museum's version of the time machine of H. G. Wells. His brief description of 1895 left us plenty of scope for imagination, and we settled on rather a quaint and comfortable vehicle for time travel: the furnishings were those of a domestic interior of the time, with a console equipped with devices appropriate to the period. At the end of their journey visitors found themselves in the exhibition of 1900, though strangely contracted from the vast area of Paris it originally occupied.

In the upper gallery, we tried to recreate something of the excitement of the original, while focusing on two of the many pavilions – the Optical Palace and the Electricity Palace. Projected images of Paris *en fête* in 1900 showed that there was much to see beyond these pavilions, but here scientific instruments and optical entertainments were the focus of attention. There was film from the very beginnings of the cinema. There were X-ray and other radiation tubes. Telescopes, microscopes, spectroscopes and other instruments from the leading European makers competed for awards from the international jury. There was a selection of the enormous literature generated by the Exposition – from souvenir postcards and photographic albums to the vast 60-volume official report. The Electrical Palace presented the hardware of an astonishing new technology and left no doubt that electric lighting and electric power would revolutionize life in the coming century.

Everywhere upstairs we tried to simulate the atmosphere of the time – in sound as well as vision. Rich materials were used wherever possible. No fluorescent tubes were allowed anywhere in the exhibition. The whole was lit by bulbs – not discreetly placed but boldly and confidently displaying the vigour and brilliance of electricity.

From the excitement of the show upstairs visitors moved to quite a different experience in the lower gallery, to the Salle Bertillon of the Paris Exposition, named after the French anthropologist and criminologist Alphonse Bertillon. Perhaps the most obvious message upstairs was one of progress and improvement – confidence in expansion and advancement, generated by the potential of new technologies. Downstairs introduced the notion that a programme of improvement might apply also to people.

Upstairs visitors examined what we presented for their instruction and entertainment. Downstairs the view was reversed, and we examined the visitors. Each person had been given a souvenir card – a record card for their personal profiles, a *portrait parlé* in the terminology of the time – and here they began to complete its different sections by going round a series of stations, where various measurements and records were noted. First a photograph was taken, followed by finger-prints and by various 'anthropometric' measurements – stature and head dimensions. A contemporary weighing machine was used to record individual weight. Aspects of the individual's phrenology were recorded, as well as their eye-colour and their performance on physiological and psychological tests of strength, reaction time and colour vision. Finally, to be true to the period, we had to represent X-ray recording, but every visitor found the X-ray booth out of order on their visit – quite a few were visibly disappointed.

All these tests were current in 1900, the regime of testing was displayed in the 1900 Exposition, and extensive surveys of populations and groups were undertaken in the period and their results published. While almost all our visitors enjoyed this novel interactive gallery, most also sensed the more sinister aspects of the human programme; they were made aware that recognizing inferior and criminal types in populations came to be associated with such recording, and that the identification of 'degenerates' could and did lead to programmes for their management and suppression.

Our visitors dutifully handed in their cards, which were processed and then posted to them: photographs were applied, measurements recorded, phrenological and other tests decoded, and so on. To remain as true as possible to the surveys of the period, after the exhibition closed each participant received a statistical report on the entire population of visitors.

HISTORY AND PUBLIC UNDERSTANDING

Whatever responses are adopted in particular museum environments to the challenge of a more inclusive and historicized approach to past science, museums must remain institutions for criticism in the proper sense. We learn science in schools, colleges and universities and go to museums not just for reinforcement but for commentary. Whatever critical perspectives they adopt, exhibitions must therefore take up the challenge of being meta-presentations with respect to science. Our visitors deserve this facility, which they will not readily find elsewhere, and history of science provides one of the most interesting, appealing and profound resources for an enriched understanding – a 'public understanding of science', to use the fashionable phrase, which goes beyond a simplified, sanitized, trickle-down account of current or – more likely – recent scientific theory.

The most authoritative statement of the philosophy of the 'public understanding' programme in relation to museums is perhaps found in the Science Museum's publication of 1992, *Museums and the Public Understanding of Science* (Durant 1992). However, there is little encouragement in this volume that the Whipple's recent approach fits easily with the aims and experience of others.

John Durant's introduction is an exception, because of his sensitivity to the dangers of presenting science as certain and unequivocal, and divorced from its social context, and because he points to the importance of portraying science in the making (ibid.: 7–11).

Other papers are less accommodating to different sensibilities. Miles and Tout, for example, are very negatively disposed to the value of what they call 'real objects' in science exhibition communication. They say that 'it is sometimes suggested that the use of real objects in exhibitions makes possible a unique understanding. There is apparently no evidence to support this proposition', and judge that 'the non-verbal language of real things is no more than museological conceit' (Miles and Tout 1992: 27). This assertion is possible only when coupled with a particular, and very narrowly focused, assumption about what constitutes the essence of science – of what is to be conveyed and understood – namely, its disembodied principles. The visitor questionnaire then measures the exhibition's achievement in this sense alone.

This attitude may derive from the special position science has constructed for itself in contemporary life, distinguished from other areas of human endeavour, one aspect of which is that its generation and use are not an essential part of what it is, and belonging outside, perhaps vaguely assigned to history or politics. Experience of these aspects does not contribute to understanding in a proper sense. Only on the basis of assumptions of that sort can Miles and Tout's assertion be made; in other museological areas it would simply be absurd. Imagine how one might react to the following claims. 'Looking at paintings contributes nothing to our understanding of Renaissance art.' 'Looking at the Houses of Parliament does not enrich our understanding of Gothic revivalism.' 'Seeing the Elgin Marbles does not enhance our appreciation of classical Greece.' 'Visiting the Pyramids tells us nothing about ancient Egyptian civilization.' 'Seeing a gable-end street painting in contemporary Belfast adds nothing to our sense of the historical imperatives of Irish conflict.' It is not difficult to construct a *reductio ad absurdum* argument of this sort, because the proposition is absurd in all contexts other than that where science is only an intellectual system of principles and rules.

In Patrick Sudbury's wide-ranging piece on techniques and approaches to museum education, he deals with some of the problems of hands-on demonstrations in science centres. 'We have experienced', he says, 'some weaknesses in the method because most experiments allow for some ambiguity which is inevitably picked up in the visitor's response. This kind of ambiguity can lead to visitor frustration and disappointment if there is no recourse to a demonstrator' (Sudbury 1992: 61). In *Empires of Physics*, on the contrary, we used such ambiguity and frustration to show the visitor that experimental science is not a straightforward affair, and to hint at the work – technical, political, social, rhetorical – which must be performed to secure it. Sudbury's response is quite different; he invokes a social and material management in the museum to head off doubt and conflict, paralleling the management originally employed in science. We have seen that he invokes the role of the demonstrator; he then says: 'The ultimate solution to this kind of problem is better scientific input, better design, and a grouping of related experiments which give a consistent and sustainable result without losing the sense of discovery' (ibid.). A different solution would be to allow, indeed to celebrate, the fact that science has more in common with other creative endeavours than this approach admits; understanding is enriched, not compromised, by its human and social dimensions and might equip us better to value science properly and use it realistically.

There is a tendency for science museums to stand at the present and from there to offer views of the past, the present or the future. A museum which takes its collections seriously as historical resources must, on the other hand, allow what is recoverable from the past to refine our understanding of both the past and the present. In the museum world, it is perhaps only in the field of science museums that so obvious a point about historic collections needs to be made, but most science museums were established for science education, not for history of science (Butler 1992). This is as true of the great historic collections – the Science Museum, the Conservatoire Nationale des Arts et Métiers, the Deutsches Museum – as it is of the modern science centres. Science museums traditionally perform the role of public showcases for science, always accentuating the positive, and they risk becoming earnest and condescending facilities for self-improvement.

Yet the older foundations were collections-based. They emphasized the applications of science, embodied in actual instruments and machinery or, where appropriate, in scale models. Familiarity with these was expected to improve the quality of everyday working life by spreading scientific utility. This at least meant that when immediate utility had passed, the museum had a collection of historic material. The shift in methodology – where specially created demonstrations have replaced the instruments and machines, and entertainment and understanding replaced utility – reflects a changed view of science – more secure now in its principles than in its assurance of universal utility. Faced with public doubt, concern and disenchantment, the science educator retreats to first principles, and the current interest in public understanding of science is at least partly motivated by the belief that if only the public *understood*, they might return to confidence.

Improving science education is important to us all, but a museum environment can encourage a richness and variety of perspectives. The lessons of history may be that all sorts of contingencies contribute to the development of science, that industrial and technological circumstances cannot be divorced from its creative context, that political and social structures and values have influenced its outcome, that it is formed in controversy as well as in consensus, and that the organization and conventions of the scientific community have helped to shape how it has emerged. Taking seriously the simple fact that science is formed in history implies a different meaning to 'the public understanding of science', but one that might engender a more realistic attitude to the vagaries of the scientific enterprise.

ACKNOWLEDGMENTS

Other teaching, research and museum staff involved with this work were Robert Brain, Kate Bycroft, Simon Schaffer, Otto Sibum, Richard Staley and Judith Thursby. A fuller account can be found in the four books published in connection with the exhibitions: J. Bennett, R. Brain, K. Bycroft, S. Schaffer, H. O. Sibum and R. Staley, *Empires of Physics: A Guide to the Exhibition*; R. Brain, *Going to the Fair: Readings in the Culture of Nineteenth-Century Exhibitions*; R. Staley (ed.), *The Physics of Empire* (public lectures by B. Brain, J. C. Maxwell, H. O. Sibum, S. Schaffer and A. Warwick); J. Bennett, R. Brain, S. Schaffer, H. O. Sibum and R. Staley, *1900: The New Age: A Guide to the Exhibition*. All were published by and are available from the Whipple Museum, Free School Lane, Cambridge.

REFERENCES

Durant, J. (ed.) (1992) *Museums and the Public Understanding of Science*, London: Science Museum.

Butler, S. V. F. (1992) *Science and Technology Museums*, Leicester and London: Leicester University Press.

Miles R. and A. Tout (1992) 'Exhibitions and the public understanding of science', in J. Durant (ed.) *Museums and the Public Understanding of Science*, pp. 27–33, London: Science Museum.

Sudbury, P. (1992) 'Linking scientists to non-science museums', in J. Durant (ed.) *Museums and the Public Understanding of Science*, pp. 57–64, London: Science Museum.

Chapter 11

Birth and Breeding

Politics on display at the Wellcome Institute for the History of Medicine

Ken Arnold

Much has been said both within and beyond the museum world about the apparent reluctance of museums to tackle politically contentious issues.[1] Conscious of this relative silence, I curated an exhibition which aimed to examine a subject of considerable political controversy, and moreover to highlight the means by which political arguments were waged by some of its most celebrated protagonists. This chapter concerns that exhibition and its reception.

The exhibition *Birth and Breeding: The Politics of Reproduction in Modern Britain* was held at the Wellcome Institute for the History of Medicine in London from October 1993 to February 1994. As became clear from peer reviews and visitor research, however, responses to the exhibition were often far removed from my own expectations and intentions. Particularly striking were the accusations that the exhibition had been 'sanitized', that it was somehow 'apolitical', and even that it was 'fascist'. In what follows, I first describe the exhibition and my original intentions; I then discuss responses to it, drawing upon reviews and visitor research carried out; and finally, I try to assess how this mismatch of perceptions arose.

THE EXHIBITION

The Wellcome Institute for the History of Medicine is primarily composed of two complementary divisions: an Academic Unit devoted to teaching and researching the history of medicine and a Library holding materials related to that history. In mounting exhibitions for the Institute, I have attempted to place them more or less in-between the two: drawing ideas for the varied menu of topics from the research undertaken in the Academic Unit, and using the extraordinary riches of the Library's collections as my primary source of exhibits – ancient and modern, Eastern and Western, unique originals and elaborate reproductions, masterpieces and ephemera. I have also been concerned to try to select medical historical topics that will be of interest to audiences beyond those already professionally concerned with medicine and its history. Exhibitions that I have presented to date include *Pills and Profits* (April–August 1994) examining the evolution of medical advertising, *Animal Doctor* (November 1994–March

1995) dealing with veterinary medicine, *Fatal Attractions* (May–September 1995) looking at AIDS and syphilis, *Abracadabra* (June–November 1996) exploring the links between medicine and magic, and a number of others tackling the overlap between medicine and art.

In frequent contact with colleagues both in and out of the Institute, the subject-matter, approach and content of all the exhibitions is inevitably based on extensive consultation and collaboration with historians (lecturers and students), curators of library collections, museum workers in other institutions, professional designers, an internal publishing department, and so forth. That said, my role as curator of the exhibitions, structurally at least, resembles nothing so much as a one-man band – albeit one which is supported by intellectually rich consultants, efficiently practical support and an enviably healthy budget. Informal consultation accompanies almost every stage of the exhibition process, but there is no official exhibition committee, no formal approval procedure and, indeed, rarely any discouraging responses to suggested exhibition themes or approaches.

Birth and Breeding was the third in a series of temporary exhibitions. The first two, to some extent thematically determined before my arrival, looked at the history of anatomical illustrations (*Picturing the Body*) and at the movements of medical ideas from one culture to another around the world (*Ever the Twain Shall Meet*). While both were very effective in their own right, neither exhibition paid much attention to the social and political contexts in which medical science and practice have existed. Also, as both exhibitions began with pre-Renaissance material, neither looked in detail at the history of twentieth-century medicine; nor did they draw on recent historiography or feminist scholarship. In material terms, the first two exhibitions mainly featured elaborately produced, finely finished works, such as printed books, framed pictures, bound and illuminated manuscripts and exquisitely carved ivory figures. Other collections in the Institute Library, however, do not consist of finely finished works but are of more haphazard and ephemeral materials such as archives and loose papers, sketches and mass-produced posters. In *Birth and Breeding* I wanted to show that these too are the stuff of medical history, reflecting and shaping it as much as the other types of exhibit previously displayed. Indeed, it was the Library's extensive holdings relating to the history of modern British reproductive politics that provided the original impetus for the exhibition.

All the exhibitions in this historical series have shared a 'traditional' object-rich presentational style. They have sought to tackle their subjects through the thematic marshalling and juxtaposition of exhibits, rather than through high-tech modes of display. Art and science, ancient and modern, beautiful and shocking, sublime and ridiculous, resonant and wonderful: these are the parameters within which I have sought to make the history of medicine seem interesting and important (Greenblatt 1991; Arnold 1993a, 1993b). Wellcome Institute exhibitions partly serve as showcases for certain sections of the Library's collections, and may draw on material kept in the various departments of the historical collections: Iconographic, Early Printed Books, Western Manuscripts, Oriental, Modern and Contemporary Medical Archive; and on three-dimensional material originally gathered by Sir Henry Wellcome now kept on 'permanent loan' in the Science Museum (Skinner 1986; Russell 1986). *Birth and Breeding* incorporated a wide range of such materials and included correspondence, book manuscripts, posters and newspaper clippings from archives as well as artefacts such as birth control devices.

The first exhibit encountered by visitors to *Birth and Breeding* was what one reviewer described as a 'tantalising dose of "living" history' (Ehrman 1993), a selection of film-clips ranging from Marie Stopes's melodrama *Maisie's Marriage* (1923) to the Family Planning Association's campaign film from the 1950s. The rest of the exhibition comprised archival collections from the following organizations and individuals, arranged in roughly chronological order: the Eugenics Society, founded in 1907 to promote education on heredity and race; Marie Stopes (1880–1958), the pioneer birth control advocate; the National Birthday Trust Fund, founded in 1928 to raise funds to promote safer and less painful childbirth; Grantly Dick-Read (1890–1959), who famously campaigned for 'natural' methods of pain free childbirth; the Family Planning Association, which, particularly during the 1950s and 1960s, had a very significant impact on both sex education and the development of contraceptive devices; and finally the Abortion Law Reform Association, which in 1967 successfully managed to change legislation regarding abortion (Arnold, Hall and Sheppard 1993).

Each set of papers from these six campaigners reflected a highly partial, often fanatically single-minded perspective on the whole range of issues tied up in the political knot of reproduction. Taken together, however, they produced a broad picture of the vigorous debates and bitter conflicts that for most of the twentieth century have surrounded issues concerning motherhood and reproduction. Set against a backdrop of ever changing personal experiences of childbirth, the exhibition presented a series of impressions of the variations in attitudes surrounding parenting. The nature and number of Wellcome archives relating to this broad constellation of issues is, however, largely a matter of chance, or rather of the particular ways in which each journeyed from the individuals and organizations involved (ibid.: 48–55). As such, the exhibition was not intended as a comprehensive overview, but as a selection of alternative historical perspectives.

Like a number of exhibitions that have looked at the history of science in its social and cultural contexts, *Birth and Breeding* mostly dealt with the science of everyday life. It focused on the processes through which politics, as the art of debate and public persuasion, was conducted rather than at the details of the scientific theories, facts or investigations. Moreover, the historical material presented was not intended to show how attitudes had changed but how a series of organizations and individuals had forcefully argued for their own ardently held points of view. All six were in their own ways highly successful at communicating their messages, and the exhibition was essentially a portrait of their

Figure 11.1 Partial perspectives: National Birthday Trust case in *Birth and Breeding* (courtesy of the Wellcome Trust)

campaigning efforts. Typical exhibits included a Eugenics Society poster headed 'Only healthy seed must be sown', a cutting from *Woman's Sunday Mirror* asking of Grantly Dick-Read 'Why try to bamboozle us . . . ?' and an Abortion Law Reform Association leaflet emblazoned with the slogan 'Women: your body belongs to you!' In short, this was an exhibition about scientific and social propaganda, and the reactions and controversies that surrounded it.

Far from diminishing since the time of the history presented, the political issues displayed in the exhibition have become increasingly contentious. As one reviewer noted of the situation today, 'at no time in womankind's history has there been so much argument about who should control the place and process of birth' (Moscucci 1993: 307). *Birth and Breeding* had nowhere near enough room to attempt a complete history of these debates; even less was it intended to resolve any of the difficult issues that underlie them. Instead, it focused on the work of six historically significant individuals and institutions to depict how some of today's controversial topics had been debated in the past.

VISITORS' REACTIONS

As with any cultural product, once released from the immediate control of the creator into the choppier seas of the public domain, the exhibition was subject to interpretations of the curatorial intent behind it. As Spencer Crew and James Sims have observed, many of an exhibition's most interesting voices 'do not emerge until after the exhibition is in place and the audience comes to view it' (Crew and Sims 1991:163). Reactions to *Birth and Breeding* were varied – 'Elitist, Dry, Inaccessible', 'Excellent-emotive', 'Food for thought!', 'FASCIST EXHIBITION'.

Visitors' views were gathered through two basic mechanisms: first, a visitors' book was provided in which a good number of those who signed added sometimes lengthy comments. Second and more substantially, over 600 visitors voluntarily filled out an 'Exhibition evaluation form'. The form asked people to rate the exhibition theme, choice of exhibits, labels and text, and design; and to record how long they spent at the exhibition, how they had heard about it and what other themes they would like to see future shows tackle. The form also asked people to add other thoughts and comments, and more than half of those who filled it in chose to do so – again, sometimes at length.

According to these data the audience of *Birth and Breeding* tended to be adult, with more than 60 per cent female. Consequently, a good proportion of the audience was clearly well-informed about the subject which directly affected them. Though the gallery is small (comprising six large show cases and interstitial spaces), visitors spent on average between 30 and 45 minutes there, some staying for up to two hours. A fair number of them clearly studied rather than just glanced at the exhibits. One described the exhibition as 'Excellent for lecturers and students', while another complained of not being able to 'read [the] whole of articles displayed because covered by other things'.

Among the reactions collected in the visitors' book and evaluation forms, three themes in particular recurred. One concerned gaps: issues, ideas and voices that had been left out of the exhibition. Broadly relating to the same issue, though arguing in more or less the opposite direction, another cluster of criticisms suggested that certain topics or organizations and individuals had been given too much space or allowed too sympathetic a hearing. The third area of concern related to the question of whether or not the exhibition had lived up to its title claim of actually dealing with the politics of reproduction at all. All three types of comment revealed frequently perceptive, often quite unexpected, reactions to the exhibition, which have provided invaluable material both with which to reflect on the audience's expectations and reactions to this exhibition and to shed light on some of the broader issues relating to the politics of presentation. What voices – personal, collective and institutional – did the exhibition project? Is balance possible or desirable when approaching explicitly controversial topics? If not, what might be the implications of deliberately presenting only part of the full story – an explicitly biased account – of a political topic?

A QUESTION OF BALANCE

'Not as extensive as is suggested by the title'. In general or specific terms, this was a disappointment expressed by many visitors. Some wished to see more science and more history along with the politics: 'thought there would be more information on birthing as well as politics'. Others felt particular aspects of the subject had been short-changed. Even though one of the exhibition's six cases concerned the Abortion Law Reform Association, at least one visitor 'would have liked to see more information concerning the history of, and political decisions made about abortions'. A more extreme, but no less justified, suggestion was that 'abortion . . . could have taken up the whole exhibition'. Somebody else was 'sorry Dick-Read's ideas leading to the formation of the National Childbirth Trust were not highlighted'.

Along with suggested additions to the sections chosen, some respondents felt that others had been missed out entirely. One individual wanted information on the population control movement, another felt that 'men's rights on birth' had been overlooked, while a third wished the theme of the history of midwifery had been tackled more fully. Ornella Moscucci in her review of the show pointed out that the voice of pro-life groups, for example, was only reflected in a minor way in the showcase displaying the Abortion Law Reform Association archive (Moscucci 1993: 307). Such gaps led one or two visitors to offer more general criticisms along the same lines: 'interesting but very incomplete', said one; and another, grasping that the size of the gallery was an inevitable limitation, thought there was 'not enough space to explore a complicated subject'. Summing up in very general terms this frustration with a sense of incompleteness, one visitor simply commented that they would have liked 'alternative views to be shown'.

The choice of dates covered by the exhibition (roughly from the beginning of the century up to the 1970s) was also challenged. 'Too much emphasis on past, not present'; 'What about something more contemporary, e.g. issues around reproductive technologies?'; and 'Reference to current situation would have put exhibition in focus', were just three typical suggestions. Writing in the *Social History Curators Group News*, Edwina Ehrman similarly felt that it was unfortunate that 'the exhibition [did] not choose to bring the debate up to date. A text panel reviewing recent developments and their ethical and social implications could have filled this gap' (Ehrman 1993: 9). The fact that no explicit reference was made to the present did not, however, stop at least one visitor from coming to her own conclusions about the relationship between then and now: 'Amazing how things don't change', she wrote.

If some visitors thought that a decade or two had been missed, many more felt that the people most closely concerned with all the issues debated had not been given appropriate space. 'What about the experiences of the women themselves?', wrote one indignantly; while another would have preferred to see 'women's *experience* of *childbirth* (not men talking about it!)', a comment echoed by another who declared that 'Gurus need to be challenged'. This same visitor went on to suggest that 'the social context needs to be explored more fully from the point of view of women and society'. While a fourth, reflecting particularly on the campaigning efforts for natural childbirth by Grantly Dick-Read, wished that the display had included some 'comment on the feelings of failure in women who didn't achieve what he – a man – proposed'. Reflecting on the same issue from a slightly different perspective, another commented that the exhibition was a 'good time capsule collection of memorabilia but need[ed] a more personal perspective of the women involved'.

In retrospect, even though I recognized this relative silence in the material as I researched it, and as a consequence tried to pre-empt such complaints by being as explicit as possible about the fashion in which the exhibition was limited by the nature of the archives it displayed, the addition of even one exhibit per case which directly conveyed the presence of a patient on the delivery end of many of these debates would clearly have considerably enriched the show. Attempts to personalize the labels, and to bring out the individual qualities of some of the more abstract-seeming exhibits, were simply too subtle a means of attempting to highlight the selectivity of the display.

Another strain of comment suggested that the exhibition had not been properly critical of individuals or organizations who respondents felt had been 'bad' influences. Thus, of the case concerning the pioneer birth control campaigner Marie Stopes, one visitor wrote that she was 'presented in an amazingly sanitised light', and feared that viewers would leave 'without any grasp of her notorious racism'. Another felt that the 'association between [the] views of Eugenics Society and those of Nazis' could have been made much clearer: 'one item from Germany portraying consequences of *applying* eugenics would have done'. Of the depiction of Grantly Dick-Read's campaigning for natural childbirth, someone unsympathetic to his viewpoint felt that he had simply been 'eulogised'. While on the abortion issue, someone else thought the presentation 'appear[ed] to be 98% pro-abortion'.

These suggestions of gaps and biases have been quoted at length to give a full sense of just how conscious of the question of bias visitors to an exhibition tackling contentious issues such as those presented in *Birth and Breeding* are likely to be. Any such exhibition has to face up to the question of whose politics is being displayed, and how. Just a few visitors to *Birth and Breeding* explicitly congratulated the exhibition on its coverage: 'Very well balanced, broad cover and good mix of material', thought one; 'very diplomatic', wrote another, somewhat ambiguously. 'Very good, tactful and tasteful treatment of an incredibly "difficult" subject', complimented a third, adding that he or she was 'Glad it wasn't sold out to "PC"'. A cynic might suspect that these were visitors who had found enough of their own pet-opinions to convince them of the show's even-handedness. One reviewer, however, felt that evident attempts to be balanced had actually compromised the energy of the presentation: 'immediacy and accessibility lose out to balance and objectivity' (ibid.: 8).

It seemed to me that it was more the hand of fate than any well-rounded fairness on behalf of the curator that gave the show whatever semblance of balance it did contain. The number of archives used were dictated by the show-cases available, and much of the selection thereafter was based on pragmatic and aesthetic criteria: exhibits had to fit the space available, and in an exhibition dominated by the printed word, any item with illustrations, colour or an interesting design was immediately likely to be at least considered for inclusion. Further, given the collections available within the Institute Library and the time allowed in which to produce *Birth and Breeding*, completeness could never have been a realistic goal, nor indeed a very attractive one. Even with all the time in the world, as Steven Lavine has said, 'the voice of an exhibition [cannot realistically expect to] reflect the evolving understandings of current scholarship and the multiple voices within any discipline' (Lavine 1991: 151). Nor indeed was the exhibition's purpose to present arguments from a representative number of points of view. As so many of the comments quoted above indicate, the range of issues raised by the subject-matter and the variety of opinions related to each was far too large ever to contemplate doing justice to them all in the display space available. Thus, in the range of possible stances taken by exhibitions, *Birth and Breeding* aimed to be very much more like an essay than a definitive monograph.

Exhibitions are inevitably selective. The consequent challenge for their curators is twofold: first, to be sure that the range of material made available through the process of selection is worth exhibiting, and second, to make the basis of that selection as transparent as possible within the exhibition. With the benefit of hindsight, I now recognize that the determination to restrict the material displayed to that kept in six Contemporary Medical Archives was based on a professional concern that the public had no reason to share; and that the public is no doubt more interested in the material on display than where it comes from. In retrospect I can also see that what I regarded as a transparent selective policy was far from clear to visitors. An explanation of the methodology – the deliberate use of just six discrete archives – did appear in the exhibition text, but it was buried in an introductory panel: a notoriously unreliable tool for communicating vital information. It might have helped to have repeated the point throughout the show, or maybe even to have reinforced the point in the exhibition sub-title, by-line – 'Six archives from the Wellcome Institute Library' – or even design. By these and no doubt other means, another version of the show would have to seek to make far more explicit the method of selection, and indeed the nature of the show's selectors. For as I shall presently go on to discuss, many visitors did, in any case, make very definite assumptions about how and why the exhibition ended up as it did.

THE EXHIBITION'S AUTHORSHIP

'How dare *you*, the Wellcome Institute', wrote one irate visitor, 'hold all this up as ideal in the society we live in today. Frightening.' Another felt that the institutional context had mandated 'a very sanitised version of events, especially viz. Abortion law reform'. These and a number of similar comments made by visitors to *Birth and Breeding* reveal two strongly held assumptions shared by many visitors to museums and exhibitions, which their creators, funders and facilitators ignore at their peril. The first is that exhibitions somehow embody the views of the institution in which they are seen – that they broadcast the institutional voice. And second, that no matter how contradictory the range of material presented seems, the fact that it is put on show at all carries with it the institution's stamp of approval.

Much of the institutional identity imposed on an exhibition is supplied by the physical environment in which it is set. Visitors are very literally that – away from their homes, on unfamiliar territory as guests in someone else's space. As such, they take their cues of what to expect, how to behave and how to interpret what is presented to them from the building, the furniture, the comfort, the ambience, the staff, the smell – that is, from any number of factors additional to the content and presentational style of the exhibition they are visiting. In the case of *Birth and Breeding* the Wellcome Institute itself provides particularly important cues.

Occupying part of the Wellcome Building, the Institute provides library resources and research and teaching facilities for those interested in the history of medicine (Rhodes James 1994; Symons 1994; Turner 1980).[2] The building itself has an imposing neo-classical limestone facade adorned with ionic columns; and inside its large revolving doors is a wide set of marble stairs leading to a spacious stairwell, embellished with reproduced art-deco lights and other decorative details rendered in dark bronze. There is an inescapable air of wealth, confidence, solidity and tradition: it does not seem like a place for the casual visitor in search of entertainment. Visitors to the building are met by immaculately turned out security personnel, who direct them towards reception staff who give out coded security badges. The gallery itself is situated on the fourth floor of the building next to a lecture theatre.[3]

It is a truism in cultural analysis to assert that the selection and presentation of ideas, images and information can only take place within a context that imparts its own messages about power (Karp 1992: 1). Although *Birth and Breeding* was inevitably caught up both in the nexus of relationships between individuals inside the organization and in the influences of donors and evaluators, visitors tended to view it as emanating not from a team of collaborators but from a single entity: the Wellcome Institute (or 'The Wellcome'). For while, within the Institute, exhibitions are very much associated with the individuals who work on them, once opened and visited by the public, the 'voice' behind them comes to be perceived instead as that of the Institute itself. For many visitors, the much-debated question of authorship in museums is answered quite unambiguously: the author of a given show is the institution that puts it on (cf. Arnold, 1994; Macdonald 1996).

As the visitor comments quoted at the opening of this section make clear, the question of exhibition authorship almost inevitably goes hand in hand with that of the exhibition's 'point of view'. *Birth and Breeding* tried to avoid giving a single point of view, presenting instead a series of alternative viewpoints, some of which were unequivocal propaganda, and as such were crude, bold and sometimes even offensive. It also sought to highlight the very 'stuff' of conviction-based political campaigning: letters from MPs, voting lists, material from fund-raising campaigns, leaflets, artwork for posters, petitions, hate-mail, lecture-tour scrapbooks and banners. The intention was that by presenting this material and juxtaposing alternative political stances – pro-choice and anti-abortion, championing of medical science and criticism of unnatural interference, support for personal autonomy and for state intervention – the exhibition itself would transcend any of the individual stances.

However, the exhibition was often not regarded in this way because the institutional context itself suggested a didactic and authoritative stance – 'the Wellcome' was assumed to be presenting some kind of definitive, authoritative picture. Moreover, visitors themselves have their own opinions through or against which they interpret an exhibition. They tend, therefore, either to confirm their own opinions or to read in the biases that they suspect will be broadcast by an organization such as the Wellcome. This gap between my intentions and visitor interpretations can be seen further in the different perceptions of the extent to which the exhibition was 'political'.

THE 'POLITICS' IN *BIRTH AND BREEDING*

Some visitors applauded *Birth and Breeding* for tackling politics head on: 'Fascinating. Congratulations on dealing with the "politics" of reproduction.'

And for at least one visitor, the exhibition had been 'Interesting but a bit too political'. A good number of others, however, lamented that reproductive politics had not figured prominently enough: one, for example, wished that there had been a more vigorous 'interpretation of various race/class bias[es] in [the] early material'; another similarly wanted 'more political analysis of the material (with its concentration of fascists)'; a third thought 'the comments could have been expanded & more critical'; while another still indicated that the exhibition was 'rather wooden and doesn't draw us into the political issues at stake'. 'Classism, racism, sexism, heterosexism are not addressed', he or she added. 'Missed opportunity to develop an interesting theme', declared another, who had hoped for 'something more controversial'. Yet another visitor seemed to speak for many when he or she wrote: 'The subtitle of this exhibition, "the politics of reproduction in modern Britain" is misleading.'

The process of trying to understand how an exhibition, whose curator meant it to deal with the everyday details of politics, could be so roundly criticized by members of its audience for being 'apolitical', reveals much about the implications of putting politics on show. From my curatorial point of view, *Birth and Breeding* succeeded in presenting reproductive politics in a particular historical period; but some of its critical visitors clearly had found a history without the politics. While I had intended to mount a display of exhibits arranged according to logical sub-sections, through which the complex processes of politic persuasion could be observed; its critics either found this of little significance or took the point for granted. And where I had hoped that a range of inflammatory but contradictory exhibits would make obvious both the lack of 'objectivity' in any given opinion and the role of propaganda in all the surveyed campaigns, exhibition critics felt that in adopting this sitting-on-the-fence pose I had missed the opportunity presented of really engaging with the politics of reproduction. In short, while I regarded the exhibition as showing that politics has always been an untidy and multi-vocal process of persuasion, many of its visitors felt instead that *Birth and Breeding* had not done what an exhibition on 'the politics of reproduction' should: namely, to expose the implicit values buried within individual exhibits, which otherwise were in danger of remaining frozen in a politically neutral past. These evidently different conceptions of what politics might mean within an exhibition shed interesting light on two particular aspects of the nature of exhibitions: their relevance and their attitude.

A number of visitors clearly felt that in dealing with the past – the most recent exhibit dated from the late 1970s – the exhibition necessarily lacked present-day relevance. For them, the chronological gap between then and now indicated an absence of meaningful political commentary. In an age in which most people digest their politics through newspapers, radio and moving images on the very day it happens, it is not too surprising that for many politics and history are seen as separate – politics happens today, history is the past.[4] Although some visitors made links or contrasts between past and present reproduction politics, many more seemed to feel that the displays in *Birth and*

Breeding were dry and distant – lacking in contemporary relevance. A number of museum commentators have argued that exhibitions need to address visitors' current concerns and 'speak to their experiences' if they are to be successful (Wallace 1989: 32; cf. Kavanagh 1990: xii; Weil 1988: 34). However, 'being relevant' is not enough. As well as acting as focal-points for a reflection of the visitors' own culture and society, museums must surely also provide something else – something unknown, unrealized, unimagined and even unpopular. Resolving this tension between the simultaneous needs for familiarity and surprise, and indeed using each to highlight and explore the other, is crucial to producing an effective historical exhibition (cf. Molella and Stephens 1996: 97–8).

Birth and Breeding, like the majority of science, medicine and history exhibitions today, attempted to take a 'neutral' or 'objective' approach – in this case by presenting a variety of different perspectives and avoiding adjudicating between them. As we have seen, however, many visitors nevertheless interpreted the exhibition as having a particular viewpoint;[5] while others, recognizing that it had not, clearly wished it had taken an explicit stance. An intriguing strategy suggests itself: for perhaps rather than trying to present a 'balanced' picture and leaving visitors to 'decide for themselves', exhibitions might instead explicitly adopt a particular 'attitude' or 'standpoint'. Thus, in addition to conceptualizing exhibitions as forums, magazines, shops and contested terrains, we might also now have to think of them as soap-boxes. In this form of display curators would not just reflect and balance different ideas relating to a theme but would 'sound off' for or against a particular position (cf. van Lakerveld 1994: 34; Suggitt 1994: 30). Visitors could then formulate their own views in relation to a particular, and explicitly stated, position. Such an approach might also provide a means of trying to disrupt the expectation that an exhibition is necessarily the voice of the institution that houses it.

My own curatorial assumptions about where the politics lay in the material I displayed in *Birth and Breeding*, and the conclusions which I thought followed logically from this, were unexpectedly and instructively not shared by many of its visitors. This showed that to mount an exhibition on a subject that is currently controversial and 'political' does not guarantee that it will necessarily be regarded as 'relevant' or political. Nor will avoiding adjudicating between viewpoints necessarily mean that an exhibition is regarded as 'objective'. Clearly, in trying to put politics on display museum curators need to take into account, but also in some cases to challenge, assumptions that visitors may make – assumptions about such matters as the relevance of history, the meanings of 'politics', and most intriguingly of all, about the role of exhibitions within politics itself.

NOTES

1 There is a growing number of exceptions to this general rule. For example, after decades of virtual neglect, in Britain we now have a healthy and respectable museum of the labour movement in Manchester. In Holland, a series of exhibitions on politically charged subjects were mounted at the Amsterdam Historical Museum throughout the 1980s. While more recently, a museum in Derry in Ireland has been brave enough to tackle 'The Troubles'.

2 Sir Henry Solomon Wellcome (1853–1936) was a pharmaceutical entrepreneur, philanthropist and patron of medical research, through whose will, the medical research charity the Wellcome Trust was set up. The building that presently houses the Trust was finished in March 1932, and was originally intended as the headquarters for its founder's research interests. The top floors housed scientific laboratories, the second, third, and fourth were fitted out with galleries for his Historical Museum, while a Museum of Medical Science was arranged on the ground floor. Though the balance of interests has shifted considerably, the form of the Wellcome Institute today is a direct descendent of the interests of its eponymous founder.

3 For more on the history of the relationship and effect of contextual architecture on museum displays see Sophie Forgan 1994 and Thomas Markus 1993.

4 Carry van Lakerveld has similarly described the difference between one exhibition project that dealt with social history safely in the past, when the issue of urban poverty was scrutinized with a close but detached interest that upset no one, and an attempt, in another exhibition, to look at contemporary development plans for the same city (Amsterdam), over which the curator almost lost his job (van Lakerveld 1994: 33).

5 In the past museums and exhibitions have been used much more frequently as tools of persuasion. The Eugenics Society (founded 1907), for example, often used exhibitions in the early twentieth century as a means of disseminating information about heredity and propounding its views on the national importance of reproductive selectivity (Arnold, Hall and Sheppard 1993: 18–20). More generally, health and hygiene have often been presented in a spirit of public education. From the nineteenth century national states and local governments throughout Europe and America used medicine, and very occasionally its history, as a tool in educating the public on matters of health, sanitation and hygiene. The best-known example in Britain was the Parkes Museum of Hygiene, founded in 1879, designed, as a 1953 *Guide to London Museums and Galleries* described it, 'for instruction in all matters connected with public health'. Even when these museums made use of historical matter, it was done for the same purpose of moral education and personal improvement: thus, for example, the Smithsonian Institution's medical exhibition in Washington, DC presented a whole historical section in order 'to warn the public against the perils of quackery and the faults of folk medicine' (Skinner 1986: 414). Art museums have also in the past played a much more didactic role than they do today, often aiming to educate the public in good taste, and to steer it clear of 'bad' art and design (Suggitt 1994: 27).

REFERENCES

Arnold, K. (1993a) 'Mysterious museums and curious curators', *Museums Journal*, 93 (8), pp. 20–1.
—— (1993b) 'Object lessons from seventeenth-century museums?', *Social History in Museums: Journal of the Social History Curators Group*, 20 (8), pp. 37–41.
—— (1994) 'Authoring chaos', *Museums Journal*, 94 (3), pp. 27–9.
Arnold, K., L. Hall and J. Sheppard (1993) *Birth and Breeding: The Politics of Reproduction in Modern Britain*, London: The Wellcome Trust.

Crew, S. and J. Sims (1991) 'Locating authenticity: fragments of a dialogue', in I. Karp and S. Lavine (eds) *Exhibiting Cultures: The Poetics and Politics of Museum Display*, pp. 159–75, Washington, DC and London: Smithsonian Institute Press.

Ehrman, E. (1993) 'Review of "Birth and Breeding"', *Social History Curators Group News* (Winter), pp. 9–10.

Forgan, S. (1994) 'The architecture of display: museums, universities and objects in nineteenth-century Britain', *History of Science*, 32 (6), pp. 139–62.

Greenblatt, S. (1991) 'Resonance and Wonder', in I. Karp and S. Lavine (eds) *Exhibiting Cultures: The Poetics and Politics of Museum Display*, pp. 42–56, Washington, DC and London: Smithsonian Institute Press .

Karp, I. (1992) 'Introduction' in I. Karp, C. Kreamer and S. Lavine *Museums and Communities: The Politics of Public Culture*, pp. 1–19, Washington, DC and London: Smithsonian Institute Press.

Kavanagh, G. (1990) *History Curatorship*, Leicester and London: Leicester University Press.

van Lakerveld, C. (1994) 'Sensitivities on display: dealing with controversial subjects in a museological context', *Social History in Museums*, 21, pp. 32–5.

Lavine, S. (1991) 'Museum practices' in I. Karp and S. Lavine (eds) *Exhibiting Cultures: The Poetics and Politics of Museum Display*, pp. 151–58, Washington, DC and London: Smithsonian Institute Press.

Macdonald, S. (1996) 'Authorizing science: public understanding of science in museums', in A. Irwin and B. Wynne (eds) *Misunderstanding Science?*, pp. 152–71, Cambridge: Cambridge University Press.

Markus, T. (1993) *Buildings and Power: Freedom and Control in the Origin of Modern Building Types*, London: Routledge.

Molella, A and C. Stephens (1996) 'Science and its stakeholders: the making of "Science in American Life"', in S. Pearce (ed.) *Exploring Science in Museums*, pp. 95–106, London and Atlantic Highlands, NJ: Athlone.

Moscucci, O. (1993) 'What about the women?', *British Medical Journal*, 307, p. 1218.

Rhodes-James, R. (1994) *Henry Wellcome*, London: Hodder & Stoughton.

Russell, G. (1986) 'The Wellcome non-medical material', *Museums Journal* (supplement), 86.

Skinner, G. (1986) 'Sir Henry Wellcome's Museum for the History of Science', *Medical History*, 30, pp. 383–418.

Suggitt, M. (1994) 'Doctors in taste?', *Social History in Museums*, 21, pp. 26–31.

Symons, J. (1994) *Wellcome Institute for the History of Medicine: A Short History*, London: The Wellcome Trust.

Turner, H. (1980) *Henry Wellcome: The Man, his Collection and his Legacy*, London: The Wellcome Trust and Heinemann.

Wallace, M. (1989) 'The future of history museums', *History News*, 44 (4), pp. 5–33.

Weil, S. (1988) 'The ongoing pursuit of professional status', *Museum News*, 67 (2), pp. 30–4.

Chapter 12

Balancing acts
Science, *Enola Gay* and History Wars at the Smithsonian

Thomas F. Gieryn

A pair of still-smouldering exhibitions at the Smithsonian Institution of Washington provide the occasion to consider defensive epistemologies available to historians and curators whose scholarly representations of the past come under fire. *Science in American Life* opened at the National Museum of American History in April 1994, to mixed reviews: some believe that the exhibition superbly shows the interactions between science and American society since the 1860s; others believe that it concentrates on the risks and horrors engendered by science while giving short shrift to its benefits. Across the mall at the National Air and Space Museum, an exhibition planned as *The Crossroads: The End of World War II, The Atomic Bomb and the Origins of the Cold War* was never built. It was to have displayed the *Enola Gay* (from whose bomb bay the atomic age was born) as the pivotal moment between hot war and Cold, revisiting the justification for dropping bombs on Hiroshima and Nagasaki, while also considering its legacy – from the immediate victims to 'mutually assured destruction'. After contentious fits and starts, the *Enola Gay's* fuselage eventually made it into the Air and Space Museum in June 1995, but relatively naked, wrapped only in a video showing pilots and crew.

These controversial museum exhibitions are strategic sites for exploring bothersome epistemological-cum-political issues of metahistory because, in the end, only one Smithsonian exhibition of science (or of the *Enola Gay*) could be built.[1] The negotiation of contents could not be a permanent solution, and while it is surely the case that finished exhibitions always lend themselves to diverse readings, those readings must be extracted from only one finite collation of artefacts and captions. In this sense, history in museums becomes a kind of zero-sum matter:[2] who decides what is to be shown about science or about the *Enola Gay*, on what grounds, and what happens when selections are contested?

Absent from these debates is big Truth: facts whose transcendent validity is grounded in their unmediated correspondence to historical reality before we got back there with concepts, theories and interpretative frames. Everywhere instead are little truths whose legitimacy rests not on reality but on normatively enforced standards of evidence, argument and purpose consensually shared among a bounded community of knowledge makers. But museum exhibitions like *SAL* and *Crossroads* bring into play *several* epistemic cultures (Knorr Cetina 1997) from within and outside the academy – historians and sociologists of science and of the Second World War, natural scientists, veterans' associations – each with a stake in how our pasts are represented. Ensuing controversies shift from debates about what really happened to debates about the conditions of legitimately knowing the past and about the fidelity of its knowers. The two cases raise troubling thoughts about the vogue relativism implied when 'facts' are replaced by 'stories'. How *will* history be represented in public museums when it must become the conjoint product of several competing epistemic cultures with incongruent standards of evidence, argument and purpose?

It may never have been possible for museum curators to defend a certain representation of history with appeals to 'the way it really was'; I don't know.[3] I do know that such realist or positivist or essentialist discourse disappears almost completely from efforts by Smithsonian curators at *SAL* and at *Crossroads* to legitimize the artefacts they chose to include and the interpretative scripts they wrote to give meaning to things. But, interestingly, neither is an appeal to 'what really happened' found much in passionate efforts by *critics* of these exhibits to change their content or interpretative spin – for *SAL*, its erstwhile patron the American Chemical Society, along with other professional associations of scientists; for *Crossroads*, the Air Force Association, allied veterans' groups and journalists enrolled to the cause. When the language of historical realism does enter the fray, it gets inverted – as an invective stuck to one's adversaries in the 'Museum Wars'. *They* (curator, critic) insist that the Smithsonian tell only one history, what actually happened. *We* (critic, curator) seek a *balanced* display that reflects the diversity of opinions and beliefs about what happened and why, invites multiple readings of artefacts and encourages museum visitors to decide history for themselves. *Their* insistence on True history, getting all the facts straight, when set down next to *our* modest request for balance, shows *them* for what *they* really are: an interest group seeking to ram some political or professional agenda disguised as History down the throats of Smithsonian audiences. Once, maybe, facts entered such controversies as support for the legitimacy of a historical representation; now they enter only to delegitimize opponents' claims.

I am intrigued both by these post-realist attempts to attach authenticity to a particular representation of history, and by the symmetry in rhetorical moves by curators and critics. War may indeed be a dance, where enemies are forced by the requirements of combat to become alike. One side responds to charges that they have imposed History by claiming to seek only balance – just what their opponents claim to seek. This mutual embrace of balance creates problems of an Orwellian kind: some exhibits evidently are more balanced than others. How do curators and critics legitimize their preferred exhibit as balanced while persuasively showing the adversaries' exhibit to be off-balance – without a historical reality that seemingly could decide the matter simply by the facts alone? Both sides replace Truth with hues of objectivity: *we* can be trusted, *they* deceive; *our* perspective is unfettered, *they* wear blinkers; *we* are disinterested, *they* are political. When history as it happened is no longer available to settle contests over its public representation, curators and critics in these controversies turn to other registers of authenticity and credibility: trust, privileged perspective, disinterest. Decisions about exhibitions must, it seems, be reached via decisions about exhibitors.[4]

I cannot gloss the contents of *SAL* and those proposed for *Crossroads* without appearing to take sides in battles that never reached consensus and where few were persuaded by good argument or reason to change their minds. I prefer to let the exhibitions emerge from and through debates among curators and critics while I remain agnostic about the verity of anybody's claim to what the exhibition really is or should be. I pursue a symmetric analysis of the symmetric rhetoric, using the same interpretative concepts from the same outside un-attached epistemic standpoint to explain identical positionings and moves of both curators and critics.[5] Such agnosticism and symmetry will be hard for me to enforce. I was a member of the advisory committee for *SAL*, appointed by Smithsonian curators to bring in a sociological or science studies perspective (i.e., to provide them with ammunition to lob back at advisers appointed by the American Chemical Society (ACS) who might wish to make *SAL* into better living through chemistry).[6] And, as a resident of academe for two decades, I find the standards of truth-telling in 'my' epistemic culture of sociologists and historians far more compelling than those of the Air Force Association or American Legion (I petitioned for conscientious objector status as a pacifist during the Vietnam War).

Can I avoid doing an inside job on *SAL* and *Crossroads*? You decide, after reading this agnostic analysis of the Museum Wars. I offer a textual display[7] of both sides (in each case) seeking balance, putting opponents off-balance by accusing them of ersatz Real History, securing authenticity via registers of trust, perspective and disinterestedness. I end pessimistic about the possibility of consensual representations of history in museum settings where stakeholders (i.e., everybody involved) live in rival epistemic communities and lack trust in the credibility and sincerity of the other side. Little truths are no match for power, which carried the day both at *SAL* and at *Crossroads*. To conclude that the survival of the curators' preferred exhibition at *SAL* is a triumph of good scholarship over power, and that the *Enola Gay* is a story about how good scholarship was crucified by political power, is exactly the asymmetric reading I hope to avoid.

'EVERYBODY WANTS BALANCE'

'Desperately seeking balance' becomes the mantra of Smithsonian curators charged with the task of telling tales of American science and the *Enola Gay* – and of their critics. To repeat and repeat again what *SAL*'s lead curator and

historian of science Arthur Molella said of his exhibition would quickly bore –
'it is true that we deal with some controversial topics, but "Science in American
Life" presents them in a balanced way'.[8] Roger Kennedy, Molella's former boss
at the National Museum of American History, chants: 'The NMAH exhibition
team reaffirms its commitment to the goals and balanced tone of the exhibition'.[9] As does I. Michael Heyman, who became Secretary of the Smithsonian
Institution *tout court* in September 1994, and who promised that changes
in response to criticism by the American Physical Society would 'render the
exhibition a lot more balanced' (in Macilwain 1996: 95).

'Balance' seems to refer both to the substance of materials to be displayed in
the exhibition and to the process through which they were selected. Looking at
the finished product, Molella and his assistant Carlene Stephens write that
SAL represents 'not only the benefits but also costs, consequences and social
responsibility' (Molella and Stephens 1996: 99) that attend the growing
significance of science in America. A member of the advisory board, its only
sociologist, says much the same thing in a letter to *The New York Times*:

> For every example of where . . . science [is] tied to unspeakable horrors,
> visitors will find an example of accomplishment and human betterment . . .
> In this exhibition, science does not come off to us as [a] . . . demon behind
> environmental degradation, nuclear fear and social injustice, but neither does
> it become a blameless panacea for these and other ills.
>
> (Gieryn 1995: 14)

A balanced representation of the good and evil wrought by science is said to
result from a process of exhibition-negotiation that was itself balanced – in
appreciating and reflecting diverse interpretations of the past. Molella says that
'the final narrative was the product of open and vigorous debate' (Molella 1994a:
13) among curators, advisory board members and scholarly consultants. It
was important to arrive at an exhibition that 'avoids taking sides', even though
'consensus among the curators on the team was not easily achieved' (Molella and
Stephens 1996: 97, 100). Molella is at pains to suggest that the issues covered
by *SAL* are 'highly debatable', and that respect for the multiplicity of framings
was achieved by enlarging the number and background experiences (and interests) of those who participated in its making. Neither 'members of the American
scientific community' nor 'scientists, sociologists, historians and educators on
our exhibit's advisory committee' (Molella 1994b: 13) believe that there can be
only one reading of science in American life, but their presence at occasionally
contentious deliberations about the exhibition ensured that it would depict both
the up-side of science, and its down.

For *SAL* curators, a balanced exhibition is also one which invites visitors to
draw their own conclusions from a rich display of materials that does not steer
them in only one direction. The goal is to raise questions rather than provide
answers: 'the exhibit does . . . force the visitor to confront questions about
the relationship between science and society – questions that were, presumably,

precisely the ones that the curators wanted us to consider' (Lewenstein 1996: 12). Molella suggests that *SAL* invites visitors themselves to participate in controversies over the place of science in American society, as he draws a self-exemplifying connection between science as an orderly debate about reality and democracy as an orderly debate about political principles: 'our goal was not to stir up controversy but to provide challenging and balanced information about the fascinating entanglement of science in society' (Molella 1994b: 2); 'Far from being detrimental, dissent and debate are essential to scientific progress, as they are to the health of a democratic society' (Molella 1995). Audience surveys conducted since the exhibition opened suggest that *SAL* may have succeeded in its goal to provide a display so balanced that visitors would be able to make their own informed judgments. Most visitors enter the exhibition feeling generally positive about science, and 'their views were reinforced rather than changed in either a positive or negative direction' (in Macilwain 1996: 95). One reviewer found *SAL* so successful in reaching what (evidently) everybody wanted for it that it came out 'balanced to the point of being innocuous' (Kleiner 1995).

Identical themes turn up in defence of the never-built *Crossroads* exhibition, with its *Enola Gay*. Martin Harwit, astrophysicist and historian of science, was 'relieved' of his position as Director of the National Air and Space Museum in the wake of the controversy, and has been the most vigorous defender of both the aims and achievements of the exhibition. In one of many letters that he wrote to explain the aims of *Crossroads* to increasingly hostile critics from veterans' organizations and eventually Congress,[10] Harwit suggests that 'this exhibit will give a balanced account of the decision to drop the bomb, the 509th Composite Group, the missions themselves and the aftermath' (Harwit 1996: 137). The proposed script went through many revisions and the exhibition changed its name more than once as balance proved to be elusive.[11] Secretary Heyman was, early on, convinced that a revised script 'now strikes the appropriate balance' (in ibid.: xii), although he would later kill the elaborate display of the *Enola Gay* in favour of a stripped-down version. In the wake of mounting criticism that *Crossroads* lacks balance (discussed shortly), Harwit formed a 'Tiger Team' review to 'be certain that the exhibition we mount is indeed balanced' (ibid.: 280). At times, even military historians such as Alfred Goldberg, Historian for the Secretary of Defense, could endorse *Crossroads* as a 'balanced presentation' (in ibid.: 307); or former Air Force historian Richard H. Kohn, who praised the text as 'cautious and balanced' (Kohn 1996: 148).

As with *SAL*, the goal of balance blurs substantive content and process: incorporating diverse perspectives becomes the means for telling a whole story. For its defenders, *Crossroads* is substantively balanced because it anchors the *Enola Gay* in the history that came before and in the future that was to come. Harwit replies to his arch-critic John T. Correll, editor in chief of *Air Force* magazine: 'it will show the circumstances that led to the development and ultimate use of the atomic bomb. It will show the immediate consequences of the bombings, the rapid increase of nuclear arsenals over the forty-year-long Cold War, and the present-day dismantling of nuclear weaponry' (Harwit 1994: 4). Such a balanced tale cannot be told from the vantage-point of one but only from those of many: scholars, documents, diplomatic eye-witnesses, veterans, the Japanese. Thomas L. Freudenheim, Assistant Secretary at the Smithsonian, puts the *Enola Gay* squabble in a broader context of the political mandate of the museum, which, 'as a national museum . . . cannot therefore take only one point of view on this question, given the diversity of opinion in this country' – and ends with the predictable invocation of 'balanced and thoughtful' (in Harwit 1996: 130). Harwit 'wanted to make sure we also included the point of view of the vanquished as well as the point of view of the victors' (in Correll 1994a: 28), and not just to avoid a diplomatic incident in then-declining relations between the United States and Japan. He knew 'how careful we would need to be to respect Japanese sensitivities' (Harwit 1996: 56). But balance also demanded that Harwit respect the sensitivities of veterans' groups and historians, something he was surely willing (but, in the end, unable) to do. In a letter hoping to cool out Donald Rehl, a B-29 pilot in the 509th Composite Group that was trained to deliver the atomic bomb, Harwit writes: 'This exhibit will give a balanced account of the decision to drop the bomb . . . All points of view will be represented, including of course the viewpoint of veterans such as yourself' (ibid.: 137). *Crossroads* was to have featured video-taped recollections from various players, including Paul Tibbetts (pilot of the *Enola Gay*, named by him after his mother), Japanese and American soldiers, scholars, survivors of the blast and – to emphasize interpretative diversity – Curtis LeMay and Kurt Vonnegut (ibid.: 107, 181).

A balanced exhibition invites visitors to participate in scholarly and political debates over the bomb, by providing them with the historical wherewithal to decide for themselves. Questions are posed; answers always hedged. In the earliest proposal for an *Enola Gay* display, Michael Neufeld (he and Tom Crouch were the curators in charge) admits that 'controversy is nonetheless unavoidable', but the purpose of the exhibition remains 'to convey to the general public some of the moral and political dilemmas of the decision to drop the bomb' (in ibid.: 121). Harwit assures Robert McC. Adams, Heyman's predecessor at the Smithsonian's helm, that 'the exhibit will deliberately avoid judgement or the imposition of any particular point of view, but will give visitors enough information to form their own impressions' (ibid.: 108). Evidently concerned that his curators did not get the point, Harwit wrote to Crouch: 'Where is it that a visitor ever has a chance to formulate an independent opinion? Where does a visitor have a chance to see for himself whether the war in the Far East differed from that in Europe, or for that matter from other wars throughout history? . . . But the headings seem to be overly dramatic and one-sided . . . If anything, the labels must be dispassionate, perhaps even bland . . . so that visitors will not be forced into one particular line of thinking' (ibid.: 184).

There is little news, I suppose, in hearing that scholars/curators hope to achieve exhibits that reflect a diversity of opinion about science and the *Enola Gay*, that refrain from imposing a party line on museum visitors, that present events as having both good and evil consequences. Such attitudes towards the representation of history are enshrined as norms governing this community of scholars and knowledge makers – disinterestedness, scepticism, detachment and multi-valency. It may be more surprising for historians and sociologists in particular to learn that they have no monopoly on such an appreciation of balance. Chemists who criticized *SAL* and veterans' organizations which criticized *Crossroads* took up the same language in defence of the different exhibitions they hoped to see at the Smithsonian (and, in the case of the *Enola Gay*, did see). Neither curator nor critic fought these battles with the weapon of Truth, or History as it really was: everybody pursued balance.

Very little criticism of *SAL* has yet made it to print. Unlike the controversy over *Crossroads* (which quickly moved into the mass media), organizations of scientists unhappy with the Smithsonian's emerging portrait of science voiced their concerns in letters to curators and museum executives or in meetings behind closed doors. The American Chemical Society did not believe that it received a good return on its $5 million investment in *SAL*, and one year after the exhibition opened the ACS formed a special committee of its Board of Directors to negotiate changes. After another year of apparently futile efforts to reframe *SAL*, Joan E. Shields (chairman of the Special Board Committee on the Smithsonian Exhibition) wrote in *Chemical and Engineering News* that the ACS had in effect washed its hands of *SAL*: 'further negotiations would be unproductive'. All along, the ACS desired only balance in the public representation of science in American life. The 'specific changes' requested by the ACS 'would provide more balance', but when left unchanged 'the Smithsonian still does not provide the desired balance in the exhibition' (Shields 1996).

This hope for balance echoes what critics of *SAL* had been saying from the start. Minutes of the first meeting of the *SAL* Advisory Board show several members arguing that 'the script needed more balance'.[12] At the ceremonial opening of the exhibition, ACS chairman of the Board, Paul H. L. Walter, was constrained by norms of celebration to declare in his after dinner remarks that *SAL* presents 'millions of people with a balanced view of what science and chemistry have done'.[13] Later assessments by scientists were less charitable: Burton Richter, president of the American Physical Society, volunteered the assistance of his society to work with the Smithsonian toward refashioning 'a more balanced portrayal of the impact of science and technology on American life' (in Holden, 1994).

Critics suggest that the as-built *SAL* plays up the unwanted and often disastrously unanticipated by-products of science at the expense of its many salutary accomplishments – and so lacks balance in its substance. Robert Park of the APS gently reminds the Smithsonian 'that advances in science have a potential for harm as well as benefits' (Park 1994: 209), while chemist Ned

Heindel of the Advisory Board is less gentle: 'there are a handful of places in *SAL* where the negative impact is not adequately balanced by good things' (in Nemecek 1995: 2). Park then pulls off his gloves for some serious slugging: 'The atomic bomb [*SAL* has a mushroom cloud] is the ultimate symbol of science as an instrument of death and terror. What could an exhibit possibly offer to "balance" nuclear weapons? Surely not nylon stockings. Perhaps the development of antibiotics . . . No hint that penicillin, along with the other antibiotics that followed, has saved many thousands of lives for every life taken by nuclear weapons and radioactive waste' (Park 1994: 208). To rebalance *SAL* as an even-handed display of good and bad outcomes of science would accomplish what Shields presents as the ACS's interest in becoming financial backer of the exhibition: 'to improve the public understanding of science' (Shields 1996). Just as curator Molella conceived of balance as providing the opportunity for museum visitors to reach their own informed conclusions about science in American life, so does Heindel believe that the point of *SAL* is 'to give the public at least some of the basics to help it make informed decisions about such issues as recycling, safety of genetically engineered foods, and the risks and benefits of having a manufacturing plant in its community' (in Ross 1994: 4). But it failed, says biologist Paul Gross, who sees *SAL* as sickened by the same anti-science virus that afflicts academic science studies, because 'people were not given the chance to judge for themselves'.[14]

The same theme emerges from the more voluminous criticisms of *Crossroads*. Editor Correll's exposé of goings-on at the National Air and Space Museum elicited a letter to his *Air Force* magazine: 'We had been assured that the *Enola Gay* exhibit sought only to show a balanced view of the events of Hiroshima and Nagasaki – the horrors of war for all participants' (Lambert 1994: 5). But such was not on the drawing board: Air Force historian Richard Hallion believes that the reason Harwit, Couch and Neufeld 'came under heavy pressure' was 'because the *Enola Gay* script was not in balance nor context' (in Correll 1994b: 64), and because they offered 'a vastly unbalanced visual presentation' (in Harwit 1996: 262). Well after Harwit and his curators sought to accommodate changes requested by the Air Force Association, the AFA's Executive Director Monroe W. Hatch, Jr. believed that 'the exhibit still lacks balance and context . . . You can't give visitors to the museum and students of history a balanced perspective of World War II if you only show the "last act"' (in ibid.: 303). In a letter to Harwit, Hatch writes that the script 'seems even less balanced . . . than the earlier concepts were', and 'balance is owed all Americans, particularly those who come to the exhibition to learn' (in ibid.: 200). Members of Congress beat the same drum in a letter to the Smithsonian, finding 'the original exhibit and accompanying script to be lacking in balance and context' (in ibid.: 257); and on the Senate floor: 'the script continues to lack balance and context' (Senator Kassebaum, in Thelen 1995a: 1137).[15]

For critics of *Crossroads*, balance most often refers to equivalent displays of potent images and artefacts that would recreate the whole moment in which the

Enola Gay was asked to make its historic run: if photographs of atomic bomb victims are shown, so too must the atrocities of Japanese war camps; if numbers of lives lost at Hiroshima and Nagasaki are reported, so too must the numbers of Allied lives lost in the Pacific campaign and the numbers of lives saved (both American and Japanese) by the bomb's bringing the war to a quick end. After an early meeting with museum officials, Correll writes in a memo to file:

> We said the concept paper was not balanced, and that it did not provide adequate background or accurately depict the context in which the decision to drop the bomb was made . . . We made an issue of the emotional impact of the school child's lunch box [retrieved from Hiroshima, with charcoal food in it] and pointed out that there was nothing on the other side for balance.
>
> (in Harwit 1996: 207)

Plainly, veterans' organizations hoped the exhibition would provide a sufficiently balanced historical context so that the decisions to drop atomic bombs would at least appear reasonable, legitimate, justifiable and perhaps even necessary – avoiding the unbalanced inference that they were (definitively) atrocities or a second Holocaust. Navy historian Kathleen Lloyd proposed several changes to bring the proposed script into greater balance:

> For balance, more details should be included on the Japanese treatment of the Asian countries that they conquered and of the Allied prisoners of war . . . Also for balance it should be made clear that no one knew the effect that the bomb would have or the lasting effect that radiation would have on individuals.
>
> (in ibid.: 264)

Consistently, critics call for balance, for completeness of the story, rather than for accuracy or fidelity to what happened in fact. The critics appreciate as much as *Crossroads*' curators that artefacts to be displayed and the captions attached to them are chosen *now* rather than determined by events *then*.

Neither do Correll and his allies insist that the exhibition tell just one story about the *Enola Gay*: as with *SAL*, a balanced display would allow visitors to reach their own judgments about what happened, how and why. Hubert R. Dagley II of the American Legion's Internal Affairs Commission said that the aircraft should be 'put . . . in context and let the erudite visitors make some decisions themselves' (in ibid.: 333). Everybody in the controversy over *Crossroads* seems to agree that the decision to drop the atomic bomb invites a variety of interpretations, and critics emphasize that interpretations by those who made that choice then may not square with the several interpretations available now. W. Burr Bennett, Jr., a Second World War veteran, asked in a letter to Adams of the Smithsonian: 'Is it honest to judge what happened in 1945 by the morality of today?' (in ibid.: 131). As the dispute wore on and as a common understanding of balance proved enduringly elusive (the Air Force Association concludes that 'a fair and balanced presentation of the *Enola Gay* is not possible with the present director-curator team' [in ibid.: 391]), critics came to prefer a display of the aircraft in minimalist interpretive dress – precisely because they did not want to impose any particular reading on museum visitors. Pilot Tibbetts prefers a naked *Enola Gay*: '"This airplane was the first one to drop an atomic bomb". You don't need any other explanations. And I think it should be displayed alone' (in Correll 1994b: 64).

I do not mean to suggest that the word 'fact' never appears in debates over these exhibitions, nor is it the case that a concern for 'accuracy' is altogether absent. My point is this: just as matters of fact did not precipitate the controversies, neither could History as it happened (rendered accurately) settle them. The contentious issue is always balance, or its lack: is the story an impartial whole and does it allow visitors to reach their own interpretations? Rare instances of realist discourse stand out against the pervasive background of arguments over balance, as when Harwit wants *Crossroads* 'to provide the public as accurate a historical picture as we can' (Harwit 1996: 205) or when B-29 pilot Benjamin Nicks wants the *Enola Gay* to be shown 'as an artefact of history as it was – not as some would have it' (in ibid.: 70). Even when accuracy becomes the concern, it is situated in the context of a perspectival epistemology in which what-really-happened radically underdetermines the representations of it. For Harwit, museums assume the scholarly responsibility 'to teach the truth' – but 'as best they understand it' (ibid.: 341); for Dagley of the American Legion, the goal was 'to achieve an exhibit that was historically accurate' – but one that 'could be evaluated from all perspectives' (in Linenthal 1996: 53).

At least in the *Crossroads* case, both sides evince ambivalence about whether matters of accuracy can be separated neatly from those of balance. Harwit seems to know the distinction in principle: '*Accuracy* concerns factual information. Are the facts, figures, names, ages, dates, weights, measures, all correct? . . . *Balance* refers to the selection of facts and objects included in the exhibition' (Harwit 1996: 52; emphases in original). The Air Force Association's Hatch is also able to differentiate a just-completed '"technical" review of the script' from remaining 'issues of context and balance [which] need to be addressed' (in ibid.: 306). But what could be more factual – raising the technical question of accuracy – than a *number*:[16] the number of American casualties from the planned invasion of Japan that was obviated by the two atomic bombs. A higher number makes the bombs all that much more justifiable in terms of American lives saved; a lower number, especially when coupled with casualty figures from Hiroshima and Nagasaki, makes alternatives to the bomb more reasonable. The heated debate between curators and critics over this number was not framed in terms of getting it right, but in terms of balance – it became a matter of negotiation, not discovery or veracity. In a meeting memo to his files, Correll notes that Neufeld had admitted that his low (20,000–30,000) casualty estimate referred to the 'invasion of the southern island only', but added that 'higher casualty estimates – such as the often-cited 500,000 – could not be used because veterans groups use a figure of 1–2 million (??!!) and would not be satisfied with anything lower'. Correll believes that Neufeld's proposed solution at that meeting – to mention no casualty estimate at all – eliminates 'the impact of a key point in the decision to drop the bomb', and – significantly – 'just happens to tilt the balance toward the point we believe they [the curators] are trying to make' (in ibid.: 208). Edward T. Linenthal, scholar of battlefield memorializations and a member of the Advisory Board, also makes the number into a question of balance: 'The August 1994 revised script offered a new label, "Invasion of Japan – At What Cost?" and tried to balance lower and higher estimates ("from 30,000 to 500,000")' (ibid.: 55). Historian Stanley Goldberg, a Smithsonian curator displeased by the process through which history was horse-traded, was discouraged that 'Harwit and the American Legion representatives eventually *negotiated* a figure – 229,000 – for the expected number of U.S. casualties' (Goldberg 1995: 32; emphasis in original).

In general, and not just in the case of casualty estimates, it seems that even if curators and critics could agree on every instance of accuracy, the controversy would scarcely cool, as Harwit realizes after it is over:

> I believed the historic facts brought out in the exhibition script to be largely correct . . . The exhibition's opponents instead appeared upset by the way these facts were presented, the choice of laudatory or pejorative wording, the juxtaposition of evidence implying certain conclusions, and the choice and balance of artefacts, images, and factual material.
>
> (Harwit 1996: 274)

'EVERYBODY ELSE IS OFF-BALANCE'

To defend a proposed exhibition, or attack it, curators and critics present the show they prefer as balanced – and that of the other side as dangerously off-balance. Off-balance seems to mean a display that is one-sided because it steers visitors towards only one of several available interpretations of historical events and processes. Despite otherwise huge differences between *SAL* and *Crossroads* – differences in subject-matters, organizational cultures at the two Smithsonian branches, personalities, interested parties, stakes, symbolic significance and, most notably, outcomes – the substantive content of 'being off-balance' is remarkably consistent. Critics accuse curators of preparing an exhibition tipped towards a demonic representation of science and of the *Enola Gay*. Curators accuse critics of seeking to replace the proposed script with something unabashedly heroic. The scale used to weigh the two exhibitions is more or less the same:

Critics accuse curators of • ———————————— • Curators accuse critics of
DEMONIC HISTORY   Λ   **HEROIC HISTORY**

Everybody involved puts themselves in the safe middle – Harwit and the Air Force Association, Molella and the American Chemical Society. But everybody also gets accused by somebody else of being inclined towards a partial history (in both senses: incomplete and biased).

Philosopher Christina Hoff Sommers helped bring the controversy over *SAL* into the public eye with an editorial in the *Wall Street Journal*, which prompted an exchange of letters. She joins the ACS and other professional associations of scientists in criticizing 'the perverse decision to highlight the failures of American science and to downplay the triumphs'. Sommers believes that *SAL* presents an 'overwhelmingly negative view of American scientific achievement', and that 'head curator Arthur Molella was unmoved by the ACS's complaint that the exhibit lacked balance' (Sommers 1995a, 1995b). Richter of the American Physical Society (APS) 'directed a formal blast' at *SAL* in *Science* magazine, 'on grounds that it "trivializes [scientific] accomplishments and exaggerates any negative consequences"' (in Holden 1994: 1327). Robert Park, also of the APS, catalogues the woes blamed on science: 'pesticide residue, air pollution, acid rain, ozone holes, radioactive waste, food additives and nuclear bombs' – but 'no mention that life expectancy in the United States has more than doubled in the last century' (Park 1995a: 15).

Other critics suggest that this demonic science is not in History but only in the minds of Smithsonian curators granted the authority to tell it. The problem is not science but Molella, who is said to want 'pollution and death' (in Flam 1994: 729), whose exhibition 'betrays hostility to natural science . . . in the form of horror stories' (Gross 1996: 118), and whose staff included those 'in influential positions . . . who . . . wanted to thumb their noses at the scientific establishment' (in Gifford 1996: 6). The language of balance pervades criticism of *SAL*, as from Advisory Board member Marcel LaFollette: 'the lead curators seemed so fearful of building a "pro-science" exhibit . . . that they wound up creating a largely negative one' (LaFollette 1995: 237). Those critics, though, are wary of tipping too far the other way: 'Richter denies that the APS insists that science should be portrayed heroically. "Of course, science can be misused . . . what's missing here is balance"' (in Macilwain 1995).

Curators for *Crossroads* are accused of doing much the same thing to the *Enola Gay*. Sacrificing subtlety for impact, one member of a review panel said that he would leave the proposed exhibit 'with a strong feeling that Americans are bloodthirsty, racist killers who after beer parties and softball go out and kill as many women and children as possible' (in Correll 1994c: 12).[17] In the *Crossroads* seen by its critics, the United States military (and its government) is demonized for its decision to use the hydrogen bomb, becoming by turns 'brutal, vindictive' (in Correll 1994a: 26), 'ruthless invaders, bent on revenge' (Correll 1994c: 8), and 'the culprits' (Correll 1994b: 64). *Air Force* editor Correll divorces this representation from History and marries it to the Smithsonian, whose curators had previously displayed their 'hostile view of air-power' in an exhibition on the First World War, which emphasized 'carnage on the ground and the unwholesomeness of military aviation . . . the military airplane as an instrument of death' (Correll 1994a: 26).

So off-balance is *Crossroads* that its only heroes are Japanese. Kamikaze pilots are portrayed as 'valiant defenders of their home land' (ibid.: 29), and, generally, for the AFA's Hatch, the exhibition 'gives the benefit of opinion to Japan' (in Correll 1994a: 26).[18] When the Japanese are not depicted as heroes, they become victims of American ruthlessness. The Air Force Association believes that the curators 'are so sensitive to the *Hibakusha* (survivors of the atomic bombs) that a museum visitor might think these Japanese are the only ones for whom suffering continued after the war' (in Correll 1994c: 10). Correll suggests that balance could be achieved if images of the *hibakusha* were counterpoised with those of disabled American veterans. The Japanese who are given voice in exhibition videos and captions are, Correll says, those who had 'suffered injuries', and who 'talk about pain and suffering' (Correll 1994a: 28). William M. Detweiler from the American Legion identifies the missing counterweight – Japan's own aggressiveness:

> It prompts the unmistakable conclusion that America's enemy in the latter days of World War II was defeated and demoralised, ultimately the victim of racism and revenge, rather than a ruthless aggressor whose expansionist aims and war fervour yielded more than a decade of horror and death for millions of the world's people.
>
> (in Linenthal 1996: 47–8)

In the earliest scripts, little was said about 'years of aggression and wanton atrocities and brutality' (Correll 1994b: 64) by the Japanese, and even when something was added: 'aggressiveness on their side is depicted as the province of a few military fanatics' (ibid.: 62). All this added up to the 'distinctive ideological tilt' (ibid.: 62) of the script.

Curators' defences of their preferred exhibitions mirror all this: it is the *critics* now who are off-balance, weighted down by desires for a one-sided *heroic* tale of American science or the *Enola Gay*. It is quickly apparent that critics are not the only ones to stereotype the others' tilt, to exaggerate balance into skew. Molella and Stephens write that critics of *SAL* 'press their cause for their own version of history' (Molella and Stephens 1996: 97), and, according to Bruce Lewenstein (who reviewed the exhibition from the perspective of science journalism), the ACS was never really comfortable with the balanced idea that 'history is precisely the telling of multiple stories about the past' (Lewenstein 1996: 12). In exchange for $5 million, chemists (as constructed by defensive curators) hoped for 'heroic science' and a 'trade show' (in Gifford 1996: 6). Even though museum officials were 'very frank in telling them [the ACS] that the exhibit we had in mind was not celebratory, but analytic',[19] critics still seemed disappointed that *SAL* did not become 'something about the triumphs of science' (Molella in Flam 1994: 729) and that the Smithsonian Institutions did not become 'boosters' of American science (Macilwain 1995: 207). The curators' goal instead, was, of course, balance: 'to show how society has changed and use that to show something about how science works' (Flam 1994).

Ditto, for the failed defence of *Crossroads*. The veterans' groups would settle for one story only, their story, precluding the multiple readings invited by the curators' script – or so said the Smithsonian people. Critics 'would never be satisfied with a dispassionate exhibit reflecting a variety of perspectives' (Harwit 1996: x) – but, remember, Correll and friends accused Harwit, Crouch and Neufeld of exactly the same partisanship (while denying that they insisted on 'only one history' [Bernstein 1995: 215]). In contrast to Harwit's advisers and staff, who admitted their differences of opinion and sought to work those disagreements into the exhibition itself, the military historians and other critics are said to demand consensus to a party line: 'if there was even one dissenting voice . . . every one else fell in line' (Harwit 1996: 270). Curators had proposed a series of displays featuring 'Historical Controversies', which would emphasize historians' multiple and merely provisional understandings of events. MIT professor John W. Dower, author of several books on Japan and the Pacific theatre during the Second World War, suggested that these displays of controversy were, for the American Legion, 'the very antithesis of simply telling history "like it was", and obviously suggested that no single "truth" could be proclaimed regarding the decision to drop the bombs'. That was an anathema for the veterans: 'Heroic narratives demand a simple unilinear story line' (Dower 1996: 80).

And that is what the Air Force Association and American Legion expected from the *Enola Gay* exhibition, as these desires were constructed by Air and Space Museum curators – who feared (and loathed) 'straightforward celebration' (Harwit 1996: 184). As Harwit saw it, the American Legion 'wanted their membership to feel heroic and have the nation's enthusiastic approval for the atomic bombings' (ibid.: 398). 'They want the Museum to tell their story the way they have always told and retold it . . . a story of a powerful new aircraft, designed, built and first flown in just 24 months; a story of ordinary citizens, men and women, working together to defeat a ferocious enemy' (ibid.: 311). Harwit collapses his critics' exhibition down to a simple tale lacking polysemy: 'the *Enola Gay* had not only ended World War II, but had also saved millions of lives' (ibid.: 148). Critics wanted to 'force [this] view of the war . . . on fellow Americans . . . American virtue and victory *were* to be celebrated' (Sherry 1996: 103). But that heroic tale already required curators to censor history, hiding details from the public who would be less able to draw informed lessons. Tom Crouch was quoted in a syndicated column, talking about the veterans' criticisms: 'What we're really looking at here is a reluctance to really tell the whole story . . . They want to stop the story when the bomb leaves the bomb bay . . . [censoring] what happens when it hits the ground'. In a rhetorical tour de force, Crouch (via a letter to Harwit) seizes the balanced middle ground for the curators while pushing the veterans' associations off on the extreme: 'Do you want to do an exhibition intended to make veterans feel good, or do you want an exhibition that will lead our visitors to think about the consequences of the atomic bombing of Japan? Frankly, I don't think we can do both' (in Harwit 1996: 309, 189). Missing is the other extreme, the demonic story of what Americans did with their bombs, which turns up of course only as critics' characterization of what Crouch really wanted.

'NOBODY BUT US IS OBJECTIVE'

Stalemate? Real History is nowhere around for either curators or critics to use in efforts to dismiss as just *wrong* the exhibitions favoured by the other side. Assertions of historical accuracy are deconstructed by opponents into evidence instead of off-balance – they reveal a desire to compel just one True story in the name of what really happened, precluding the possibility that visitors could make their own informed judgments about artefacts, events and their significance. Nobody's claim to balance goes unchallenged, but rather all are equivalently torpedoed by charges that a proposed exhibition tends towards the heroic (if we listen to curators) or demonic (according to critics). Are there any useful arguments left still standing – with historical realism only a liability, and balance rhetorically undermined with apparent ease – through which curators and critics might still legitimize and justify the exhibitions they prefer? The discourse of objectivity in its manifold meanings – trust, uniquely privileged perspective, disinterestedness (pinned to oneself but denied to foes) – moves the Museum Wars further from History and even beyond its balanced accounting. Victory hinges on the credibilities of the *people* who would make *SAL* and *Crossroads* into very different representations of the past.

Trust

It is usually difficult to declare without irony, in public or academic debate, 'trust me – I'm honest'. Instead, curators and critics provide grounds for denying trust to their opponents by describing them as dishonest, double-dealing and duplicitous scoundrels who will stoop to the unethical in defence of a certain exhibition they like. Arthur Molella accuses Robert Park, loud critic of *SAL* from the American Physical Society, of 'obviously [having] never seen the exhibit at all'.[20] To defuse Sommers's criticism that *SAL* plays up the débâcles of science, Molella says that she 'utterly distorts the exhibit', and ends with: 'I hardly recognized the show [she] attacked' (Molella 1995). Some of the attacks on *SAL* occurred in cyberspace, and Molella and Stephens suggest that the internet version of the exhibition – in his judgment, 'an electronic straw man' – justifiably angered scientists with its misrepresentations. On the Web, even the exhibition's title was routinely miscast as 'Is Science the God that Failed?' (a label introduced by Park 1995b: A11). Turnabout is fair play. Sommers writes that Molella and other Smithsonian officials stonewalled *SAL* by refusing to negotiate in good faith: 'Molella was unmoved by the ACS's complaint that the exhibit lacked balance' (Sommers 1995a: 414), and Park writes that 'advisory committee members complain bitterly that their recommendations were ignored by the chief curator' (Park 1995b). More evidence of bad faith is given by the ACS's Shields, who suggests that the ACS trumped up the cost of making requested changes in the exhibition: adding one sentence to an extant label would cost $4,205.

Accusations of untrustworthy conduct become high art in the controversy over *Crossroads*. Harwit 'was convinced that General Tibbetts had never read our script' (Harwit 1996: 290), but relied on deliberately massaged but bogus versions provided him by the Air Force Association – a serious problem for the museum because of Tibbetts's symbolic authority as the *Enola Gay's* pilot. But Tibbetts was not alone in criticizing what he putatively had not read. Harwit justifies his desire to have the full text of *Crossroads* published (indeed it was, but only after the final decision to kill the exhibition), because 'so much had been written and said about this exhibit, by people who had never read the script or who quoted it out of context' (ibid.: 415). 'Significant misinformation and unfounded rumor' (ibid.: 246) constituted the foundation for the veterans' criticisms of *Crossroads*, a point made as well by one of Harwit's few allies in the military. Lt.-Gen. C. M. Kicklighter, Executive Director of the 50th Anniversary of WWII Commemoration Committee argues that 'the NASM's opponents have gone out of their way to misrepresent the Museum's intention' (in ibid. 1996: 305). Harwit gives one instance of this: having been accused of trying to mount an exhibition that would portray the United States and Japan as having had 'morally equivalent' positions in the Second World War, he says that this idea 'would clearly be outrageous and never entered any of our minds' (ibid.: 203).

Critics' supposed misrepresentations of the evolving *Enola Gay* script take several forms. Some critics seek to manipulate legislative charters defining the mission of the Smithsonian Institutions in order to show that the proposed exhibition falls outside its mandated purview. But Harwit points out that Second World War veteran W. Burr Bennett relied on 1961 enabling legislation for a 'National Armed Forces Museum' which was authorized but neither funded nor built (ibid.: 148). Another tactic is to fabricate misleading images of *Crossroads* by statistical legerdemain. In response to Correll's assertion that the still-unbalanced revised script contained 97 images of Japanese suffering, not the 32 actually in the script, Harwit writes: 'how he obtained those particular numbers was not clear' (ibid.: 253). But even if Correll and other critics had read the proposed script accurately, they would still be prone to misleading misrepresentation because they would not be able to take into account the specific juxtaposition of differently-sized images and artefacts (or lighting, the videos, voice-overs) – which may be more consequential for visitors' take-home messages than details on a label (ibid.: 215).

Deceitful misrepresentations of the curators' intentions and of the exhibition's contents do not exhaust the sins of the critics. Air Force historian Hallion is in effect accused by Harwit of double-dealing when – in the course of later denunciations of the exhibition as unbalanced – he denied that he had praised the proposed script. In the posthumous defence of *Crossroads*, Harwit includes the full text of Hallion's favourable assessment, in which three type-script pages of minor suggestions are followed by the handwritten note: 'Again – an impressive job. A bit of "tweaking" along the lines discussed here, should do the trick' (in ibid.: 224). When Harwit learned later that the Air Force Association had enlisted Hallion to its camp of critics, Harwit assumed at first that they must 'surely be misquoting' him (ibid.: 249). Harwit also accuses the Air Force Association of 'stirring up public protest' (ibid.: 277) by falsely accusing the curators of wilful bias, and worse, by disclosing the substance of delicate negotiations to the mass media. 'We no longer could openly talk with each other without fear of having our conversation reported and analyzed in the newspapers the next day' (ibid.: 305).

Critics see just this issue in a different light. For them, timely access to information is vital for accountability, ensuring democratic accessibility to the negotiations over the public's museum in Washington. Correll accuses curators of stonewalling when – under protection of copyright – they would not allow photocopying of a revised script for *Crossroads* 'without permission from the Smithsonian Institution' (Correll 1994b: 61). Charles D. Cooper, editor of the *Retired Officer*, specifically regrets the curators' 'early stonewalling' (in Harwit 1996: 334) which fast became a perennial theme in efforts to depict Harwit and other museum officials as unwilling to compromise in good faith. Curators 'waved off the rest [of the criticisms] as "disinformation"', 'were not to be dissuaded' (Correll 1994c: 8, 12), offered up 'the usual regimented response' (Nicks in Harwit 1996: 71) and generally were 'unwilling to repair' (Hallion in ibid.: 262) an obviously broken script. In response to a *New York Times* editorial that presented curators instead as adjusting the script responsively to diverse criticism, Correll denies their co-operativeness by pointing out that 'the curators shrugged off appeals for change until the pressure became too much to ignore' (Correll 1994c: 9). This admission by critics of their ability to put pressure on the Smithsonian opens the door for Harwit's defence: they 'do their best to hide from the public the enormous influence they wield' (Harwit 1996: vii). Harwit declares that he has nothing to hide from the public, and that it is the Air Force Association really who 'never did cite . . . that the script had already undergone five months of revisions' involving veterans' organizations as well as scholars (ibid.: 301). For Correll, Harwit's stonewalling is not the result of a principled defence of a better exhibition, but rather a feature of his customary duplicitous conduct designed only to keep critics at bay. After Harwit admitted that the script contained too many gruesome ground-zero photographs from Hiroshima and Nagasaki, and after directing his curators to remove about two-thirds of them: 'that did *not* happen' (Correll 1994b: 60; emphasis in original). When Harwit revised casualty estimates back downwards – after 'previously agreed language' – he is accused by the AFA of a 'breach of faith' (in Harwit 1996: 386). Following an agreement on 7 June 1994 to take 'about a year' to remove perceived imbalances, Harwit announces but two weeks later that the curators had reached 'a final product, minor wording changes aside' (Correll 1994b: 60). Such double-dealing is of a piece with Harwit's 'imaginative interpretation of what we [the Air Force Association] actually said', and with his conjuring of a mythical exhibition when describing *Crossroads* for public audience (ibid.). Worst of all, Harwit is accused of defaming the iconic General Curtis Lemay – whom he attempts to use, 'without merit', 'as a crutch' (Lambert 1994). Diogenes and lantern would have been frustrated walking among those who argued the fate of the *Enola Gay*.

Privileged perspective

The very idea of objectivity implies that not all standpoints are equally well-vantaged for looking out at nature or back on history. Some perspectives are clouded, either by ignorance or prejudice – and the two Smithsonian controversies are fat with both accusations. Here I consider just the first sort: the standpoint of the other side lacks perspicuity – which is located uniquely in scholarly *expertise* for the curators and in personal *experience* for the critics. In the end, there probably is no Archimedean point from which one could decide that 'being well read' is a more privileged perspective on the past than 'being there' (or vice versa) – and so the argument went unquelled.

Curators ground their defence of the scripts on what they have the most of – skill in deciphering meaning from historical documents and artefacts, and fluency in ever-contentious academic interpretations of them. That already-introduced sociologist on the *SAL* Advisory Board wrote a letter to Molella's predecessor, historian Jeffrey Stine, to say that he 'shall write as a practitioner of science and technology studies [STS] seeking to shift the main messages of that line of inquiry from the pages of scholarly journals to corridors of the Smithsonian', because 'STS opens up new ways of looking at science in American life'.[21] He was evidently convincing, for Lewenstein – in a review of the completed *SAL* – praises it for its ability 'to inject insights of recent scholarship in history and sociology of science' (Lewenstein 1995: 3). But it was a struggle to fend off the know-nothings on the Advisory Board and elsewhere – those who lack the penetrating insights of recent academic scholarship *about* science. Molella and Stephens write that 'stakeholding interest groups' 'will not tolerate a "master narrative" crafted behind the scenes by "experts" who exclude their experiences' (Molella and Stephens 1996: 105). The implicit contention is that *SAL* is a better exhibit precisely because it incorporates the views of STS and other scholarly research, and would only be weakened if criticisms were heeded from those who are ignorant of it.

In the same way, *Crossroads* is defended as embodying the latest scholarly understandings of the Second World War and of the atomic bomb. Harwit distances the exhibition from his own personal opinions, anchoring them instead 'in a committee that includes some of the nation's leading military historians and experts on the war' (Harwit 1994: 4).[22] Curator Michael Neufeld says that a revised script is 'consistent with the latest scholarship' (in Harwit 1996: 300), as it exploits an academic expertise that is distinguished (in the early proposal for an *Enola Gay* exhibition) from private views held by exhibition critics: 'Almost everyone has an opinion on this matter, but these opinions are often shaped by limited knowledge and personal prejudices' (ibid.: 122). To replace mere opinion with certified knowledge is in the Smithsonian's charge: '"The increase and diffusion of knowledge", [and] to make this scholarly research accessible to the public' (Neufeld in ibid.: 281).

The exhibition is improved by the accumulated wisdom of historians who have unearthed previously unknown or inaccessible documents that 'show the problem to be more complex' (ibid.: 134). Scholars have been able to revise their understanding of events in light of new empirical materials: 'Often a much clearer view of events is available years later, when many secret actions and documents have come to light' (ibid.: 132). Availability of a previously classified 'Memo discussed with the President, April 25, 1925. Top Secret: Original and 3 carbons made', written by Truman's Secretary of War Henry Stimson (which lays out in hazy but frank ways what the post-atomic world might be like), is for Harwit 'like breaking through the fog of historian's opinions to personally glimpse fragments of the truth' (ibid.: 225). The significance of these recently released documents would be lost on veterans and others outside academe, who are more concerned about protecting traditional tales of glory: 'declassified information must not be permitted to change the way this story has always been told' (ibid.: 427). At first, Harwit seems blissfully optimistic that veterans too would get excited about new interpretations allowed by these documents, holding out for the possibility that knowledge based on personal experience might be corrigible: 'We were sure that veterans would find such an exhibition revealing of detail they had never known' (ibid.: x). The hindsight of Stanford historian Barton Bernstein, after *Crossroads* was killed, is closer to the mark: '[Correll] seemed unconcerned, and perhaps largely uninformed, that the scholarship of the last thirty years . . . had challenged important parts of that orthodox history' (Bernstein 1995: 215). That Correll would persist in his critique of *Crossroads*, choosing to ignore historical evidence that subverted his views, is a 'chilling broadside' threatening 'the lifeblood of serious intellectual inquiry . . . a constant willingness to entertain serious challenges to entrenched and orthodox views' (Dower 1996: 76). The stakes in this Museum War for curators and academic historians are becoming more clear: not just personal ambition or improved public understanding and certainly not Truth, but professional authority over history: 'For better or worse', writes Wisconsin historian Paul Boyer, 'it is the historians, at the end of the day, to whom society delegates its custodianship of the past' (Boyer 1996: 139).[23] Only on some days.

On the other side, exhibition critics (also) valorize what they have the most of: personal experience with events and processes to be displayed, and first-hand memory of how things were. It is altogether unexceptional (and even boring) to hear curators and historians insisting that the declassification of pertinent documents has forced historians to develop new interpretations of the end of the Second World War – until this rhetoric is set aside another discursive register that challenges the connection between such expert readings of empirical evidence and truth. Veterans are endowed with a presumptive authority to recall correctly what happened when they were there. 'We're vets, we've actually been in a Cold War – they haven't' (Giese in Sherry 1996: 100). Typical is a letter to *Air Force* magazine from retired Lt.-Gen. James V. Edmundson:

> I commanded a B-29 group on Tinian . . . As an American who was stationed at Hickam Field on December 7, 1941, who fought at such places as Midway, Tulagi and Guadalcanal . . . I deeply resent an agency of my government telling the American people that the war aims of the Japanese were more noble than those for which so many of my friends died.
>
> (Edmundson 1994)

Paul Fussell's essay 'Thank God for the Atom Bomb' is invoked by *Crossroads* critics – for example, B-29 reconnaissance flight photographer Burr Bennett – as possessing the privileged insider's insight:

> There are two mutually exclusive positions on the *Enola Gay* and its bombing mission. There are those assigned to wade ashore in the scheduled invasion of Japan, and those who were unborn, too young, or back home in their job. Paul Fussell . . . doesn't demand that the anti bomb folks 'experience having their ass shot off, I merely note that [they] didn't'. Those on their way to the invasion *knew* that the *Enola Gay*, *Bockscar*, the hasty entry of the Russians, and the atomic bombs saved their lives.
>
> (in Harwit 1996: 145; emphasis added)

So unbalanced is *Crossroads* that its producers must surely have had 'light regard for military perspectives . . . on a military subject' (Correll 1994b: 63), choosing to ignore or dismiss 'firsthand reports from veterans who fought the war' (Hatch in Harwit 1996: 307).[24] If curators had listened to the eye-witnesses, they would not have proposed an exhibition that became for Paul Tibbetts 'a package of insults' (in ibid.: 243).[25] Senator Ted Stevens from Alaska asked Linenthal during committee hearings: 'On what basis do you justify an interpretation of the history of this event so different from those of us who lived through it?' (in Thelen 1995b: 1034).

The expertise of scholars is delegitimized: those who were not there to see and feel cannot know what happened, no matter how carefully they pore over documents.[26] The deep currents of anti-intellectualism in American life rise to the surface in criticisms of *Crossroads*. Edmundson continues in his letter (started above) to say that he does not blame the Smithsonian Secretary personally for the off-balanced script, because 'after all, he is the product of his environment and typical of some of the educated idiots who crawl out from under the wet rock of academia from time to time' (Edmundson 1994). Such a blanket criticism of academic expertise elsewhere gives way to *ad hominem* attacks on the supposed credentials of Neufeld ('a Canadian citizen who spent his years at the University of Calgary between 1970 and 1974, when Americans were fleeing to Canada to escape the Vietnam war') and Crouch ('took his graduate courses at Miami University and Ohio State during the Vietnam War') (Ringle in Nobile 1995: xxxvi). The wrongs of the exhibition are traced back to one credential of supreme value to critics but absent in these two curators: experience at war.

Insiders are also accorded a privileged perspective in the controversy over *SAL*: it takes a scientist to know science. Chemist Marvin Lang described his time on the *SAL* Advisory Board as a 'gut wrenching experience' because he was asked to work in close company with 'social scientists and pseudo-scientists who had no idea how science worked' (in Macilwain 1995: 207). *Scientific American* reporter Sasha Nemecek notes that although the history of science was 'once the province of scientists with an interest in the past, the field has evolved into one in which practitioners may know more about society than about, say, chemistry' (Nemecek 1995: 24). Such a demographic transition helps Robert Park of the APS to account for the failures of *SAL*: social constructivists believe that 'science is just another narrative and has no greater claim to authority than any other narrative. On that basis, a Native American folk legend of the origin of humans should be taken as seriously as the theory of evolution' (in ibid: 24). *SAL* Advisory Board member Marcel LaFollette uses scare quotes to ironize the supposedly privileged perspective afforded insiders: 'The scientists "know" what science is all about; the veterans "know" what they remember from World War II' (LaFollette 1995: 238). Veterans and chemists would just as easily put scare quotes around LaFollette's academic 'knowledge', if her expertise conflicted with their experiential memory.

Disinterested apolitics

A final strategy for denying authenticity and credibility to others' claims is to reveal their ulterior motives of a political kind, to suggest that behind the script they prefer lies a hidden agenda that goes beyond the pursuit of balance or improved public understanding. Those on the other side have these political or economic interests that compel them to push for an exhibit not necessarily congruent with the interests of the general public and, moreover, they are part of some wider political or intellectual movement that leans precipitously to the Right (when curators attack critics) or to the Left (when critics attack curators). At the same time, everybody accused of playing politics displays the empty hands they bring to the controversy, and insist that they have only one goal – a balanced exhibition. With all the symmetry found in the rhetoric of curators and critics alike, it is important not to lose sight of the asymmetries on which each argument depends: *they* have politics, *we* don't; *we* can be trusted, *they* cannot.

The language of 'political correctness' runs throughout criticism of *SAL* and of *Crossroads*. Curators are said to toe the liberal line, as they sully American achievements in science or in war by recalling without end the many who suffer beneath the triumphs. For the *Wall Street Journal*, the National Air and Space Museum was 'now in the hands of academics unable to view American history as anything other than a woeful catalog of crimes and aggressions against the helpless people of the earth' (in Correll 1994c: 8). A boundary is placed between the politics of *Crossroads'* curators and the high-minded disinterestedness of its critics. Correll writes that the exhibition is 'more political than aeronautical' (ibid.: 8), while veteran Benjamin Nicks is 'suspicious that the Smithsonian is more interested in sending a political message about strategic defense and nuclear weapons' and concludes that the proposed exhibition would 'deal not with history, the eminent domain of any museum – but instead, pure politics' (in Harwit 1996: 69). *Crossroads* is impugned as a 'politically rigged horror show' (Correll 1994c: 12), a 'countercultural morality pageant put on by academic activists' (Correll in Wallace 1996: 173) organized by 'bleeding hearts who have belabored us . . . with the message that it was immoral to drop the bomb' (Edmundson 1994) and who will 'not give up on their radical political agenda' (AFA in Harwit 1996: 391). Veteran Burr Bennett makes explicit the risks the Smithsonian takes in 'its decision to join the "PC forces"': 'as disgust of this rewriting of history builds, it could erode both your credibility and your financial support' (in ibid.: 131).

Critics seek to show that the curators' politics are extreme and at variance with the mainstream American flow, while at the same time suggesting that their own views are widely and enthusiastically shared. Republican Bob Stump (Arizona) is quoted in the *Washington Post*: the museum has elevated 'a vocal but tiny minority of politically correct opinion to the level of the beliefs of an entire generation' (in Correll 1994c: 12). Historian Newt Gingrich wants this revisionism to get back to the ivory towers where it belongs: 'Political correctness may be okay in some faculty lounge, but . . . the Smithsonian is a treasure that belongs to the American people and it should not become a plaything for left-wing ideologies' (in Harwit 1996: 394). An oft-cited *Washington Post* editorial from February 1995 simultaneously denies political motives to critics of *Crossroads* while attaching them to its curators, securing (it hopes) truth and authenticity for the views of veterans and their spokespersons:

> It is not, as some would have it, that benighted advocates of a special-interest or right-wing point of view brought political power to bear to crush and distort the historical truth. Quite the contrary. Narrow-minded representatives of a special interest and revisionist point of view attempted to use their inside track to appropriate and hollow out a historical event that large numbers of Americans alive at that time and engaged in the war had witnessed and understood in a very different – and authentic – way.
>
> (in Correll 1995: 21)

As evidence of the broad-based disaffection with *Crossroads* among the American people, 'more than 11,400 signatures on petitions of protest' (Correll 1994b: 64) were presented to the Smithsonian.

And so it is with critics of *SAL*. Robert Park believes that visitors to the exhibition will take home this message: 'Ring the bell of evil, and . . . automatically blame a scientist' (in Nemecek 1995: 21). *SAL* is full of 'politically correct, postmodern social constructivism' says Park (1994: 207), a view endorsed by Shields speaking for the ACS: the 'deconstructionist view of history' leads to a 'politically correct, revisionist historical display of science as a litany of moral debacles, environmental catastrophes, social injustices and destruction by radiation, while at the same time ignoring the many triumphs, achievements and contributions of science to our lives' (Shields 1996: 40). Henry Allen, staff writer at the *Washington Post*, says that the 'god of science' is 'largely forgotten in favour of paying homage to environmentalism and political correctness' (Allen 1994: B1). Paul Gross suggests that the curators were swept away by 'ideological fervor' (Gross 1996: 119), and Christina Hoff Sommers asks rhetorically: 'who, pray tell, will save us from the self-righteous politics of Smithsonian curators?' (Sommers 1995b: A11).

The American Chemical Society, however, admits to no political stake in *SAL*. Its $5 million was donated, Shields reminds everybody, for noble ends. 'The society's goal in providing the financial sponsorship for the exhibition was to improve the public understanding of science and encourage young people to pursue careers in science' (Shields 1996: 40). As evidence of its disinterestedness (or its misplaced trust in *SAL*'s curatorial team), the ACS has 'always acknowledged that the Smithsonian has control over the content of any exhibition that it produces' (ibid.).

In accusations of playing politics with history, it takes two to tango: curators insist that it is them – the critics – who have hidden agendas, not us. Sophia Vackimes, reviewing *SAL* positively for the *American Anthropologist*, suggests that tucked behind the ACS's $5 million was more than altruism:

> At the Smithsonian Institution, special interest groups are seeking to eliminate the questioning of scientific research and its consequent technological applications. The gifts of money the American Chemical Society has given for the exhibit are being used as a lever with which to force the curators to change the exhibit.
>
> (Vackimes 1996: 391)

Exactly the same point is made by Harwit about the critics of *Crossroads*: 'For whatever it costs to buy influence, you can now have your own version of our nation's history displayed and opposing views suppressed at the Smithsonian Institution' (Harwit 1996: viii). The Air Force Association is labelled by Harwit a 'competing interest group' who 'sought to impose their views and perspectives on the exhibition, the museum, the Institution, and ultimately, the visiting public' (ibid.: 193). Professional historians were appalled at the fate of *Crossroads*, calling the orchestrated criticism 'a transparent attempt at historical cleansing' (in ibid.: 345).

Harwit knew he was at war with a 'partisan campaign' that would pursue 'victory by any means' (ibid.: vii). The means chosen by Correll were the routine stuff of American politics: scare tactics, ad campaigns, publicity and lobbying on Capitol Hill. The AFA enlisted allies by 'fanning the fears of aging veterans by telling them that [*Crossroads*] would dishonor their wartime service to the nation' (ibid.: 427). A 'media blitz' was launched to elicit broad public support: 'twenty-eight radio interviews . . . international CNN coverage . . . thirty further television interviews . . . print coverage [exceeding] 330 articles' (ibid.: 239, 250). Correll successfully buttonholed members of congress: speaking of a letter that came to him straight from the Hill, Harwit suggests 'the hand of the Air Force Association could not have been clearer if this letter had been written on AFA stationery' (ibid.: 257). All of this politicizing was said to be in the service not of balance but of perpetuating a 'conservative mood' or an 'extremist right wing' (ibid.: xi, 198) by 'patriotic bullies who used words like *liberal* a bit the way Nazis had once used *Jew*' (Sherry 1996: 113; emphasis in original).

But such politics stop at the door of the Smithsonian, or so its curators would have us believe. Harwit does 'not consider himself "politically correct"' (in Correll 1994a: 27), and would not admit to 'any deliberate bias' (Harwit 1996: 63) in making *Crossroads*. The Smithsonian is 'not an organization that made political statements' such as calling 'for the abolition of all bombs' (ibid.: 165). The exhibition would not 'take a stance in the debate' over whether it was justifiable to drop the bombs, nor does it 'intend to pass moral judgement' (ibid.: 236, 205). Historian Mike Wallace defends *Crossroads* by writing that 'the only political correctness . . . was the censorship that shut down the real exhibition and prevented people from judging it for themselves' (Wallace 1996: 133). With that outcome, says Harwit, 'the losers . . . are the American public' (Harwit 1996: vii), not Truth, his career or professional authority: his motives are altruistic. Nowhere is the asymmetry between our truth and their power so neatly exposed than by Harwit looking back on the exhibition that never was: 'true knowledge is not determined by votes, or money or power; it is shaped by careful research, respect for facts, and dispassionate discourse. I like to believe that we fought valiantly but were badly outgunned' (ibid.: 318).

'SO MUCH FOR TRUTH'

I have tried to step outside of the controversies over *SAL* and *Crossroads*, better to see what they consist of – but I have failed. My failure is not to do with an inability to shed epistemic attachments to the community of knowledge makers I belong to: scholars, on the curators' side. I believe that I have delivered, as promised, a symmetric analysis of the symmetric rhetoric used by curators to defend their exhibition – and by their critics to attack it. I may have found something out about the framing of debates over public representations of history at museums like the Smithsonian: curators and critics alike claim to seek balanced exhibitions, where sufficient materials are displayed for visitors to reach their own informed judgments about the place of science in society or the justifiability of dropping atomic bombs. But it is a precarious balance, undermined rather easily by counter-assertions that one is really using History to push a party line, squelching multiple interpretations in order to legitimize a reading that advances political interests.

It is instead the very idea of an agnostic standpoint that fails me – Mannheim's free-floating intellectual (1936) is a chimera not even worth pursuing, Haraway's god-trick (1991: 191) is something for mortals to avoid. Stepping outside gets me nowhere.[27] Out here, there is nothing *in the rhetoric of anybody* that enables me to assign virtue, credibility, honesty, fair play, interpretative prowess, objectivity, sincerity and balance to one side or the other. Every defence of an exhibition – and every attack – has been deconstructed down to dust. When the rhetoric of curators and critics is laid down like double-entry bookkeeping, as I have done, it does seem to cancel itself out. But this of course overlooks what the rhetoric was designed to accomplish from the start and what really settled things: to get more powerful allies on your side than your enemy has – which is what veterans' organizations were able to do, and the American Chemical Society was not. It is a delusion, in other words, for 'us' to think that it was noble principles or objectivity or truth that permitted Molella to resist the chemists' assault: persuasive rhetoric and powerful allies did as much for *SAL* as it did for veterans' organizations.[28]

It is only from some epistemic inside that Good Guys and Bad become visible,[29] that truth is separable from power or method from politics, that trust can be extended or denied, that History is worth fighting for. So I go home, to an unruly community of sociologists and historians, some of whom (like me) study scientists, plying our trade at museums and universities, most of the time disputing among ourselves. I return unconvinced that the inevitable world of multiple epistemic communities is something to celebrate (but rather, to struggle through), depressed by the realization that none of our sometimes well-intentioned rhetorical weapons (objectivity, interpretative skill, dispassion) are fail-safe in convincing everybody else to accept our stories over different ones better aligned with their interests and faiths,[30] discouraged about the prospects for common ground or deliberative democracy or universal principles of reason,[31] cheered only by the score at half-time: a one-to-one draw.

NOTES

1 In the burgeoning scholarly literature on museums, I have found especially useful: Bud (1993, 1995); Crew (1996); Crew and Sims (1991); Harris (1995); Macdonald (1996); Finn (1990); Fyfe (1996); Macdonald and Silverstone (1992); Silverstone (1992); Clifford (1997).

2 Although historian Gerald Zahavi could at least imagine a 'multiple script' exhibition of the *Enola Gay*, with one corridor representing the views of critical revisionist

historians and another representing the views of conservative veterans' organizations (Zahavi 1995).

3 'The notion that once upon a time there were "neutral" museum exhibits or artefacts that "spoke for themselves" is, of course, illusory' (Linenthal 1996: 26).

4 'OUR KNOWLEDGE of what the world is like draws on knowledge about other people – what they are like as sources of testimony, whether and in what circumstances they may be trusted' (Shapin 1994: xxv–xxvi).

5 Such symmetry is part of the 'strong programme' in the sociology of knowledge developed initially by David Bloor. In seeking causal explanations for how and why different groups hold to different representations of reality (natural or historical), analysts must refrain from starting out with *a priori* assumptions about which claims are true or false, factual or ideological, rational or irrational (Bloor 1991).

6 I have elsewhere (Gieryn 1996) published an account of my experiences on the *SAL* Advisory Board, written from within the epistemic culture of sociologists, historians and professional curators of science – and frankly unagnostic about chemists' criticisms, which I dismissed as an exercise in scapegoating and blaming (obviously impotent) science studies for the apparent decline in public enthusiasm for the support of big science. I did not, in that piece, level my critical guns at defences of *SAL* by its curators and by me, so that the controversy comes off as our Truth against their Power. Because of that, I was able to end the paper optimistically if Pollyanna-ishly, by inviting the critical chemists and physicists to work with us, with our obviously superior standards of evidence, argument and purpose, toward a consensual representation of science in American life.

7 My own analysis will be 'unbalanced' in seeming to give greater attention to *Crossroads* than to *SAL*. This is a measure of how much more ink has so far been spilled over the *Enola Gay* (three books [Nobile 1995; Linenthal and Engelhardt 1996; Harwit 1996], two theme sections of journals [Thelen 1995a; Hein 1995], along with hundreds of articles and editorials) than over *Crossroads* (no books and a handful of articles). The extracts come from a mixed bag of texts: confessionals, quotations in the mass media, reminiscences, meeting minutes. It would be quite wrong to assume that battle lines are necessarily as neatly drawn as this analysis would make them seem. The American Chemical Society did not always agree with the American Physical Society, nor did the American Legion necessarily pursue the same goals as the Air Force Association (Goldberg 1995), nor was consensus reached among the historians on the Enola Gay Advisory Board (Sherwin 1995: 1088). On the dangers of exaggerating polarization and essentializing 'sides' in scientific/political debates, see Wynne 1996. Zolberg 1996 provides a different sociological analysis of the *Enola Gay* flap, centring on American vs. Japanese constructions of national narratives.

8 This comes from a posting by Molella on the History of Technology newsgroup titled 'Smithsonian Institution response to "What's New" by Robert Park, American Physical Society', 1 July 1994.

9 Kennedy is quoted in 'Science in American Life: a management review', prepared by the *SAL* Exhibition Development Team, December 1990, p. 2, typescript.

10 An accessible reprint of Senator Nancy Landon Kassebaum's resolution on the *Enola Gay* exhibit, followed by excerpts from testimony and debate, may be found in Thelen (1995a: 1136–44).

11 In a 1993 planning document, the proposed exhibition was titled *Fifty Years On . . .* After settling on *Crossroads* for the first draft script in January 1994, the exhibition idea evolved into *The Last Act: The Atomic Bomb and the End of World War II* by May 1994 (after much material about the Cold War implications of Hiroshima and Nagasaki was deleted). To keep matters simple, I shall refer to the exhibition consistently as *Crossroads*, even when this is anachronistic. I do so because

the published version of the script (Nobile 1995) comes from the time when the exhibition was known as *Crossroads*.

12   'Minutes: Exhibition Advisory Board Meeting', 1 June 1991.

13   Paul H. L. Walter, 'Remarks: Opening of Science in American Life', Washington, DC, 25 April 1994. In my insider's account of *SAL* (Gieryn 1996), I suggest that Walter's speech was in fact damnation with faint praise, as he uses the occasion to warn gathered dignitaries of the spectre of postmodernism and anti-reason – which, in the ensuing controversy, would be used as scapegoats blamed for *SAL*'s enduring unbalance.

14   Gross is co-author with Norman Levitt of *Higher Superstition: The Academic Left and its Quarrels with Science* (1994). From posting on Science and Technology Studies newsgroup, titled 'Who Owns History?', 8 May 1995.

15   In questioning historian Edward T. Linenthal during hearings of the Senate Committee on Rules and Administration, Senator Wendell H. Ford from Kentucky says that 'the role of the Smithsonian management, I think, [is] to balance the perspectives' (in Thelen 1995a: 1141).

16   This impassioned dispute over a number does not conform to historian of science Theodore Porter's argument that 'reliance on numbers and quantitative manipulation minimizes the need for intimate knowledge and personal trust'. Indeed, neither curators nor critics trusted the others' numbers, and for that reason it was impossible to produce knowledge independent of the particular people who make it' (which, says Porter, is what the 'highly disciplined discourse' of quantification should yield) (Porter 1995: ix).

17   In less heavy-handed language, Correll writes in *Air Force*: 'Another theme of this postwar section is to show the American victors celebrating merrily in contrast to the anguish and suffering of the defeated Japanese' (Correll 1994b: 63).

18   'The new script, like the last one, avoids showing warlike images of the Japanese armed forces . . . Indeed, they are the only military members on either side who appear in heroic roles in this exhibit' (Correll 1994b: 63).

19   Stanley Goldberg, historian at the National Museum of American History, posting on the Science and Technology Studies newsgroup, 11 July 1995.

20   Posting on History of Technology newsgroup, titled 'Smithsonian Institution Response . . . ', dated 1 July 1994.

21   Personal correspondence, Gieryn to Stine, 12 October 1990.

22   At least one member of *Crossroads*' advisory committee agrees that the task of the project 'was to reflect, in part, the nature of scholarly thinking – and not to impose the curator's own historical judgement' (Bernstein 1995: 225–6).

23   'those who make history and those who write it are, or should be, two different kinds of people' (Sodei 1995: 1122).

24   Harwit, of course, suggests the opposite: that in spite of veterans' typical unawareness of the latest scholarship and recently available documentary evidence, the exhibition would include 'the voices of those who have special knowledge based on having been there' (Harwit 1996: 214).

25   As an illustration of the curators' obliviousness to the sensitivities of veterans who were there, Correll writes: 'The new script . . . no longer says that the B-29 aircrews who flew the atomic bomb missions against Japan were "only following orders." Dr. Harwit told *Air Force Magazine* in August that it never occurred to the curators that this line might suggest an insulting parallel to the classic war crimes defence at Nuremburg' (Correll 1994c: 10).

26   Scholars too sometimes use the language of 'being there' to legitimize their accounts – as in ethnographic fieldwork – but Geertz reminds us that the credibility of anthropologists' stories is not inherent in their experiential contact with the other

but a literary accomplishment of skilful rhetoric practised back home, e.g. 'We were surrounded by crowds of naked chattering youngsters' (Geertz 1988: 12; here quoting from Raymond Firth's *We, the Tikopia*). Joan W. Scott identifies risks in essentializing 'experience' as a privileged source of authoritative knowledge, and restates in a different way what was at issue between curators and critics: 'What counts as experience is neither self-evident nor straight-forward; it is always contested, always therefore political' (Scott 1992: 37). See Linenthal 1995 for more discussion of this issue in the *Enola Gay* controversy.

27 The idea of analysing competing representations of reality agnostically and symmetrically took hold in the sociology of scientific knowledge during the 1970s, but it took almost two decades for my tribe to consider systematically the political implications of our constructivism and (shades of) relativism. A special issue of *Social Studies of Science* (volume 26, no. 2, May 1996) gathers up a provocative set of papers which suggest that situating beliefs in social contexts makes for good sociology but impotent politics, and that agnostic detachment may make a sociologist of science vulnerable to having one's research exploited for ends that the author might not endorse.

28 If this is so, then (sociologically speaking) historians or curators may be placed into the same analytic category as veterans' organizations or the ACS: interest groups all (a point made by John Rumm, historian at the Smithsonian, before the Organization of American Historians [Rumm 1995: 1116]).

29 Evidently, this conclusion will come as no surprise at all to professional politicians: Senator Ford, noting that Linenthal was writing a paper about the *Enola Gay* controversy, said during committee hearings: 'Whoever reads it is going to have his interpretation of who the bad guys are and who the good guys are . . . I think I have a pretty good idea from listening to your comments this morning who the white hats are going to be and who the black hats are going to be . . . You start interpreting what happened here from all the reading, and we have some information, you have other information. Maybe we both do not have the same information. *So you write yours from yours, and we make our judgements from ours*' (in Thelen 1995a: 1142–3; emphasis added).

30 'What if a realist theory of the correspondence between history as written and the actual past is abandoned for a constructionist view of history as a form of representation? . . . [Answer:] If disciplines and written histories are socially and temporally located, then their ability to persuade others of their representations of texts, events, or subjects is severely constrained or eliminated' (Berkhofer 1995: 3). Other works in metahistory (not elsewhere cited) that take up the implications of Berkhofer's question include: Davis 1996; Le Goff 1992; Novick 1988; Scott 1997, who mentions the *Enola Gay* case.

31 Some readers will no doubt believe that I have ended this essay just when it got interesting. I do not know how Gutmann and Thompson's (1996): 1 'core idea' of deliberative democracy – 'when citizens or their representatives disagree morally, they should continue to reason together to reach mutually acceptable decisions' – could have provided guidance for resolving differences between curators and critics, when reason was always in short supply and mutual satisfaction never achieved.

REFERENCES

Allen, H. (1994) 'Science is Golden', *Washington Post* (April 27), p. B1.
Berkhofer, R. F., Jr (1995) *Beyond the Great Story: History as Text and Discourse*, Cambridge, MA: Harvard University Press.

Bernstein, B. J. (1995) 'The struggle over history: defining the Hiroshima narrative', in P. Nobile (ed.) *Judgment at the Smithsonian*, pp. 127–256, New York: Marlowe.

Bloor, D. (1991) *Knowledge and Social Imagery* (2nd edition), Chicago: University of Chicago Press.

Boyer, P. (1996) 'Whose history is it anyway? Memory, politics, and historical scholarship', in E. T. Linenthal and T. Engelhardt (eds) *History Wars: The Enola Gay and Other Battles for the American Past*, pp. 115–39, New York: Metropolitan Books/Holt.

Bud, R. (1993) 'The museum, meaning, and history: the case of chemistry', in S. H. Mauskopf (ed.) *Chemical Sciences in the Modern World*, pp. 277–94, Philadelphia, PA: University of Pennsylvania Press.

—— (1995) 'Science, meaning, and myth in the museum', *Public Understanding of Science*, 4, pp. 1–16.

Clifford, J. (1997) 'Museums as contact zones' in J. Clifford (ed.) *Routes: Travel and Translation in the Late Twentieth Century*, pp. 188–219, Cambridge, MA: Harvard University Press.

Correll, J. T. (1994a) 'War stories at Air and Space', *Air Force Magazine* (April), pp. 24–9.

—— (1994b) '"The Last Act" at Air and Space', *Air Force Magazine* (September), pp. 58–64.

—— (1994c) 'The three doctors and the *Enola Gay*', *Air Force Magazine* (November), pp. 8–12.

—— (1994d) 'The decision that launched the *Enola Gay*' *Air Force Magazine* (April), pp. 30–4.

—— (1995) 'The activists and the *Enola Gay*' *Air Force Magazine* (September), pp. 18–25.

Crew, S. R. (1996) 'History in the museum', *Perspectives: American Historical Association Newsletter*, 34 (October), pp. 6–8.

Crew, S. R. and J. E. Sims (1991) 'Locating authenticity: fragments of a dialogue', in I. Karp and S. D. Lavine (eds) *Exhibiting Cultures: The Poetics and Politics of Museum Display*, pp. 159–75, Washington, DC: Smithsonian Institution Press.

Davis, N. Z. (1996) 'Who owns history? History in the profession', *Perspectives: American Historical Association Newsletter*, 34 (November), pp. 1, 4–6.

Dower, J. (1996) 'Three narratives of our humanity', in E. T. Linenthal and T. Engelhardt (eds) *History Wars: The Enola Gay and Other Battles for the American Past*, pp. 63–96, New York: Metropolitan Books/Holt.

Edmundson, J. V. (1994) 'Displaying the *Enola Gay*' (letter), *Air Force Magazine* (July), p. 5.

Finn, B.S. (1990) 'The Museum of Science and Technology', in M. S. Shapiro (ed.) *The Museum: A Reference Guide*, pp. 59–83, New York: Greenwood.

Flam, F. (1994) 'Privately funded exhibit raises scientists' ire', *Science*, (5 August), p. 729.

Fyfe, G. (1996) 'A Trojan Horse at the Tate: theorizing the museum as agency and structure', in S. Macdonald and G. Fyfe (eds) *Theorizing Museums*, pp. 203–28, Oxford: Blackwell.

Geertz, C. (1988) *Works and Lives: The Anthropologist as Author*, Stanford, CT: Stanford University Press.

Gieryn, T. F. (1995) 'Smithsonian science' (letter), *The New York Times*, (15 July), p. 14.

—— (1996) 'Policing STS [Science and Technology Studies]: a boundary-work souvenir from the Smithsonian exhibition on "Science in American Life"' *Science, Technology and Human Values*, 21, 1, pp. 100–15.

Gifford, B. (1996) 'Bad chemistry', *Lingua Franca* (July/August), pp. 6–7.

Goldberg, S. (1995) 'Smithsonian suffers Legionnaires' disease' *Bulletin of the Atomic Scientists* (May/June), pp. 28–33.

Gross, P. (1996) 'Reply to Gieryn', *Science, Technology and Human Values*, 21, 1, pp. 116–20.

Gross, P. R. and N. Levitt (1994) *Higher Superstition: The Academic Left and its Quarrel with Science*, Baltimore, MD: Johns Hopkins University Press.

Gutmann, A. and D. Thompson (1996) *Democracy and Disagreement*, Cambridge, MA: Harvard University Press.

Haraway, D. (1991) *Simians, Cyborgs and Women: The Reinvention of Nature*, New York: Routledge.

Harris, N. (1995) 'Museums and controversy: some introductory reflections', *Journal of American History*, 82, pp. 1102–10.

Harwit, M. (1994) 'Harwit Responds' (letter) *Air Force Magazine* (May), p. 4.

—— (1996) *An Exhibit Denied: Lobbying the History of the* Enola Gay, New York: Copernicus/Springer-Verlag.

Hein, L. (ed.) (1995) 'Remembering the bomb: the fiftieth anniversary in the United States and Japan', theme issue of *Bulletin of Concerned Asian Scholars*, 27 (April–June).

Holden, C. (1994) 'History slights science', *Science*, (25 November), p. 1327.

Kleiner, K. (1995) 'Fear and loathing at the Smithsonian' *New Scientist*, (8 April), p. 42.

Knorr Cetina, K. (1997) *Epistemic Cultures: How Science Makes Sense*, Cambridge, MA: Harvard University Press.

Kohn, R. H. (1996) 'History at risk: the case of the *Enola Gay*', in E. T. Linenthal and T. Engelhardt (eds) *History Wars: The* Enola Gay *and Other Battles for the American Past*, pp. 140–70, New York: Metropolitan Books/Holt.

LaFollette, M. C. (1995) 'Editorial: wielding history like a hammer', *Science Communication*, 16, 3, pp. 235–41.

Lambert, J. W. (1994) 'Displaying the *Enola Gay*' (letter) *Air Force Magazine* (July), p. 5.

Le Goff, J. (1992) *History and Memory*, New York: Columbia University Press.

Leo, J. (1994) 'Visiting a politically correct Smithsonian', *The Indianapolis Star*, (5 October), p. A10.

Lewenstein, B. V. (1996) 'Shooting the messenger: understanding attacks on Science in American Life', http://scicomm96.unimelb.edu.au/scicomm96/.

Linenthal, E. T. (1995) 'Can museums achieve a balance between memory and history?', *Chronicle of Higher Education* (10 February) pp. B1–B2.

—— (1996) 'Anatomy of a controversy', in E. T. Linenthal and T. Engelhardt (eds) *History Wars: The* Enola Gay *and Other Battles for the American Past*, pp. 9–62, New York: Metropolitan Books/Holt.

Linenthal, E. T. and T. Engelhardt (eds) (1996) *History Wars: The* Enola Gay *and Other Battles for the American Past*, New York: Metropolitan Books/Holt.

Macdonald, S. (1996) 'Theorizing museums – an introduction', in S. Macdonald and G. Fyfe (eds) *Theorizing Museums*, pp. 1–18, Oxford: Blackwell.

Macdonald, S. and R. Silverstone (1992) 'Science on display: the representation of scientific controversy in museum exhibition', *Public Understanding of Science*, 1, pp. 69–87.

Macilwain, C. (1995) 'Smithsonian heeds physicists' complaints', *Nature* (16 March), p. 207.

—— (1996) 'Chemists sound warning on sponsorship of exhibitions', *Nature*, (14 March), p. 95.

Mannheim, K. (1936) *Ideology and Utopia*, New York: Harcourt Brace Jovanovich.

Molella, A. P. (1994a) 'Smithsonian science exhibit' (letter), *Science* (7 October), p. 13.

—— (1994b) 'Science in American Life: an exhibition', *History of Science in America*, 11, 2 (Fall–Winter), pp. 1–2.

—— (1995) 'We're not scientific heretics' (letter), *Wall Street Journal*, 31 July.

Molella, A. P. and C. Stephens (1996) 'Science and its stakeholders: the making of "Science in American Life"', in S. Pearce (ed.) *Exploring Science in Museums*, pp. 95–106, London: Athlone.

Nemecek, S. (1995) 'Out of the lab and into the fire', *Scientific American* (February), pp. 21, 24.

Nobile, P. (1995) 'On the steps of the Smithsonian: Hiroshima denial in America's attic', in P. Nobile (ed.) *Judgment at the Smithsonian*, pp. xvii–xcvii, New York: Marlowe.

Novick, P. (1988) *That Noble Dream: The "Objectivity Question" and the American Historical Profession*, New York: Cambridge University Press.

Park, R. L. (1994) 'Is science the god that failed?', *Science Communication*, 16, 2, pp. 206–10.

—— (1995a) 'The danger of voodoo science', *The New York Times*, (9 July), Section 4, p. 15.

—— (1995b) 'Science and the Smithsonian' (letter), *Wall Street Journal* (17 August), p. A11.

Porter, T. M. (1995) *Trust in Numbers: The Pursuit of Objectivity in Science and Public Life*, Princeton, NJ: Princeton University Press.

Ross, L. (1994) 'Science in American Life: ACS-backed exhibit opens at Smithsonian', *Chemical and Engineering News* (2 May), pp. 4–5.

Rumm, J. (1995) 'Comments at the Organization of American Historians Meeting', *Journal of American History*, 82, pp. 1116–7.

Scott, J. W. (1992) 'Experience', in J. Butler and J. W. Scott (eds) *Feminists Theorize the Political*, New York: Routledge.

—— (1997) 'After history?', *Common Knowledge*, 5, pp. 9–26.

Shapin, S. (1994) *A Social History of Truth*, Chicago: University of Chicago Press.

Sherry, M. S. (1996) 'Patriotic orthodoxy and American decline', in E. T. Linenthal and T. Engelhardt (eds) *History Wars: The Enola Gay and Other Battles for the American Past*, pp. 97–114, New York: Metropolitan Books/Holt.

Sherwin, M. J. (1995) 'Hiroshima as politics and history', *Journal of American History*, 82, pp. 1085–93.

Shields, J. (1996) 'Science in American Life revisited', *Chemical and Engineering News*, (11 March), p. 40.

Silverstone, R. (1992) 'The medium is the museum: on objects and logics in times and spaces', in J. Durant (ed.) *Museums and the Public Understanding of Science*, pp. 34–42, London: The Science Museum.

Sodei, R. (1995) 'Hiroshima/Nagasaki as history and politics', *Journal of American History*, 82, pp. 1118–23.

Sommers, C. H. (1995a) 'The flight from science and reason', *Wall Street Journal*, (10 July), p. A14.

—— (1995b) 'Science and the Smithsonian' (letter) *Wall Street Journal*, (17 August), p. A11.

Thelen, D. (ed.) (1995a) 'History and the public: what can we handle? A round table about history after the *Enola Gay* affair', theme section in the *Journal of American History*, 82 (December), pp. 1029–144.

—— (1995b) 'History after the *Enola Gay* controversy: an introduction', *Journal of American History*, 82 (December), pp. 1029–35.

Vackimes, S. (1996) 'Exhibit review essay: Science in American Life', *American Anthropologist*, 22, 2, pp. 388–91.

Wallace, M. (1996) 'Culture war, history front', in E. T. Linenthal and T. Engelhardt (eds) *History Wars: The Enola Gay and Other Battles for the American Past*, pp. 171–98, New York: Metropolitan Books/Holt.

Wynne, B. (1996) 'SSK's identity parade: signing-up, off-and-on', *Social Studies of Science*, 26, pp. 357–91.

Zahavi, G. (1995) 'Comments at the Organization of American Historians Meeting', *Journal of American History*, 82, pp. 1116–7.

Zolberg, V. (1996) 'Museums as contested sites of remembrance: the *Enola Gay* affair', in S. Macdonald and G. Fyfe (eds) *Theorizing Museums*, pp. 69–82, Oxford: Blackwell.

Afterword: from war to debate?

Sharon Macdonald

The Science Wars, History Wars and Culture Wars have been characterized, not surprisingly, by a sharp polarization into adversarial 'sides'. Each of these 'sides', fuelled by media representations that always seem to favour neat oppositional controversies, has produced a stereotype of the other. So, on the one side, we are presented with a bunch of narrow minded social conservatives, fiercely holding on to elitist ideas of Truth and tradition, talking a language of transcendent rationality and positivism that serves to pretend away political interests and implications. Scientists tend to be lumped *tout court* into this category. On the other side, is supposedly a gaggle of sloppy-thinking left-wingers, more concerned with political correctness than accuracy or achievement, setting out simply to bash science or tradition because of the authority that these have had. Those working in social and cultural disciplines often find themselves nailed willy-nilly with this 'anti-science' label. This is a battle which often sounds rather like a generational squabble: the inflexible, bigoted/sensible, wise grand-parents on the one hand; and the naive, rebellious/socially aware, free-thinking adolescents on the other.

Such polarization, of course, does a good deal of symbolic violence to the sophisticated and complex positions which individuals may adopt (cf. Rose 1996). This is not to say, however, that such polarization is somehow imaginary: on the contrary, it is a very real feature of much contemporary debate and shapes relations not only between those who spar at a distance through the media but also between those who may work in the same institutions, such as in museums. It is a response partly to contexts where the stakes are high – where the types of representations may affect the allocation of scarce public funding and of space within the public arena. The rhetorical battles are themselves, of course, also more complex than the gross stereotyping of the 'other side' (though this certainly goes on). As Thomas Gieryn has described, neither 'side' these days tends to argue its cause in terms of greater truth status; instead the language is one of 'balance' and 'redressing the imbalance' of the opposition. Such liberal discourse is, perhaps, more difficult to challenge. Various other rhetorical moves that draw on a more multi-vocally tolerant discourse can also often be seen. For example, both sides may represent themselves as a threatened minority trying to speak in the public interest. Science and social criticism are depicted as minority pursuits besieged respectively by the forces of 'anti-science' or 'anti-intellectualism', both of which are regarded as controlling the media and are charged with creating a public more unsympathetic to their cause than it surely would be if only education could be improved. Such moves, however, while they may alter the language in which the battles are fought, do little, as Gieryn laments, to bring us any nearer to opening up what seem to be increasingly entrenched positions.

In this Afterword I comment briefly on some of the implications of a book such as this for science and for museums of science. In doing so, my aim is to show why the cultural, political exercise in which this book has engaged is not necessarily antithetical to scientific endeavour and nor to the tasks of science museums. My hope is that the book can contribute to a debate about the relationship between science and cultural criticism, and about the politics, roles and techniques of museums of science; and, more broadly, that such debate might replace the unproductive fencing of the Science, History and Culture Wars (cf. Martin 1996).

The studies in this book have been particularly concerned with situating knowledges – exploring their locations, motivations, specificities and effects. Such an approach does not, however, entail that we regard knowledge as reducible to its social or political context. Knowledge is not simply an epiphenomenon of social and political interests. The studies in this book have highlighted, for example, the fact that political intentions do not always translate neatly into knowledge statements (such as exhibitions). Rather, they have shown how the political worlds in which knowledges are situated are complex and multivalent, and populated not only by ambitions and plans but also by materials and other, maybe conflicting, beliefs and positionings, including those of 'the public' (or, better, 'publics'). Public displays, this book suggests, while clearly political, are not necessarily clear-cut triumphs of political will with determined political effects. Both before and after an exhibition is deemed finished, visions are subject to revision. To acknowledge revision, complexity and the incompleteness of analysis, should not, however, be regarded as a weakness. On the contrary, I suggest that it can help to lead towards more sensitive and finely tuned accounts. Moreover, such accounts can, perhaps, provide conceptual 'bridges' between scientific and cultural approaches.

Contributors to this volume have made their arguments on the basis of detailed analysis which engages directly with empirical data (from documentary research or direct observation, or both) and brings this into a dialogue with theoretical perspectives. Although in the various epistemological 'wars', cultural perspectives are sometimes regarded as being based on a simplistic assertion of political motives, the studies here show the careful analytical readings on which cultural arguments may be made, and the challenges and revisions to which particular expectations may have been subject. Just as exhibition-makers may have to rethink their ambitions in light of material or conceptual intransigencies (e.g. an artefact which is too heavy for the floor-loading, an abstract principle which seems to evade graphic depiction), and just as scientists may have to reformulate hypotheses in light of unexpected results or observations, so too may cultural critics rework their analyses through engaging with the rich and often awkward detail of empirical data. To acknowledge this, and its importance, is not to turn positivist, though it is to avoid an exaggerated social constructionism (and accompanying form of relativism) which sees the social as the only motive force of knowledge and practice. It is to recognize the possibly disruptive agency of that which is studied – the 'intervention' of the world (Hacking 1983), the demand for 'revisioning' that the empirical may make. Such a perspective, as Donna Haraway puts it, 'require[s] that the object of knowledge be pictured as an actor and agent, not a screen or a ground or a resource, never finally as a slave to the master that closes off the dialectic in his unique agency and authorship of "objective" knowledge' (Haraway 1991: 198). Such a perspective acknowledges the agency of that which we study while all the time striving for critical awareness of the significance of the categories, forms and contexts of analysis. If we wanted purposefully to blur the battle lines in order to promote dialogue, we might reasonably call such a perspective both 'cultural' and 'scientific'.

The argument that exhibition-makers' intentions may be thwarted by other players, including material objects, time, space, money, boards of trustees, and visitors, should not be taken as an argument that exhibition-makers can throw responsibility to the winds in the knowledge that their plans may not be realized and that visitors may read the exhibition in unexpected ways. It is precisely here that more sensitive, nuanced accounts can surely help to illuminate the kinds of processes, assumptions and political alternatives which may reshape exhibitors' visions. Studies in this book have identified the multiple players and sometimes contradictory agendas which may be involved in exhibition-making, the socio-political milieux within which exhibitions take on their meanings, ways in which particular display strategies may articulate with these, and perspectives from which visitors may interpret displays. Although the chapters here were not written with policy intentions to the fore – and indeed perhaps the breadth of their insight derives partly from the fact that they were not instrumentally focused – they provide a body of research which can surely productively inform debate about the aims and likely effectiveness of public display. This is not to say that they will provide easy answers: on the contrary, what they raise are difficult questions. These are, however, questions that need to be addressed if museums of science are to play significant roles in public debate about science.

Tony Bennett (1992a; 1992b) has suggested that it is to such questions of cultural policy and its technologies of implementation that cultural criticism might be particularly directed. Rather than aiming primarily to alter conscious-ness or 'modify the relationship between . . . text and reader' (Bennett 1992a: 24), as is the political project of much cultural studies, Bennett's argument is that cultural institutions, such as museums, would be a more politically effective focus, for it is through such technologies that 'culture' is constituted. Bennett's arguments have drawn criticism because they have been interpreted as relinquishing the role of the critic as an independent thinker, untainted by policy concerns, and because they do not spell out the criteria according to which cultural policies should be judged or the directions in which cultural modification should go (McGuigan 1996: 14–24). Nevertheless, there is surely no reason why attention to cultural policies and their techniques should not be coupled with debate over their situation, role and ambitions.

It would be a mistake to imagine that critical perspectives on institutions such as museums come only from the academy or from elsewhere 'outside'. In the Science Museum, London, where I carried out field work, there were certainly plenty of often impassioned debates about the politics of certain directions that the museum was taking, how best to empower visitors, how to represent different communities, what to collect, how to deal with controversy over science, whether to depict science as just 'one way of knowing', and just what a national museum of science and industry should be doing as a new millennium loomed. The final four chapters in this book all describe museum exhibitions which, to varying extents, drew upon and incorporated critical ideas within public display. While they may, to varying extents, have been subject to criticism, it is nevertheless significant that they were devised and mounted within museums of science.

There are a number of exhibitionary strategies, suggested by various chapters here, which could provide a means through which museums might promote more public debate about science. I prefer the idea of public *debate about* science to 'public understanding of science' because the latter seems so often to be rather narrowly focused on getting the public to know more scientific facts and to appreciate science better (cf. Collins and Pinch 1993). Public debate about science should entail a proper understanding of the nature, workings and achievements of science. It should also, however, enable the public to evaluate its validity and consider its implications and politics. While this would incorporate attention to negative as well as positive aspects of science, such increased public debate might, paradoxically, help encourage greater public interest in science.

In order to provoke more debate about science, various chapters in this book suggest that museums consider disrupting something of the culturally authoritative role which they have tended to assume through strategies such as standpoint displays, the display of controversy, and reflexive and experimental exhibitions. All of these hold promise, though none is without its problems.

Standpoint exhibitions

Science museum exhibitions are typically not assigned specific individual or group authorship. That is, there is usually no billboard announcing the name of the curator or curators responsible for creating an exhibition; and this despite the fact that names of design companies, sponsors and benefactors are usually displayed. By eliminating mention of any individual or individuals responsible for the content (designers tend to be thought of as dealing with the 'packaging'), museums inevitably give the impression that exhibition content – its 'storyline' – is somehow disconnected from personal agency: it is 'objective'. Exhibitions are authored by an invisible figure which visitors may regard as 'science' or the museum in which the exhibition takes place (e.g. 'the Smithsonian', 'the Wellcome'). Again, as both these institutions – science and the museum – tend to be regarded as authoritative, the effect is to close off debate. This may also create problems – at least in a climate where most museums do present authoritative accounts – for exhibitions which try to present more open and questioning displays.

In light of the experience of visitors misunderstanding his intentions in *Birth and Breeding*, Ken Arnold suggests that museums might consider more explicitly authored exhibitions. These would acknowledge and speak from a particular perspective. Visitors would be encouraged to regard them as partial and positioned perspectives and to read them in this light. It is an approach which could be coupled with another of museums' contemporary aims, to widen access and allow a broader representation of 'voices' within museums.

This approach is not, of course, without its problems, which museums would need to address carefully if thinking of adopting it. There is the important question of how far visitors would be enabled to read exhibitions critically and assess their partiality. If presented with only a single angle, what would they evaluate it against, how would they be provided with the information with which to situate it? Clearly, having an author's name alone might not mean much. Perhaps museums should provide multiple perspectives or standpoints on the same issue, though this raises delicate questions of balance and selection over which museums will still, of course, remain the arbiters. This is, nevertheless, a format which is clearly better suited to the notion of debate than is a single uni-vocal authoritative representation.

Representing controversy

Partly because many museum displays are *in situ* for years, because their own planning time tends to be fairly lengthy and because they draw on extant collections, science museums often steer clear of ongoing controversies. The fear is that these will be over or outdated before or soon after the exhibition is complete. Yet this, of course, excludes many of the topics which are most likely to engage the public in debate about science.

In recent years science museums, such as the Science Museum in London, have experimented more with exhibitions which deal with ongoing controversial subjects (e.g. cold fusion, genetic engineering), usually by using temporary exhibitions and perhaps making use of audio-visual material. It is an approach that raises some of the same problems as do standpoint exhibitions, though through use of multimedia technologies there is perhaps the opportunity to provide visitors with a resource for further background and information about the subjects within the exhibition. One could imagine an approach to the *Enola Gay* and *Science in American Life* which might have included the controversies over the representations within the exhibition space itself – an approach which might have created fascinating and provocative public displays. Another question for museums here, however, is one of how far they are to be, and the public wants them to be, distinguished from other media. What can they provide – and provide within the context of what is usually a fairly brief visit to an exhibition – that cannot be provided better by newspapers, books and television? While museums may be able to provide a distinctive breadth of scope and coverage within one space, they surely need also to draw on their three-dimensional capacities (including their capacity to stage dramas, use interactives, present 'real' artefacts and so forth) in the creation of engaging exhibits about controversy.

Reflexive exhibitions

The exhibitions mounted by Mary Bouquet and Jim Bennett included within them reflection about the nature of certain kinds of science and certain kinds of exhibitions. This reflexivity was not performed primarily through words but through the juxtaposition of pictures, reconstructions and artefacts. The aim was to raise questions for visitors through the exhibits themselves rather than to convey particular facts. How far they succeeded in this is, of course, open to question, and Jim Bennett acknowledges that there were problems on this score in the exhibitions which he curated. Nevertheless, exhibitions which disrupt typical science museum formats through, perhaps, including representations from popular culture alongside scientific evidence or juxtaposing the measurement of scientific processes with that of people, as did the exhibitions described here, can surely help, potentially, to create for visitors a more interrogative spirit in which to approach exhibitions.

In creating such reflexive exhibitions, science museums might profitably draw on cultural research and perspectives, and on ideas in disciplines (such as social anthropology) which have sought to analyse and recast their own traditional formats for the representation of their research. This is not to say that all exhibitions should come critically to address the phenomenon of exhibition (such a move would be as tedious as all ethnographies only talking of the format of ethnography) or to address scientific process. However, by introducing more reflexive perspectives within science museums this may help to promote the notion of museums of science as forums not just for being educated in science but for reflection on, and debate about, it.

These are just some of the suggestions which might be drawn from this book. Such innovative moves are, as examples here show, already under way, and we are surely going to see increasing numbers of interesting experimental exhibitions in museums of science in the years ahead. Museums of science are undoubtedly going to face challenges and be the subject of controversies as they struggle to redefine their roles in the face of cultural and political change. As such, they are a significant cultural space – and cultural agency – to watch. This book will, we hope, help to provide some questions and provocations in the debates about the politics of public display which are sure to continue.

REFERENCES

Bennett, T. (1992a) 'Putting policy into cultural studies', in L. Grossberg, C. Nelson and P. Treichler (eds) *Cultural Studies*, pp. 23–37, London: Routledge.

—— (1992b) 'Useful culture', *Cultural Studies*, 6 (3).

Collins, H. and T. Pinch (1993) *The Golem: What Everyone Should Know about Science*, Cambridge: Cambridge University Press.

Hacking, I. (1983) *Representing and Intervening: Introductory Topics in the Philosophy of Natural Science*, Cambridge: Cambridge University Press.

Haraway, D. (1991) *Simians, Cyborgs and Women: The Reinvention of Nature*, London: Free Association Books.

McGuigan, J. (1996) *Culture and the Public Sphere*, London: Routledge

Martin, E. (1996) 'Meeting polemics with irenics in the science wars', *Social Text*, 46–7 (1&2), pp. 43–60.

Rose, H. (1996) 'My enemy's enemy is – only perhaps – my friend', *Social Text*, 46–7 (1&2), pp. 61–80.

Science as Culture

26 Freegrove Road London N7 9RQ, England

tel. 0171-609 0507 fax 0171-609 4837
email pp@rmy1.demon.co.uk

Science as Culture explores the role of expertise in shaping the values which contend for influence over the wider society. The journal analyses how our scientific culture defines what is rational, and what is natural. *SaC* provides a unique, accessible forum for debate, beyond the boundaries of academic disciplines and specializations.

Contributors have included: Vincent Mosco, Donna Haraway, Richard Barbrook, Langdon Winner, Michael Chanan, Sarah Franklin, Michael Shortland, Steve Best & Douglas Kellner, Roger Smith, Mary Mellor, Scott L. Montgomery, Roger Silverstone, Bruce Berman, Ashis Nandy, Jack Kloppenburg, Jr., Les Levidow, Christopher Hamlin, Philip Garrahan & Paul Stewart, Maureen McNeil, Barbara Duden, Andrew Ross, Dennis Hayes, Kevin Robins & Frank Webster, David Pingitore, Jon Turney, Stephen Hill & Tim Turpin, Chunglin Kwa, Joel Kovel, David Hakken, Robert M. Young.

The journal has published articles on mass-media representations of expertise, the political role of radio, human and agricultural biotechnologies, cultures of workplace automation, the metaphors central to scientific knowledge, artificial intelligence, images of the scientist in film and theatre, etc.

Index